# THE PROMISE AND
# PRACTICE OF
# BIBLICAL THEOLOGY

# THE PROMISE AND PRACTICE OF BIBLICAL THEOLOGY

*Edited by*
JOHN REUMANN

*Preface by*
JOHN W. VANNORSDALL

Fortress Press                    Minneapolis

Library of Congress Cataloging-in-Publication Data

The Promise and practice of biblical theology / edited by John Reumann ; preface by John W. Vannorsdall.
    p. cm.
    Includes bibliographical references and index.
    ISBN 0-8006-2495-5
    1. Bible—Theology. 2. Theology, Practical. I. Reumann, John Henry Paul.
    BS543.P76  1991
    230—dc20                                                91-18794
                                                            CIP

Manufactured in the U.S.A.                                          AF 1-1560

95    94    93    92    91    1    2    3    4    5    6    7    8    9    10

# Contents

# Contributors

ROBERT BORNEMANN is Burkhalter Professor for Old Testament and Hebrew at the Lutheran Theological Seminary, Philadelphia (LTSP), where he has taught since 1953. He has directed the seminary choir, at times in the performance of his own compositions. His edition of *5 Hymns from the Hymn Book of Magister Johannes Kelpius* was published in 1976 (Philadelphia: Fortress). He has also taught Hebrew Scriptures at LaSalle University, Philadelphia.

DANIEL J. HARRINGTON, S.J., is Professor of New Testament at Weston School of Theology, Cambridge, Massachusetts, and editor of *New Testament Abstracts*. He is the author of *God's People in Christ: New Testament Perspectives on the Church and Judaism*, Overtures to Biblical Theology (Philadelphia: Fortress, 1980), among other books.

ROBERT G. HUGHES is St. John Professor of Practical Theology (Homiletics) at LTSP and is founder and director of the Academy of Preachers. He has published *A Trumpet in Darkness: Preaching to Mourners*, Fortress Resources for Preaching (Philadelphia: Fortress, 1985). In 1991 he became the tenth President of LTSP.

MARGARET A. KRYCH is Professor of Christian Education and also teaches systematic theology at LTSP. Her book *Teaching the Gospel Today: A Guide for Education in the Congregation* was published in 1987 (Minneapolis: Augsburg).

ROBERT KYSAR has been Adjunct Professor in New Testament at LTSP and, with his wife, Myrna, pastor at Upper Dublin Lutheran Church near Philadelphia. Among his published works are *John* and *I, II, III John* in the Augsburg Commentary on the New Testament series (Minneapolis: Augsburg, 1985 and 1986, respectively). In 1991 he was elected Professor of Homiletics and New Testament at LTSP.

ULRICH MAUSER has been a dean at Pittsburgh Theological Seminary and is editor of *Horizons in Biblical Theology* as well an editor of the

*Jahrbuch für Biblische Theologie.* In September 1990 he became Professor of New Testament at Princeton Theological Seminary.

JOHN REUMANN, Ministerium of Pennsylvania Professor, New Testament and Greek, has taught at LTSP since 1950. His most recent book is *Variety and Unity in New Testament Thought* (New York: Oxford University Press, 1991).

ROBERT B. ROBINSON has taught at the University of Missouri and in 1989 became Associate Professor of Old Testament and Hebrew at LTSP. His study, *Roman Catholic Exegesis since* Divino Afflante Spiritu: *Hermeneutical Implications,* appeared in the Society of Biblical Literature Dissertation Series 111 (Atlanta: Scholars Press, 1988). He is co-chair of the seminar on "Theological Implications of Biblical Hermeneutics" in the Catholic Biblical Association.

JAMES A. SANDERS is Professor of Intertestamental and Biblical Studies at the School of Theology, Claremont, California, where he also founded and directs the Ancient Biblical Manuscript Center for Preservation and Research. His published works include *Torah and Canon* and *Canon and Community,* Guides to Biblical Scholarship (Philadelphia: Fortress, 1972 and 1984, respectively).

GEORG STRECKER has been Professor of New Testament at the Georg-August-University, Göttingen, Germany, since 1968. He has been visiting professor in the United States, South Africa, Australia, and Korea. His extensive publications have especially dealt with Matthew and the Sermon on the Mount, the Johannine epistles, and the Pseudo-clementine literature. He edits the series Göttinger Theologische Arbeiten.

PHYLLIS TRIBLE is Baldwin Professor of Sacred Literature (Old Testament) at Union Theological Seminary, New York, where she has taught since 1979. Among her published works are two in the Fortress Press Overtures to Biblical Theology series, namely, *God and the Rhetoric of Sexuality* (1978) and *Texts of Terror* (1984); and "Genesis 22: the Sacrifice of Isaac," Gross Memorial Lecture, 1989 (Valparaiso, Ind.: Valparaiso University Press, 1990).

JOHN W. VANNORSDALL, widely known for his preaching, former dean of the chapel at Yale College, was President of LTSP from 1986 until his retirement in 1990. A collection of his sermons, *Dimly Burning Wicks: Reflections on the Gospel after a Time Away,* was published in 1982 by Fortress Press.

# Preface

Those who have little opportunity to read much of the current literature in biblical theology will be impressed by the lively ferment evident in this book of essays. It becomes clear that what is happening in biblical theology reflects the broader changes in the whole field of biblical studies. This book provides not only a window to these changes, but also a unique opportunity to explore the implications of new insights for the various aspects of the practice of ministry. The Lutheran Theological Seminary at Philadelphia is grateful to those who have made the book possible, and commends it to all who cherish the Holy Scriptures and find in them the Word of the Lord.

This book had its beginnings when the seminary committee planning the school's 125th anniversary asked the biblical faculty to develop a series of lectures on biblical theology for the spring semester of 1989. It was not an unusual request, because the theology of the Testaments has long been a part of the seminary's curriculum. Professors Robert Bornemann and John Reumann established a program of five guest lecturers, each with a different approach and most working at the current frontiers in biblical studies. Each presentation was well received by the seminary community and numerous visitors. The lively discussions that arose from these lectures prompted their organizers to seek publication of the texts of the lectures. We are grateful to the lecturers, for they granted permission to be published, and their work constitutes Part One of this book.

At the suggestion of Drs. John A. Hollar and Marshall D. Johnson of Fortress Press, we invited faculty members, especially of the practical area, at the Lutheran Seminary at Philadelphia to prepare essays that draw from the original lectures the implications for the daily work of the parish pastor. Their assignment was to show how biblical theology, as this discipline is variously understood, finds application in the practice of ministry. Their work forms Part Two of this book.

We are thus also grateful to those faculty members who have prepared materials specifically for this book, and offer special thanks to Dr. Reumann, who gracefully importuned us until he received the manuscripts. Ms. Laurie E. Pellman, Coordinator/Secretarial Services, and Ms. Leslie Weisser reworked some manuscripts on the word processor. The publishers have patiently provided the extensions of deadlines by which both students and professors cope with the flight of time.

Thanks to the seminary's John C. and Kathryne M. Fisher Lectureship endowment, similar lecture series are regularly presented on the campus and are made available to parish pastors, college and university religion departments, and to interested people in the congregations. One such series, *Reading and Preaching the Book of Isaiah,* edited by Christopher R. Seitz, was published by Fortress Press in 1988. Other series are available on videotape through the Krauth Memorial Library of the seminary, still others through the Select program at Trinity Lutheran Seminary, Columbus, OH 43209. Among the more recent series are "Where Are We Ecumenically Today?" (1985), "Spotlight on Systematic Theology and Ethics" (1986), "A Year of Remembering" (Anglican, Lutheran, African Methodist Episcopal, and Russian Orthodox Legacies, 1987), and "Ministry: Where Theology and Human Sciences Meet" (1988). There were also lectures on Mark in 1985 and on Romans in 1987.

We are pleased to add this book to our growing list and hope that it will serve its readers well.

*John W. Vannorsdall*

JOHN REUMANN

# Introduction
## Whither Biblical Theology?

The questions have been asked many times and in varied ways over
the years: What is "biblical theology"? Is a biblical theology possible?
How shall its promise be realized? Is there a future for this discipline-in-
process-of-definition, which has had so many ups and downs?

There were times in the 1950s and early 1960s when people spoke of
biblical theology as the Cinderella of theological studies and as a beacon
for ecumenical advance, especially in the form of *Heilsgeschichte* (salvation history) or in the theology of the Second Vatican Council, as
*mysterium salutis*. But again and again the claims of its practitioners, for
example, members of the American "biblical theology movement" of the
1950s, were reduced to cinders and ashes. Terms such as crisis, demise,
and rebirth figured in descriptions of this confused and changing scene.
Each time the death certificate for biblical theology has been displayed,
signs of new life have appeared. Like the ancient, legendary phoenix or
like a Transylvanian vampire—depending on one's perspective—biblical
theology rises again.

For the last decade or so biblical theology, especially in the forms in
which it had been known in the past, has been in eclipse. Yet harbingers of
revival or metamorphosis again exist. Voices that describe varied trends
that may affect biblical theology are found in Part One of this book.
Ways in which biblical theology could relate to practical theology in the
life and work of individual Christians, parishes, preachers, liturgy and
lectionary, and education, as well as in relation to systematic theology and
pastoral care, are described in Part Two. This approach, in Part Two, to
the practice of biblical theology does not wish to waive the academic and
scholarly considerations; it simply concentrates on aspects often intended

1

but never fully delivered in many previous incarnations of the discipline. Promise and praxis ought to relate, practically!

## AN OLD DISCIPLINE

The emergence of biblical theology as a distinct discipline is usually traced to the year 1787 when Johann Philipp Gabler gave an inaugural address in Latin as he assumed the chair in theology at the University of Altdorf, some 12 miles southeast of Nürnberg, Germany. The world then took little notice of Gabler's claim that "biblical theology" should mediate between "biblical religion" and "dogmatic theology" by providing a systematic description of biblical religion. The result would be that the pure, unchanging concepts of this biblical theology that Gabler was confident could be articulated might inform how dogmaticians philosophize, with their contemporary restatements for each age. In time the university moved from Altdorf to Erlangen-Nürnberg, and the buildings in Altdorf became a school and clinic. But Gabler's proposals, which in those revolutionary days reflected and challenged Protestant Orthodoxy's dogmas, Pietism's fervor for the Bible, and Rationalism's efforts to distinguish "word of God" from "words of Scripture" (as J. S. Semler put it), set in motion problems that are still debated.

Rudolf Bultmann traced the term "biblical theology" further back, to a 1708 book entitled *Biblische Theologie,* in which Pietism sought to sever scriptural teachings from dogmatics.[1] Others hailed Luther and the Reformers, or Joachim of Flora around C.E. 1200, or Origen in the third century as "biblical theologians" (each in his own way). In any case, biblical theology is at least two hundred years old, based on the date of Gabler's essay, and has thus recently marked a largely unnoticed bicentennial. As a discipline situated between the religions of Israel and early Christianity, on the one hand, and systematic theology, on the other (so Gabler), or as a subdivision within the study of the Hebrew Scriptures and Christian origins, it is far older than source criticism (especially for the Gospels and J, E, P, and D), *Formgeschichte,* or redaction criticism. It is not surprising that biblical theology has had a complex history and many definitions.

It is not necessary here to trace again this history of biblical theology. Phyllis Trible sketches Old Testament aspects of biblical theology from Gabler through its nineteenth-century flowering, then "40 years of wilderness wanderings (1880–1920)," Eichrodt and von Rad as *'aleph* and *taw* of the movement, and subsequent influences (chap. 2). Ulrich Mauser notes some New Testament aspects, from Gabler through Ernst Troeltsch and the movement in the 1950s (chap. 5). Other excellent accounts exist, including such brief ones as that for the Old Testament by Coats, and those for the New Testament by Fuller, Boers, Donahue, Bultmann, and Goppelt; as well as more detailed ones for each Testament (Old Testament: Hasel, Hayes and Prussner, Reventlow, Zimmerli; New Testament: Neill, Schnackenburg, Hasel, Morgan, Strecker, Merk) and for the entire Bible (O. Betz, Stendahl, Smart, Childs, Reventlow, Strecker, Morgan and Barton, Kraus, Birch and Harrington).[2]

Notwithstanding all these accounts (or perhaps because of them), conflicting views exist even over how to classify types of approach or to decide whether the discipline was flourishing or in decline during a specific period. For example, Gerhard Hasel, who has for some two decades reported on trends in biblical theology, has listed some nine approaches to the Old Testament, but only four for the New,[3] and these are often difficult to align with each other. The chart below represents Hasel's list, with arrows added to suggest connections.[4]

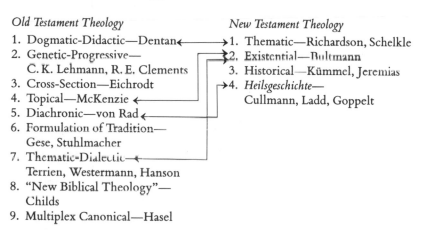

*Old Testament Theology*
1. Dogmatic-Didactic—Dentan
2. Genetic-Progressive—
   C. K. Lehmann, R. E. Clements
3. Cross-Section—Eichrodt
4. Topical—McKenzie
5. Diachronic—von Rad
6. Formulation of Tradition—
   Gese, Stuhlmacher
7. Thematic-Dialectic—
   Terrien, Westermann, Hanson
8. "New Biblical Theology"—
   Childs
9. Multiplex Canonical—Hasel

*New Testament Theology*
1. Thematic—Richardson, Schelkle
2. Existential—Bultmann
3. Historical—Kümmel, Jeremias
4. *Heilsgeschichte*—
   Cullmann, Ladd, Goppelt

The chart implies that scholars of the Hebrew Scriptures have been twice as innovative methodologically as their New Testament colleagues. Is this true? Or does the larger amount of material in the Old Testament necessarily bring about a more varied methodology? Is Hasel himself more familiar with the Old Testament? An update of the New Testament list would add the approach of Peter Stuhlmacher and others, one that reflects the "formulation of tradition" or *traditionsgeschichtlich* approach. Which Old Testament approaches correspond to what Hasel termed the historical approach in the New? (Perhaps all of them!) Cannot "diachronic" describe some New Testament approaches? Cannot *"Heilsgeschichte"* refer to von Rad's approach? To Hasel's list of four approaches to the New Testament (all exemplified by Protestant scholars), Donahue[5] has added that of the Roman Catholic systematician Edward Schillebeeckx. This addition raises the question of an entire dogmatic tradition uncatalogued by Hasel which has increasingly treated Jesus and Christology in a responsibly exegetical, biblical-theological manner, as evidenced in the works of Walter Kasper and the Latin American liberation theologians Juan Luis Segundo and Jon Sobrino, among others.[6]

Regarding eras within the history of biblical theology, the period of Protestant liberalism (1880–1920) can rightly be called a wilderness sojourn (Trible). Nevertheless, textbooks for courses on Old and New Testament theology continued to appear in Europe and America in those decades.[7] Although many have written about the death of biblical theology in the late 1960s, others refer to a "third wave" that came in the 1970s, following the "golden age" of the 1950s and the halcyon days of Eichrodt and von Rad and the debates of the 1920s and 1930s.[8] In contrast to the bleak picture that Smart or Childs painted of the 1970s, Hasel[9] could cite the decade from 1967 to 1976 as a high point in the publication of Old Testament theologies. One may therefore say that, except in the case of a particular, American variety, "biblical theology never really fell into crisis but has continued in fairly full productivity on the continent, in the Roman Catholic world, and in the developing countries, if not in the United States."[10] Indeed, Houlden sees biblical theology's influence in the Second Vatican Council, in lectionary reform after the Council, and in ecumenical dialogues such as that of the Anglican–Roman Catholic International Commission as signs of its vitality.[11]

The swirling scene for biblical theology is so kaleidoscopic that chroniclers can honestly disagree over past trends, recent history, and predictions of what will ensue. When, however, one considers the history of the discipline as a whole and the last four decades in particular, several observations stand out.

1. By and large, scholars dealing with the *Old Testament* have customarily made *syntheses* of the huge and diverse materials in the Hebrew Scriptures, often organizing everything around a master theme such as "covenant" (Eichrodt) or the development of Israel's traditions about salvation, law, and other themes (von Rad) or more recently around the two poles of blessing and deliverance (Westermann), the aesthetic and the ethical (Terrien), the cosmic and the teleological vectors (Han-

son), the legitimation of social institutions and the embracing of pain (Brueggemann).[12] It is difficult, however, to find one book that treats the theology of the Yahwist, then those of the Deuteronomist school, the Priestly Writer(s), and "Zion theology"—let alone the possible theologies of the Elohist, Isaiah of Babylon, wisdom literature, and the apocalyptists—separately between two covers.

*New Testament* scholars, on the other hand, have tended to give us chapters on the *separate theologies* of Paul and of John (Bultmann), perhaps those of Matthew, Luke-Acts, and Hebrews (Stevens, Conzelmann, Morris) in a volume called "New Testament Theology" (singular), but never a synthesis of any sort (except for such writers as Stauffer and Richardson).[13] Why is there such disparity in organizing "the theology" of each Testament? Is Old Testament theology conceived to be more sharply in contrast to Old Testament religion and history than New Testament theology is to early Christian history and varieties of religion?

2. *Theologies of the entire Bible are rare* and can be counted on two hands. One thinks of Burrows, Vos, and Lehmann (but chiefly as collectors of data on a series of topics, topics often drawn from later theology or concerns) and of Dentan for lay people. Blenkinsopp's *Sketchbook,* Cordero in Spanish, or McCurley and Reumann also come to mind.[14] Terrien's *Elusive Presence* stands out as a singular case in which an Old Testament scholar has also taken up the New. But these examples are rare and not likely to grow more plentiful.

3. *Jesus* stands out as an issue of great magnitude in methodology. Is he to be treated as one of the key theologians of the New Testament (Kümmel), even as the revelation to which what follows is, though apostolic, but a response (Jeremias, Goppelt)? Or do we know so little about the historical Jesus that he remains within Judaism as but one of the "presuppositions for the theology of the New Testament rather than a part of that theology itself"?[15]

4. For Christians working on *Old Testament theology*—so far a basically Christian discipline, although some see no reason why Jews or persons of other religious traditions or of no faith conviction cannot engage in the undertaking (and sometimes have)[16]—the problem has been *linkage to the New Testament.* This issue can be posed in christological terms as the issue or the problem of "Israel and the church."[17]

For those doing *New Testament theology*—again almost always Christians of one sort or another—the problem has been not so much "Jesus and the church," for it is now recognized that our New Testament documents all bear the stamp of church communities, even if Jesus never spoke of an ongoing *ekklēsia.* The problem has been the New Testament and the sequel in *the patristic church;* how do the communities depicted in the biblical books emerge into the catholic church? This involves not only debate about "early (and later) catholicism" or the tendency to read the New Testament in light of patristic "norms," especially regarding ministry and sacraments (Richardson), but, above all now, the questions raised by *feminist theology* about (re)patriarchalization of the Jesus movement in the church.[18]

5. Finally, it is obvious that biblical theology has from its beginnings been *affected by currents in church life, theology generally, and academic trends.* This was true in Gabler's day, regarding views he opposed and in his own assumption that, consistent with the Enlightenment, biblical theology could present "certain and universal ideas" that will be "appropriate to the Christian religion for all times."[19] Likewise with influences from Protestant liberalism, neoorthodoxy, liberation or black theology, and a host of other trends in our day. The attempt to objectify biblical theology into "what it meant" in contrast to "what it means"[20] has more and more been criticized. But the hazard remains that biblical theology may be subservient to and led about by present-day concerns and currents.

In light of this past history one cannot be sanguine in forecasting what will come next in biblical theology; there have been too many surprises. Reginald H. Fuller speaks of how "Wrede tried to kill the discipline" ninety years ago and how James M. Robinson in 1974 "exalted over its impending demise as a historical discipline," although Robinson went on to speak of the future for New Testament theology as lying in extensions of its (anthropological) language, "in terms of sociology," " 'theologically,' 'ontologically,' 'cosmologically,' 'politically.' "[21] Fuller himself sees "other possibilities" in Roman Catholicism and "churchly oriented Protestantism" and notes also Robert Funk's hope that "departments of religion in secular universities" might pursue "the claim of Christianity as part of the religious past of humanity" and hence of American humanism.[22] Such proposals can be seen in Ulrich Mauser's modest venture: "Biblical theology has a chance again today" (chap. 5).

## NEW METHODS ON THE "CUTTING EDGE"

All five chapters in Part One below reflect the current situation, as seen by each essayist, within some aspect of contemporary biblical studies. Whether dealing with the historical Jesus, source and redaction criticism, biblical theology itself, or new emphases such as feminist hermeneutics, the impact of Judaism on the New Testament, or canonical criticism, everything in Part One reflects some of the change that is claimed to be taking place in biblical studies. As Peter Macky has put it, "we are moving from the *historical* era to the *literary* era in biblical studies." This he calls "a paradigm shift," which presages "the coming revolution."[23]

During the Reformation and the Enlightenment there was movement from a philosophical-theological approach to an increasingly historical one. The shift now, it is claimed, is a move away from historical criticism to a new and quite expansive literary approach. The shift is attributed in part to a host of new techniques, often developed in general literary studies and then applied to the Bible, such as narrative criticism, rhetorical approaches, structuralism, and emphases on social setting and sociological explanations of phenomena. The new mood also arises from a certain satiety with historical criticism and its alleged inability to provide a consensus regarding results and useful findings. This stance also coincides with new emphases on "story" in theology and the kind of canonical criticism that stresses each finished book in the Bible in its "intertextuality" with all others in the agreed collection or canon (Childs). Those in a "Catholic tradition" can take delight in the way the church's decisions on canon and authority are thus recognized; Conservative Evangelicals can delight in the emphasis on the final text and not on putative sources or earlier oral traditions, the text having authority and indeed a life of its own.

Such a shift from "history" to "literary narrative" needs to be pondered. Many trained in biblical studies over the last thirty years will find themselves in a strange new world, with old landmarks missing and different markers or clues to meaning exalted. For the present, in seminaries and graduate schools, through popular paperbacks on religion or treatments for Sunday church schools, most students of Scripture and casual readers are still getting both the historical and literary emphases. But in time the former emphasis may recede, the latter take over. Macky suggests the result will be that "we will see history as preliminary."[24] That will surely reverse the biblical theology of the 1950s, at least the American brand, about "the God who acts in history."[25] History is not then "His story"; God is instead to be discerned in the yarns of storytellers. For ecumenism this change could mean the need to overcome past differences other than by careful examination of texts historically. The result of such methods, long in use, is that nineteenth-, sixteenth-, or first-century problems have often been interpreted differently and old impasses transcended historically. Indeed, the nature of doctrine itself would be differently viewed under the impact of, among other things, language analysis and world religions with their stories.[26] As reader and audience interpretation grow (at the expense of emphasizing the author's intent), the way is clear for seeing multivalent meanings in texts, a variety of levels of meaning that are open to the concerns of today's interpreters. Or is this a new kind of "wax nose," like the one Luther protested the allegorists imposed on Scripture, in order to twist it in any direction they desired, like silly putty?

That is to paint the scene quite broadly, perhaps lumping too much together. But the literary approach is broad. The simple fact is that many Jews, Christians, and others, steeped in traditional methods or trained along nineteenth-century lines of the interpretation of history as "what really happened"—a mood dominant in biblical studies until recently— are now confronted by a new world of narrative and literary approaches alongside of or in the stead of history. The outcome is not yet clear, but all these developments are hailed as a major change. That shift lies not far from the awareness of most who write in the chapters of Part One below.

Given such changing currents in scriptural scholarship, what are some of the future possibilities for biblical theology? It is necessary, first of all, to hear the view that there is or should be *no such thing as "biblical theology,"* for it represents a dogmatic intrusion into scientific study of the literature of Israel and early Christianity and is an impossible construct from later theologies.

The essay by Georg Strecker, on the Sermon on the Mount as law (chap. 1), reflects the view of one who is critical of the concept of biblical theology. Professor Strecker's presentation had been arranged as part of his North American lecture tour before the biblical theology series at the Philadelphia Seminary took shape. In dealing with Jesus' own critical view of the Old Testament law, the loyalty to the law of Jewish Christianity (as in the Q document and community), and then Matthew's strengthening of "the ethical lines of interpretation of the Old Testament-Jewish law," Dr. Strecker exhibits how complex New Testament positions are on just one issue (law) from one segment (Matthew 5–7) of the literature. He also shows how far all this is from the later law-gospel contrasts and how Matthew is closer to the theology of James than to that of Paul. Yet, to use Strecker's closing metaphor, the contribution of Matthew's voice can "release its full sound" only in "the multivoiced choir of New Testament writers," including Paul and John.

For his lecture in Philadelphia on April 11, 1989, Strecker added brief comments (not included below) about his critique against biblical theology. He attributes the lack of discussion on the topic in recent generations of New Testament scholars to the facts that a supposedly unified content of the two Testaments had become suspect to historical interpretation, as had "the integrity of the biblical canon," and that the "identity of biblical teachings and dogmatics" was long since abandoned. Although one may wrestle with similar problems and related contents in both the Hebrew Scriptures and the Greek New Testament, the attempt to legitimate "the unity of the canon" as an exegetical principle is a "step backwards." Strecker levels such criticisms especially at the efforts of a "New Tübingen School" (H. Gese, P. Stuhlmacher) to establish a biblical theology based on the developing traditions in the Hebrew Scriptures, Judaism, and the New Testament.[27] For Stuhlmacher this means, above all, the theme of "reconciliation," arising from Jesus and central in Paul, and a hermeneutic of "hearing" the text (*Vernehmen;* cf. Schlatter's "perception," *Wahrnehmen*) and then "agreement" (*Einverständnis*) with the text.[28]

Strecker has criticized three elements of this program. The first is that these scholars relate Old and New Testament through an eschatological "Zion torah" at the expense of the Sinai torah; moreover, they fail to recognize that the New Testament use of the Old is often not a matter of employing the Hebrew (Massoretic) text but rather the Greek Old Testament (Septuagint), a translation that Paul, for example, interpreted christologically and soteriologically. The second is that the history-of-religions background for New Testament language and concepts is too easily adapted to Old Testament and Judaism, to the neglect of the Greco-Roman world into which Christianity so soon entered and which, indeed, permeated much of Palestinian Judaism. The third is, hermeneutically, a deficit in the program's "agreement" with the text, because the program emphasizes *documents* of the past (in the manner of Schlatter and Barth) at the expense of the "Christ *event*" and its anthropological perspective (Bultmann)—applied not "individualistically" but for interpreters in their human situations today.

A similarly negative judgment on biblical theology can be found in other writers, for example, James Barr. The U.S. movement of the 1950s and 1960s went into decline and "now belongs to the past history of biblical studies," he has written, although useful elements survive "in the world of Roman Catholic theology" where "its emphases may be more needed."[29] He allows that individual studies, notably in Germany, in a more narrow sense of biblical theology, have often transcended such convolutions. Barr continues to level arguments against biblical theology as a discipline, now in the name of systematic theology:[30] the old biblical theology was too allied with neoorthodoxy as a kind of "sophisticated fundamentalism"; theology should have God, not the Bible, as its horizon; its "material" is wider than just Scripture; the danger is a retreat from the modern world into "a biblical myth."

Of all recently emerging approaches to Scripture, *feminist theology* has probably generated the largest and most significant bibliography, especially if considered as a type of liberation theology. The lecture given in the Philadelphia series by Phyllis Trible of Union Theological Seminary, New York, was a case study on Miriam in biblical theology. It was subsequently published in the *Bible Review,* and its methods and findings provoked vehement responses from readers.[31] Listeners perceived her lecture at the Philadelphia Seminary as a positive example of both narrative and feminist theology, an example that will be more fully developed in a forthcoming book.

For the present volume (chap. 2) Dr. Trible contributed a more programmatic essay on feminist hermeneutics and biblical theology, which she deemed particularly pertinent. It appeared in earlier form in an issue on biblical studies of the Jesuit journal *Theological Studies* (50:279–95) for its fiftieth anniversary in 1989. (In 1939, she remarked, "feminist hermeneutics was an unrecognized subject" among Catholics—and elsewhere.) In interrelating "waves of feminism" and history of biblical theology, she deals with both methodology and actual exegesis (including work on Miriam) and contours and content of feminist biblical theology sure to come. For those made nervous by such developments, it is to be noted that Dr. Trible, while aware of "androcentric bias" in both scholarship and Scripture, belongs not to the feminist position that would jettison or despair of the Bible but among those who "insist that text and interpreters provide more excellent ways" (56, 58).

As noted above, *Jewish backgrounds* to the New Testament, Judaism as a living religion then in process of development, Judaism as a link between the Hebrew Scriptures (and their Greek versions) and the Christian church, and modern Christian-Jewish conversation all unite to provide another significant avenue of interpretation which any biblical theology must take into consideration. Daniel J. Harrington, S.J., in a compact survey (chap. 3) treats Judaism as context for Jesus, his teachings, life, death, and resurrection, not to mention such issues as covenant(s), types of Christology, and modern realities, including the Holocaust. One again encounters liberation theology (to which Jewish reaction is usually negative) and the suggestion of Jesus' "Jewishness" as "a way forward in Christology."

The bibliography in Father Harrington's notes gives a balanced picture of much recent work. While it may appear that analyses of the historical-Jesus question and of Paul have moved increasingly into the

Jewish realm, it must be added that "early Judaism research is in a state of flux" and that studies about this topic, including those by Jewish form critics, feminists, and even "(biblical) theologians" show the influence of many of the same trends noted above for biblical studies by Christians. But even attempts to retrieve systematically the Jewishness of Jesus for the church do not always commend themselves to experts in the field as adequate understandings of first-century C.E. Judaism.[32]

The essay on canon (chap. 4) by James A. Sanders of the School of Theology at Claremont, California, follows up on his approach over the last two decades to canon as "shape" (*norma normata,* the norm that is normed by something else) and canon as "function" (*norma normans,* the norm that serves as norm). Here he recounts autobiographically his move from working on canon as function (in terms of the process whereby the books developed) to texts and versions and the varied context of books in these, that is, the "shape" of the canon. As hermeneutic for the canon in communities of believers, Jewish or Christian, Dr. Sanders stresses the principle of "theocentric monotheizing pluralism." A series of examples from both Testaments suggest how what were originally polytheizing passages came to be (rightly) monotheized. Not all listeners agreed when he argued that in the New Testament "the canon's monotheizing thrust" should be used to speak of "*God's* Christ" and to lower the christological profile of John 14:6 ("No one comes to the Father, but by me") or Acts 4:12 ("no other name ... by which we must be saved"). This is to opt for Jeremiah or "Luke's Jesus" as canon within the canon for discerning how such verses are to function.

"*Canonical criticism*" has, unfortunately, come to be used as a blanket term for what both James A. Sanders and Brevard Childs,[33] among others, are doing in biblical theology. Childs has claimed that Sanders invented the term, but Childs now disclaims involvement in it.[34] The phrase has varied meanings, and more will be said below about Childs's approach to the importance and the role of canon.

The most difficult assignment in the lecture series at the Philadelphia Seminary may have been that chosen by Ulrich Mauser, dean at Pittsburgh Theological Seminary, on the *future of biblical theology.* As editor of *Horizons in Biblical Theology* and co-editor of the *Jahrbuch für Biblische Theologie,* he has committed himself to the unity of Scripture, knowing full well the disputed heritage of the discipline. His lecture (chap. 5) focused on the role of critical history in past biblical interpretation and asked whether "the domain of history" is "the liberator or the foe of biblical theology." The principles of Ernst Troeltsch (1865–1923) about historical research argued that the historian must be detached from the documents he or she treats, must establish truth or falsity by analogy to our modern experience, and must correlate or interconnect events so that no point in time is not "conditioned by its antecedents" (via cause and effect). Such a position is close to the Greek view of history as "inquiry," not the biblical view of God's word and work. What is said of the Hebrew phrase *dĕbar YHWH,* e.g., the word of the Lord, is more briefly carried over by Prof. Mauser into New Testament narrative and witness about God's Word, in Jesus.

Has this essay brought us full cycle, so that the future of biblical theology must of necessity embrace some features of past endeavors, and "history" for the Bible involves the word and reality of God? Before feeling a sense of *déjà vu,* one should ask not only about the nature of Scripture and whether what criticism finds *behind* texts is what matters, but also to what extent some of the new trends in criticism, favoring literary aspects instead of history, do not reshape Troeltsch's axioms. The judgments in criticism are no longer made solely by white North Atlantic males, nor are "our experiences" and the interconnection of events seen any longer exclusively from such vantage points; they are now "under new management." The new potential players for biblical theology operate—some will say, alas—with different vistas and agendas. So much so that "the threat of contextualisms" has prompted Robin Scroggs to ask, "Can New Testament Theology Be Saved?"[35]

## SORTING OUT POSSIBLE APPROACHES

The number of attempts made over the years to link the thought of the two Testaments is large. Such attempts began long before biblical theology emerged as a distinct discipline and involve proposals only now emerging for the future. They include the following:

1. *New Testament use of Old Testament Scriptures* was noted in the approach by Gese and Stuhlmacher and in Strecker's critique of it. No one would propose Matthew's development of "formula quotations" or Paul's application of the Septuagint as "what was written for our admonition" as the way to do exegesis today. But one can gain insight, by studying such usages, into how early Christians read the map of God's past dealings with Israel and humankind, in light of their experiences in Christ and future hope. Out of an immense amount of data, as to which Old Testament books or sections thereof were favored, textual history in Hebrew and Greek, and Greek-rabbinic rules (usually quite logical) for interpreting, scholars have spoken of such activity as "the substruc-

ture of New Testament theology" (Dodd), a part of Christian apologetic (Lindars), or as the constitutive rock whence Christianity was hewn, giving continuity and authority to the new movement.[36] It continues as an influence in the theme of "prophecy and fulfillment."

2. *Allegory* was adopted from the Greeks into Judaism (compare the commentaries by Philo of Alexandria) and occasionally from both into the New Testament (for example, Gal. 4:21-31). It mushroomed in the writings of the church fathers. Allegory was normative for centuries. Even the Renaissance, Reformation, and Enlightenment did not fully root out the much-beloved "spiritual sense." It is still found in some traditional lectionary combinations of lessons and in liturgy as "extended," "theological" meaning but is rejected by historical-critical analysis.[37]

3. *Typology* has had an equally long history. The term occurs at times in Paul (1 Cor. 10:6; Rom. 5:14) and elsewhere (1 Pet. 3:21; Heb. 9:24, "antitype"). It has received considerable modern attention and approval (von Rad, Goppelt).[38] Even earlier, patterns or types can be said to occur in the Hebrew Scriptures (return from the exile as a "new exodus" or new creation). In ancient and modern forms, typology has served Christology and salvation history by seeing correspondences between persons, events, and institutions in one Testament and then in the other, for example, great David's greater son; the serpent lifted up in the wilderness and the cross of the Son of Man; the sabbath rest (Gen. 2:2; Hebrews 4). In service of the gospel, it expresses God's economy or plan, all the while (in the minds of its champions) preserving the historicity of type and corresponding or contrasting antitype. A certain continuation and periodic upsurges of typology have occurred, especially in Anglicanism and Roman Catholic circles (under patristic influence), in the hermeneutics of *Heilsgeschichte* (compare some volumes in the *Biblischer Kommentar* series), and elsewhere. Conservative evangelicals often embrace allegory, consciously or unconsciously.

4. The *Sensus Plenior* or notion of a "fuller sense" implies a meaning to words in the Bible which is more than literal and goes beyond the mind of the author. This meaning, however, was what God intended, and interpreters subsequently discover it.[39] This concept, apparently coined in 1925, leaped into prominence in Roman Catholic circles in the 1950s, as the Catholic biblical movement sought to relate emerging use of critical study with traditional interpretations. Criteria were developed, but basically the fuller sense depended on a later, further revelation (so that Matt. 1:23, about the virgin birth, interpreted Isa. 7:14). Opinions varied as to whether this further insight could come about through the later authority of the post–New Testament church's magisterium. By and large

the Second Vatican Council opted for a more historical view of revelation and the mystery of salvation. Some think *sensus plenior* will be but a footnote in future histories of hermeneutics.

5. *Lectionaries* have been used week in and week out for centuries as a widespread method of relating scriptural texts from different parts of the Bible, often from the two Testaments, and that most frequently within the framework of a church-year calendar. Such orderly sequences of reading in the Bible for edification and as the basis for preaching and worship go back, of course, in some instances to the patristic centuries when pericopes emerged for use on Sundays and festivals. In the West, Roman Catholics, Lutherans, and Anglicans for years shared a similar system. The *Ordo Lectionum* worked out by Roman Catholics after Vatican II and adapted in North America and elsewhere by many Protestant churches introduced a three-year cycle consisting of first lesson (usually Old Testament) in relation to a Gospel passage for the day, and Epistle sequences read in a semicontinuous way. The hermeneutic here clearly makes the Hebrew Scriptures subservient to the four Gospels. But even among those who make no use of lectionaries, a Free Church pastor, by choosing two or three readings for Christmas or Easter, is creating an intertextual relationship along thematic lines. In one way or another the appointed (or self-chosen) readings of Scripture at worship set the pattern for biblical theology which is sometimes good, sometimes bad.[40]

6. *Word study* methods and *Bible dictionaries* have become a pervasive modern form of biblical theology. The great influence of the Kittel *Theological Dictionary of the New Testament* (1933–79) can scarcely be underestimated.[41] Its originally *heilsgeschichtlich* orientation (from Adolf Schlatter), the debate about anti-Semitism especially in some Kittel articles written in the 1930s, and the strictures by James Barr against the word study method are well known.[42] But Kittel and a host of imitators and successors[43] have in their own way determined how in many cases biblical concepts, relations between and among literary segments of the Bible, and interthematic connections are understood. Sometimes the word study method is equated with biblical theology: it is indeed the theology of the Bible!

7. The *topical approach* has long been popular and often useful. In the case of Melanchthon's *Loci communes* (1521), Calvin's *Institutes of the Christian Religion* (1539), and Protestant Orthodoxy's "proof texts" (*dicta probantia*,[44] scriptural passages were assembled in relation to the topics (*loci*) of systematic theology. Pietism and nineteenth-century biblical theology created their own more scriptural topics, often in order to oppose those of dogmatics in the name of the Bible. Millar Burrows in 1946

arranged verses and thoughts from both Testaments under 110 headings, some traditional, some reflective of liberal Protestant social ethical concerns, for use in Christian education as well as preaching.[45] Stauffer found the motifs of "the doxological," "the antagonistic," and soteriology convenient for assessing themes in New Testament theology.[46] Dentan, McKenzie, Bonsirven, and Richardson offer further examples.[47] At times the thematic approach has been attempted on more limited topics, for example, in monographs on the "wilderness" theme in Scripture or "God's glory."[48]

8. The *chronological* or, in more recent times, the *tradition-historical* approach is perhaps the most widely followed method for doing biblical theology in textbooks. Theologies of various biblical writers and schools are laid out in roughly the order in which they emerged. At times this historically sequential process has become identical with a history of Israel's religion.[49] Von Rad represents the history-of-traditions ("diachronic") school. Examples for the New Testament are as different as Stevens, Bultmann, and Conzelmann.[50] "Trajectories" has become a favored, if ambiguous, term in New Testament theology.[51] There is a sense in which all approaches reflect, at least in tracing individual themes or "the history of salvation," a chronological scheme of movement from early to later developments. The opposite would be a flatly level canon from within which material from the earliest strata might be cited, without context, in the same breath with much later authors, and responses to earlier positions in the Bible, adaptations of them, or advances in thought scarcely noted.

9. It is possible to make a case for *creedal approaches* to Israel's faith or to the gospel of early Christianity. The confessions found in the Bible itself, not the creeds of patristic or later times, structure such a theology. In some ways von Rad's use of Deut. 26:5-11 did exactly that, and other examples of "Israel's credo" can be cited.[52] Martin Albertz arranged the message of the New Testament around the themes and sequence of 2 Cor. 13:14 (the grace of our Lord Jesus Christ, the love of God, and the *koinōnia* of [participation in, fellowship brought about by] the Holy Spirit).[53] Cullmann, in *Christology*, and O. S. Barr and others trace the course of the "apostles' faith" into the Apostles' Creed.[54]

10. No list would be complete without reference to the widely practiced but often ill-defined concept of salvation history or *Heilsgeschichte*. Quite apart from attempts to find earlier examples, as in Luke-Acts or in Irenaeus's "(four) covenants theology," we must look to mid-nineteenth-century Germany, where the term characterized a distinct movement, the *Heilsgeschichte* School at Erlangen University, headed

by J. C. K. von Hofmann.[55] When Oscar Cullmann used the term in the 1950s, he claimed to be independent of this prior movement as he spelled out the key moments (*kairoi*) on God's time line or plan (*oikonomia*) of *Heil* (salvation) as significant history (*Geschichte*).[56] Many books, including the Kittel dictionary, reflect variations on such a view of biblical theology. If the test is to encompass both Old and New Testaments, salvation history meets the requirement in a way that topical, tradition-historical, and other methods at times do not.

11. *Canonical criticism* has already been noted above in connection with the work of J. A. Sanders (see also chap. 5, below) and others. Among these other exemplars, one of the most prolific writers is Brevard Childs, of Yale,[57] even though "Theology in a Canonical Context" might be a more accurate name for his enterprise. Main features in Childs's approach include: first, the canon is an authoritative "given" (it, and not a reconstructed Israelite religion or "Christian origins," is the arena of understanding). Second, any "canon within a canon" is rejected as the hermeneutical key, in favor of the whole Bible. Third, Old Testament theology is a Christian discipline, reflecting on one part of the canon but in relation to Christ, for it is testimony to the God of Israel in pre-Christian form. Fourth, New Testament theology explores the other part of the Christian canon. Finally, biblical theology is disciplined reflection on both parts of the canon, in dialogue with dogmatic theology. In all cases, what matters is first the final form of the biblical book, not supposed sources or earlier traditions; then books in their subcollections, like the Pauline corpus, within a testament; and finally all books and parts in their intertextual relationships. The result is "canonical construals" of data. This approach gives a more weighted vote to later decisionmakers (those who determined what went into the canon) in comparison with predecessor sources and traditions before a book's redactor went to work. There are ways in which church use of the Bible "intertextually" (in doctrine and the lectionary) is a corollary of this approach, so that those in a "Catholic" tradition can applaud it, for all of Childs's "early Protestant" emphasis on "the book" as text.

12. The emphasis by Childs on the finished books of the Bible relates in some ways to the *narrative approach*[58] to theology in recent criticism, noted above. Canonical criticism that puts less weight on the process of how a biblical book developed can make common cause with a literary approach that sees the finished product as a whole. The book becomes a mirror into which one looks, not a window through which one peers in order to glimpse prior events. The latter method seeks to go behind the book, the former to deal with the book and its impact. Narrative

approaches can, of course, be used to tell us what a book says about God, Christology, or the human situation. But other practitioners of the art present it as inimicable to traditional Christology, doctrine, and theology; instead the reader peruses plot, characters, and other features, and may (or may not) be drawn into a symbolical world of values which can impact on life today.

13. Current *sociological* interests and the *history of world religions (Religionsgeschichte)*[59] may produce future biblical "theologies" where societal factors and comparison with other religions shape what is said. Extant examples of articles and monographs on individual books of the Bible, biblical themes, or certain periods of biblical history are harbingers of a theology oriented to the "social world" or a theology of *Weltreligionsgeschichte*.

14. *Liberation* and *feminist theology*[60] are mentioned above as often interrelated approaches that in some forms regard the Scripture as still vital and meaningful, when interpreted in "more excellent ways." The amount of such writing that relates to biblical theologies is impressive, even if a biblical theology may perhaps never be written because of the advocacy role involved. In other words, for this approach, a biblical (or any other) theology is never "pure" or "simple" because it arises situationally out of the theologian's world on the margins of society or her experiences as one patriarchally oppressed.

*Liberation theology* has Latin American, African, and Asian varieties, as well as European and North American strands. The most impressive work has probably been accomplished by South and Central American authors, acting and reflecting, in local situations. They often have a Roman Catholic heritage, but are "church-critical," in the sense of a person's attitude toward existing structures. They also reflect much classical literature, philosophies, and traditional theology. Among the recurring themes in their work are the exodus; the historical Jesus (especially of Luke 4:16-21, with "liberty" understood sociopolitically, not as liberation from sins—an approach that voids the common understanding of Luke-Acts as an *apologia* to the Roman government); Christology; the poor and wealth; and egalitarianism. At times they have provided "materialist" (Marxist) readings of the biblical books, or historical reconstructions invoking archeology which stand Israelite history on its head, so that the crowning period was that of the popular revolt against Canaanite overlords (which conventionally we call "the conquest"), in contrast to the "fall" into monarchy under Kings Saul, David, and Solomon, who oppressed the people and destroyed the egalitarian society.[61]

Some inkling of the scope of feminist approaches to biblical theology has already been given. Elisabeth Schüssler Fiorenza's *In Memory of Her* is a landmark because it attempted in a pioneering way the hermeneutical reorientation, historical reconstruction of Christian origins (from the equality of women with men found in Jesus and Paul to a repatriarchalization of the Christian movement), and actual exegesis of passages, all in one book. Phyllis Trible retells mostly forgotten tales about women in Scripture; thereby an alternate "theology of a remnant" emerges.[62] Rosemary Ruether has broadly used the prophetic, liberating principle within the Bible to show how God vindicates the oppressed (women and others) and judges systems of power.[63]

It may be significant that the first 1989 issue of *Koinonia,* a new journal by seminary graduate students, was devoted to feminism and biblical theology.[64] In the "creative clash" now taking place, some of these students look for a hermeneutic and results to emerge out of a combination of "tradition" (the past), "experience," and "creative imagination." But the experience now involves, or at least includes as never before, the experiences of women, a long silenced majority in the church. Will there be, as one man suggests, a "perichoretic" construction (from the ancient christological idea of *perichōrēsis* or reciprocity or mutual inherence of the two natures of Christ) in this triadic combination? Or must there first be fuller assertion of how women see biblical theology?

15. Among all the new subdisciplines in the recent literary turn in biblical studies, John R. Donahue has purposed that *rhetorical criticism* "offers an important resource for NT theology."[65] The approach uses methods not simply from ancient rhetoricians (such as Augustine) but also from modern analysts of argumentation and emotional appeal (such as G. A. Kennedy). This method examines the "rhetorical situation" of a text and the writer's strategy. That leads to the "world in front of the text" and ultimately to a *theologica rhetorica.* Donahue suggests such rhetorical criticism "integrates literary criticism and social analysis," and he cites work by Schüssler Fiorenza and others moving in that direction.

16. *The history of exegesis or interpretation,* as a descriptive approach to biblical theology, describes how texts have been understood—a tradition history or trajectory, so to speak—since the passage or book was completed. Several dissertation series and independent monographs contribute to this approach.[66] Childs, among others, has shown great interest in it.[67] The patristic and rabbinic traditions reflect its course. It has been argued that church history is the history of how Scripture has been understood (or misunderstood) in the church.[68] The person doing biblical

theology who does not know the history of past interpretation may be doomed to repeat the mistakes of the past.

## ACADEMIA AND ECCLESIA

To focus, in Part Two of the essays that follow, on the promise of biblical theology in practical, day-in, day-out areas of the church's life is not to abandon biblical theology as an academic discipline. Its adherents, often in university faculties (Stevens, Burrows, von Rad, Bultmann), proceeded with utmost intellectual rigor in doing biblical theology. Some of the new approaches presented above can claim a place in the academic landscape of institutions with no connections at all to any church (or synagogue). One could make a strong case for developing descriptively a biblical theology in completely secular, pluralistic settings, as an account of what the Bible teaches (according to current scholarship), just as one might do a course on "what the Koran teaches" or on the "theology" of any other sacred book.

In the Christian community and curricula of its schools, especially seminaries, biblical theology has usually been taught as a course or segment of Old and New Testament offerings (the Hebrew Scriptures, Christian origins and literature). The Lutheran Theological Seminary at Philadelphia, committed to integrating biblical studies so that the student (or systematician or other teacher) is not left solely on his or her own to relate the findings (often atomistic) about the Hebrew Bible and the Greek New Testament, has experimented with a variety of ways to help bring these two parts of the Bible closer together. They have sometimes taught Old Testament thought or theology side by side with a similar course on the New Testament, at which time they shared student papers in discussion sections so as to gain a broader picture on "grace" (*hesed, charis*), "covenant," *torah-nomos* ("law"), or righteousness-justification in both Testaments. In recent years students in their final year have taken a required course taught by an *Alttestamentler* and New Testament professor. It has dealt with the history of the discipline, ways of doing biblical theology, and probes into selected topics, sometimes on such current issues as healing or justice concerns. Team-teaching was used at an earlier stage in the curriculum to introduce students to both Testaments at once with regard to tradition criticism or themes such as creation or "Spirit." On occasion a single instructor has dealt with both Testaments: Old Testament theologies (J, P, and others), New Testament theologies (such as Paul or John), then efforts at a theology of the entire Bible (Terrien). A professor of Hebrew Bible may do an elective on the Old Testament in the New, a *Neutestamentler* one on "Creation, Continuing and New," in all of Scripture (and the ancient world generally). What amounts to a biblical theology around the theme of "gospel" or good news, *Witness of the Word* (1986), grew out of team-taught seminary courses and ten years of an adult education program in the Lutheran Church in America and beyond.[69] On another occasion one professor's lectures on the theology of the Hebrew Scriptures (God's acts, God's people, God's will, God's purpose) were paralleled with similar or contrasting presentations on the New Testament counterpart themes. Other seminaries have doubtless engaged in similar approaches.

But the many ways of doing biblical theology as a discipline of the two Testaments will not achieve the desired impact unless related to, and done as, practical theology. Of course, there are obvious links to systematic theology which can be developed in many more ways than as traditional *sedes doctrinae* or proof-texts, as witness Barth or Schillebeeckx. But it is in connection with those church activities of scriptural proclamation in preaching, teaching, worship, witnessing, and counseling that the success or failure of any biblical theology comes home to roost.

Accordingly, in Part Two, chapters explore various aspects of biblical theology in light of the lectures in Part One. "Biblical theology as practical theology" was a leitmotif proposed by the publisher and editor in June 1989 and, we note, served as theme for the October 1990 meeting of the Association of Practical Theology.

Robert Bornemann, under the modest title of "Toward a Biblical Theology" (chap. 6), takes up the question of how to do a theology of the Hebrew Scriptures, in light of "religion" and a participant's theological commitment to the Bible. He seeks both to reflect "encounter with God through Christ" and to be sensitive to Christian-Jewish concerns, while alert to historical research and in a manner so as to contribute to church life. How we live in relation to God, ourselves, our world, and the neighbor runs through the essay as motifs.

Robert Robinson focuses, as no essay in Part One does so exclusively, on "narrative theology" as a response to a widely perceived crisis in the use of the Bible (chap. 7). Here, Dr. Robinson argues, is a way to rescue the clarity ( *perspicuitas*) of Scripture, of which the Reformation spoke, from the mismanagement of all the methods for historical-critical study which have arisen in the last two centuries or so, and thus from the hands of a professional elite, for the sake of all the laity in the church and the average reader. This essay reflects the opinion, already quoted, that a shift is taking place from historical to literary/narrative approaches. Others, of course, have issued warnings that "narrative criticism cannot provide a shortcut around the old elements of historical criticism" and that the "plurality of readings" in narrative approaches may frustrate the goal for theology to "fix the meaning of the text."[70] It must be noted also that the Robinson proposal does not represent "all narrative theology," but takes shape around the work of the late Hans Frei (1922–88), Professor of Religious Studies at Yale University.

"Preaching as Biblical Theology" (chap. 8) is Robert Kysar's proposal for a homiletical praxis that takes seriously the historical-critical method on the part of parish practitioners. Dr. Kysar's more recent work on the Fourth Gospel has sometimes made use of narrative approaches, and must be described overall as both historical-critical and literary in style. As a preacher he calls for exegesis of the community addressed as well as of the biblical text in use. He illustrates this treatment by analyzing a passage in 1 John, a letter that, like most Epistles, has not always proven popular for preaching and on which narrative approaches may not help much.

Jesus' parables, on the other hand, have long provided a popular textual basis for preaching and teaching in the church and for analysis of Jesus' message in university and other circles. Robert Hughes examines the history of parable study (chap. 9). Here a shift from historical, often socioeconomic, investigation into the Jewish world of Jesus in Galilee to more literary concerns has clearly been effected over the last forty years or so. What such shifts in scholarship can mean to the parish pastor or teacher in a congregation are the ultimate concern of this article, for Dr. Hughes writes as the founder of the Academy of Preachers, an association for study and discipline toward better proclamation which is based at the Philadelphia seminary.

In most of the chapters through Dr. Hughes's, reference is made to the pertinence of biblical theology for the church's teaching task. Anti-Semitism, for example, calls for efforts toward correction in the classroom and adult forum as well as from the pulpit. So does development of a sound attitude toward Scripture in life. A biblical theology provides the framework for understanding individual books (and passages) of the Bible within any "multivoiced chorus" of New and Old Testaments. But education and Scripture studies have not always served each other well. Margaret Krych discusses both what biblical theology has and has not done for parish Christian education, as well as what parish education has and has not done for biblical theology (chap. 10). She writes as a professor of Christian Education as well as a systematic theologian.

Biblical theology obviously can relate to worship as a whole, in liturgy as well as to lectionaries read in church. Pastoral counseling, when Christian, presumes a scriptural view of the human situation (anthropology), for which biblical theology is, in most traditions, foundational. Such areas could, opportunity permitting, be explored as well. Thus, biblical theology, an old but changing discipline which we have left undefined—or rather, have recognized in its various definitions—meets us in church life as well as in academic study. Widely influential, even determinative on some issues, biblical theology, if not done as a coherent discipline, will be done piecemeal for us. The issue is not whether, but how. Proposals follow.

## NOTES

1. See the R. Bultmann "Epilogue," which includes, "The Task and the Problems of New Testament Theology (the Relation between Theology and Proclamation)" and "The History of New Testament Theology as a Science," in *Theology of the New Testament*, trans. K. Grobel, 2 vols. (New York: Charles Scribner's Sons, 1952, 1955) 2:237–51, esp. 242.

2. **Brief surveys on the history of biblical theology:** G. W. Coats, "Theology of the Hebrew Bible," in *The Hebrew Bible and Its Modern Interpreters*, ed. D. A. Knight and G. M. Tucker (Chico, Calif.: Scholars Press; Philadelphia: Fortress, 1985) 239–62. R. H. Fuller, "New Testament Theology," in *The New Testament and Its Modern Interpreters*, ed. E. J. Epp and G. W. MacRae (Atlanta: Scholars Press; Philadelphia: Fortress, 1989) 565–84. H. Boers, *What Is New Testament Theology? Guides to Biblical Scholarship* (Philadelphia: Fortress, 1979). John R. Donahue, "The Changing Shape of New Testament Theology," *Theological Studies* 50 (1989) 314–35. Bultmann, *Theology of the New Testament*. L. Goppelt, *Theology of the New Testament*, trans. J. Alsup, 2 vols. (Grand Rapids: Eerdmans, 1981, 1982) 2:251–81.

**Old Testament:** G. Hasel, *Old Testament Theology: Basic Issues in the Current Debate*, 3d ed. (Grand Rapids: Eerdmans, 1982). J. H. Hayes and F. Prussner, *Old Testament Theology: Its History and Development* (Atlanta: John Knox, 1985). H. G. Reventlow, *Problems of Old Testament Theology in the Twentieth Century* (Philadelphia: Fortress, 1985). W. Zimmerli, "Biblische Theologie, I. Altes Testament," *Theologische Realenzyklopädie* (Berlin/New York: de Gruyter) 6 (1980) 426–55.

**New Testament:** S. Neill, *The Interpretation of the New Testament 1861–1961* (New York: Oxford University Press, 1964; *1861–1986*, 1988). R. Schnackenburg, *New Testament Theology Today* (New York: Herder & Herder, 1963). G. Hasel, *New Testament Theology: Basic Issues in the Current Debate* (Grand Rapids: Eerdmans, 1978). R. Morgan, *The Nature of New Testament Theology*, Studies in Biblical Theology 2, no. 25 (London: SCM, 1973). O. Merk, *Biblische Theolo-*

*gie des Neuen Testaments in ihrer Anfangszeit. Ihre methodischen Probleme bei Johann Philipp Gabler und Georg Lorenz Bauer und deren Nachwirkung,* Marburger Theologische Studien 9 (Marburg: Elwert, 1972). G. Strecker, "Das Problem der Theologie des Neuen Testaments," in *Das Problem der Theologie des Neuen Testaments,* ed. G. Strecker, Wege der Forschung 367 (Darmstadt: Wissenschaftliche Buchgesellschaft, 1975) 1–31, repr. in Strecker's *Eschaton und Historie: Aufsätze* (Göttingen: Vandenhoeck & Ruprecht, 1979) 260–90. O. Merk, "Biblische Theologie, II. Neues Testament," *Theologische Realenzyklopädie* 6:455–77.

**Entire Bible:** O. Betz, "Biblical Theology, History of," *The Interpreter's Dictionary of the Bible,* ed. G. A. Buttrick et al., 4 vols. (Nashville: Abingdon, 1962) 1:432–37. K. Stendahl, "Biblical Theology, Contemporary," ibid. 1:418–32; cf. also his essay in *The Bible in Modern Scholarship: Papers Read at the 100th Meeting of the Society of Biblical Literature, December 28–30, 1964,* ed. J. P. Hyatt (New York: Abingdon, 1965), with a response by A. Dulles, S.J., 196–209, 210–16. J. Smart, *The Past, Present, and Future of Biblical Theology* (Philadelphia: Westminster, 1979). B. S. Childs, *Biblical Theology in Crisis* (Philadelphia: Westminster, 1970). H. G. Reventlow, *Problems of Biblical Theology in the Twentieth Century* (Philadelphia: Fortress, 1986). G. Strecker, " 'Biblische Theologie'? Kritische Bemerkumlaut ungen zu den Entwürfen von Hartmut Gese und Peter Stuhlmacher," in *Kirche: Festschrift für Günther Bornkamm zum 75. Geburtstag,* ed. D. Lührmann and G. Strecker (Tübingen: Mohr-Siebeck, 1980) 425–45. R. Morgan with J. Barton, *Biblical Interpretation,* Oxford Bible Series (New York: Oxford University Press, 1988). H.-J. Kraus, *Die Biblische Theologie: Ihre Geschichte und Problematik* (Neukirchen-Vluyn: Neukirchen Verlag, 1970). "Biblical Hermeneutics in Recent Discussion," a review essay, "Old Testament" by B. C. Birch, "New Testament" by D. J. Harrington, *Religious Studies Review* 10 (1984) 1–10.

3. Hasel, *Old Testament Theology* 42–96; *New Testament Theology* 73–139.

4. **Old Testament theologies** noted as illustrative in the chart: R. C. Dentan, *The Design of the Scriptures: A First Reader in Biblical Theology* (New York: Seabury, 1979). C. K. Lehmann, *Biblical Theology,* 2 vols. (Scottdale, Pa.: Herald Press, 1971, 1974). R. E. Clements, *Old Testament Theology: A Fresh Approach* (Atlanta: John Knox, 1978). W. Eichrodt, *Theology of the Old Testament,* trans. J. A. Baker, 2 vols. (Philadelphia: Westminster, 1961, 1967). J. L. McKenzie, *A Theology of the Old Testament* (Garden City, N.Y.: Doubleday, 1974). G. von Rad, *Old Testament Theology,* trans. D. M. G. Stalker, 2 vols. (New York: Harper & Row, 1962, 1965). H. Gese, *Essays on Biblical Theology,* trans. K. Crim (Minneapolis: Augsburg, 1981). P. Stuhlmacher, *Historical Criticism and Theological Interpretation of Scripture,* trans. R. A. Harrisville (Philadelphia: Fortress, 1977). S. Terrien, *The Elusive Presence: Toward a New Biblical Theology,* Religious Perspectives 26 (New York: Harper & Row, 1978). C. Westermann, *Elements of Old Testament Theology,* trans. D. W. Scott (Atlanta: John Knox, 1982). P. D. Hanson, *Dynamic Transcendence: The Correlation of Confessional Heritage and Contemporary Experience in a Biblical Model of Divine Activity* (Philadelphia: Fortress, 1978); *The Diversity of Scripture,* Overtures to Biblical Theology 11 (Philadelphia: Fortress, 1982).

Childs, *Biblical Theology in Crisis,* and *Old Testament Theology in Canonical Context* (Philadelphia: Fortress, 1985). Hasel, *Old Testament Theology* 92–96.

**New Testament theologies** noted as illustrative: A. Richardson, *Introduction to the Theology of the New Testament* (New York: Harper, 1959). K. H. Schelkle, *Theology of the New Testament,* 4 vols. (Collegeville, Minn.: Liturgical Press, 1971–77). Bultmann, *Theology of the New Testament.* W. G. Kümmel, *The Theology of the New Testament According to Its Major Witnesses: Jesus—Paul—John,* trans. J. E. Steeley (Nashville: Abingdon, 1973). J. Jeremias, *New Testament Theology: The Proclamation of Jesus,* trans. J. Bowden (New York: Charles Scribner's Sons, 1971). O. Cullmann, *Christ and Time: The Primitive Christian Conception of Time and History* (Philadelphia: Westminster, 1950); *Salvation as History* (New York: Harper & Row, 1967). G. E. Ladd, *A Theology of the New Testament* (Grand Rapids: Eerdmans, 1974). Goppelt, *Theology of the New Testament.*

5. Donahue, "Changing Shape of New Testament Theology" 316–27, with reference to E. Schillebeeckx, *Jesus: An Experiment in Christology* (New York: Seabury, 1980); *Christ: The Experience of Jesus as Lord* (New York: Crossroad, 1983).

6. W. Kasper, *Jesus the Christ* (New York: Paulist, 1976). J. L. Segundo, *Jesus of Nazareth Yesterday and Today,* trans. J. Drury, 5 vols. (Maryknoll, N.Y.: Orbis, 1984–88). Jon Sobrino, *Christology at the Crossroads: A Latin American Approach,* trans. J. Drury (Maryknoll, N.Y.: Orbis, 1978). See further J. Reumann, "Jesus and Christology," in *The New Testament and Its Modern Interpreters,* ed. E. J. Epp and G. W. MacRae (Philadelphia: Fortress; Atlanta: Scholars Press, 1989) 501–64.

7. For example, A. B. Davidson, *The Theology of the Old Testament* (New York: Charles Scribner's Sons, 1904). G. B. Stevens, *The Theology of the New Testament* (New York: Charles Scribner's Sons, 1899).

8. Hayes and Prussner, *Old Testament Theology* 153, 204, 220.

9. Hasel, *Old Testament Theology* 9–13.

10. J. Barr, "The Theological Case against Biblical Theology," in *Canon, Theology, and Old Testament Interpretation: Essays in Honor of Brevard S. Childs,* ed. G. M. Tucker, D. L. Petersen, and R. R. Wilson (Philadelphia: Fortress, 1988) 3.

11. J. L. Houlden, "Biblical Theology," in *The Westminster Dictionary of Christian Theology,* ed. A. Richardson and J. Bowden (Philadelphia: Westminster, 1983) 69–71. For the ARCIC conversations, see *Anglican–Roman Catholic International Commission, The Final Report* (London: SPCK, 1982). What Houlden claims with regard to historical criticism and biblical theology for these two traditions, that earlier "inability to bring their theological traditions into fruitful relationship" was "somewhat released by common attention to biblical ideas and themes" (71), is borne out by experiences in other bilateral dialogues and the Faith and Order Movement.

12. For Westermann, see *Elements,* and his *What Does the Old Testament Say about God?* (Atlanta: John Knox, 1979) and *Blessing in the Bible and in the Life of the Church* (Philadelphia: Fortress, 1978). Terrien, *Elusive Presence.* Hanson, *Dynamic Transcendence* and *Diversity of Scripture.* W. Brueggemann, "A Shape for

Old Testament Theology, 1: Structure Legitimation," and "A Shape for Old Testament Theology, 2: Embrace of Pain," *Catholic Biblical Quarterly* 47 (1985) 28–46, 395–415.

13. Bultmann, *Theology of the New Testament*. Stevens, *Theology of the New Testament*. H. Conzelmann, *An Outline of the Theology of the New Testament*, trans. J. Bowden (New York: Harper & Row, 1969). L. Morris, *New Testament Theology* (Grand Rapids: Zondervan, 1986). E. Stauffer, *New Testament Theology* (German 1948), trans. J. Marsh (London: SCM, 1955). Richardson, *Theology of the New Testament*.

14. **Theologies of both Testaments** noted as illustrative: M. Burrows, *An Outline of Biblical Theology* (Philadelphia: Westminster, 1946). G. Vos, *Biblical Theology: Old and New Testaments* (Toronto: Toronto Baptist Seminary, 1947; Grand Rapids: Eerdmans, 1948). Lehmann, *Biblical Theology*. Dentan, *Design of the Scriptures*. J. Blenkinsopp, *A Sketchbook of Biblical Theology* (New York: Herder & Herder, 1968). M. García Cordero, *Teología de la Biblia*, 2 vols., Biblioteca de autores cristianos 335, 6 (Madrid: Editorial Católica, 1970, 1974). F. McCurley and J. Reumann, *Witness of the Word: A Biblical Theology of the Gospel* (Philadelphia: Fortress, 1986). Terrien, *Elusive Presence*.

15. Bultmann, *Theology of the New Testament* 1:3. Kümmel, *Jesus—Paul—John*. Jeremias, *Proclamation of Jesus*. Goppelt, *Theology of the New Testament*.

16. On the possibility of theologies (of the Hebrew Scriptures) by non-Christians, see the review of Childs's *Old Testament Theology* by Z. Zevit in *Catholic Biblical Quarterly* 50 (1988) 493, and consider the program of M. H. Goshen-Gottstein, "Tanakh Theology: The Religion of the Old Testament and the Place of Jewish Biblical Theology," in *Ancient Israelite Religion: Essays in Honor of Frank Moore Cross*, ed. P. D. Miller et al. (Philadelphia: Fortress, 1987) 617–44. For the past ten years Goshen-Gottstein, a professor at Hebrew University, Jerusalem, has been exploring such a theology of the law, the prophets, and the writings that would deal with "the relationship between God and Israel," "what Tanakh is about" (628).

17. Reventlow, *Biblical Theology* 10–144, presents a detailed bibliographical survey of the relationship between Old and New Testaments, especially involving Israel and the church, including interfaith documents since the Holocaust (64–132).

18. Richardson, *Theology of the New Testament* 312–13, 325–29, 380–87. On feminist theology, see esp. E. Schüssler Fiorenza, *In Memory of Her: A Feminist Theological Reconstruction of Christian Origins* (New York: Crossroad, 1984).

19. So J. P. Gabler in 1787, in J. Sandys-Wunsch and L. Eldredge, "J. P. Gabler and the Distinction between Biblical and Dogmatic Theology: Translation, Commentary, and Discussion of his Originality," *Scottish Journal of Theology* 33 (1980) 133–58, quotation from 143.

20. Stendahl, who seeks to avoid Bultmann's existentialism, "Biblical Theology, Contemporary," in *Interpreter's Dictionary*.

21.  R. H. Fuller, "New Testament Theology," in Epp and MacRae, eds., *The New Testament* 578–79, with reference to W. Wrede's essay in 1897, "The Task and Methods of New Testament Theology," trans. in R. Morgan, *The Nature of New Testament Theology: The Contribution of William Wrede and Adolf Schlatter*, Studies in Biblical Theology 2, no. 25 (London: SCM, 1973) 68–116, and to J. M. Robinson, "The Future of New Testament Theology," *Drew Gateway* (Madison, N.J.) 45 (1974–75) 175–87, also printed in *Religious Studies Review* 2 (1976) 17–23 (see esp. 22 for phrases quoted) and in *Studia Evangelica* 7 (*Texte und Untersuchungen* 126 (Berlin: Akademie-Verlag, 1982) 415–26.

22.  Cf., for the British Isles, Morgan and Barton on the universities as the hope of the future, free from the church but as a meeting place, *Biblical Interpretation* 38–42, 289–96.

23.  P. W. Macky, "The Coming Revolution: The New Literary Approach to New Testament Interpretation," *The Theological Educator* 9 (1979) 32–46, reprinted in *A Guide to Contemporary Hermeneutics: Major Trends in Biblical Interpretation*, ed. D. K. McKim (Grand Rapids: Eerdmans, 1986) 263–79, quotations from 263–65.

24.  Ibid. 279.

25.  The phrase is taken from G. E. Wright. See his *God Who Acts* (London: SCM, 1952) and *The Old Testament against Its Environment*, Studies in Biblical Theology 2 (London: SCM, 1950). The notion of God acting in history was also popularized by F. V. Filson, *The New Testament against Its Environment: The Gospel of Christ the Risen Lord*, Studies in Biblical Theology 3 (London: SCM, 1950). See also G. W. Wright and R. H. Fuller, *The Book of the Acts of God: Christian Scholarship Interprets the Bible*, Christian Faith Series, ed. R. Niebuhr (Garden City, N.Y.: Doubleday, 1957). It is important to note Wright's stance that "the narrative mode of biblical literature plays no role in shaping the theology." See D. H. Kelsey, *The Uses of Scripture in Recent Theology* (Philadelphia: Fortress, 1975) 37.

26.  Cf. G. Lindbeck, *The Nature of Doctrine: Religion and Theology in a Postliberal Age* (Philadelphia: Westminster, 1984).

27.  Cf. Strecker's "Das Problem" and his "'Biblische Theologie'?"; Gese, *Essays on Biblical Theology;* Stuhlmacher, *Historical Criticism.* Also, H. Gese, *Vom Sinai zum Zion: alttestamentliche Beiträge zur biblischen Theologie*, Beiträge zur evangelischen Theologie, theologische Abhandlungen 64 (Munich: Kaiser, 1974); P. Stuhlmacher, *Vom Verstehen des Neuen Testaments: Eine Hermeneutik*, Grundrisse zum Neuen Testament, Das Neue Testament Deutsch Ergänzungsreihe 6 (Göttingen: Vandenhoeck & Ruprecht, 1979); with Helmut Class, *Das Evangelium von der Versöhnung in Christus* (Stuttgart: Calwer Verlag, 1979); "The Gospel of Reconciliation in Christ," *Horizons in Biblical Theology* 1 (1979) 161–90; *Reconciliation, Law, & Righteousness: Essays in Biblical Theology* (Philadelphia: Fortress, 1986); and "Die Mitte der Schrift—biblisch-theologisch betrachtet," in *Wissenschaft und Kirche, Festschrift für Eduard Lohse*, ed. K. Aland and S. Meurer,

Texte und Arbeiten zur Bibel, hrsg. von der Deutschen Bibelgesellschaft, Bd. 4 (Bielefeld: Luther-Verlag, 1989) 29–56.

28. See the titles by Stuhlmacher cited above, esp. *Vom Verstehen* 156–61 on Schlatter, 205–25 on *Einverständnis,* and 225–47 on *Versöhnung.* For an appreciative summary of Stuhlmacher's "hermeneutics of consent," see R. A. Harrisville's introduction to Stuhlmacher's *Historical Criticism* 7–15, or K. Froehlich, "Biblical Hermeneutics on the Move," *Word and World* 1 (1981) 147–52, reprinted in McKim, ed., *Contemporary Hermeneutics* 185–91.

29. J. Barr, "Biblical Theology," *The Interpreter's Dictionary of the Bible Supplementary Volume,* ed. K. Crim (Nashville: Abingdon, 1976) 111.

30. Barr, "The Theological Case against Biblical Theology."

31. P. Trible, "Bringing Miriam out of the Shadows," *Bible Review* 5 (1989) 14–25, 34, with letters in the June issue, pp. 4–8.

32. On flux in the study of early Judaism and cautions about drawing implications from uncertain situations, see G. W. E. Nickelsburg with R. A. Kraft, "Introduction," *Early Judaism and Its Modern Interpreters,* ed. R. A. Kraft and G. W. E. Nickelsburg (Philadelphia: Fortress; Atlanta: Scholars Press, 1986) 25. B. J. Lee, *The Galilean Jewishness of Jesus: Retrieving the Jewish Origins of Christianity* (New York: Paulist, 1988) is rightly criticized by P. J. Hass in *Religious Studies Review* 15 (1989) 263 for using somewhat antiquated secondary literature in reconstructing pre-Mishnaic Judaism.

33. J. A. Sanders, *Torah and Canon* (Philadelphia: Fortress, 1972); *Canon and Community: A Guide to Canonical Criticism,* Guides to Biblical Scholarship (Philadelphia: Fortress, 1984); and *Canon as Paradigm: From Sacred Story to Sacred Text* (Philadelphia: Fortress, 1987) esp. 9–40; "Adaptable for Life: The Nature and Function of Canon," reprinted from *Magnalia Dei: The Mighty Acts of God, Essays on the Bible and Archaeology in Memory of G. Ernest Wright,* ed. F. M. Cross et al. (Garden City, N.Y.: Doubleday, 1976) 531–60. B. S. Childs, *Old Testament Theology; Introduction to the Old Testament as Scripture* (Philadelphia: Fortress, 1979); *The New Testament as Canon: An Introduction* (Philadelphia: Fortress, 1984) esp. 3–53.

34. B. S. Childs, "The Canonical Shape of the Prophetic Literature," *Interpretation* 32 (1978) 54.

35. R. Scroggs, "Can New Testament Theology Be Saved? The Threat of Contextualisms," *Union Seminary Quarterly Review* 42 (1988) 17–31. The "threat" is seen in the "new forms" of sociocultural, literary, rhetorical contextualization, both ancient and modern (18), amid a "hermeneutics of paranoia" about Paul and a narrative criticism of the Gospels which precludes "theology or christology in the traditional sense." Unable to accept Stuhlmacher's "hermeneutics of consent" (see above, n. 28) on the right or the left-wing rejection of the Bible as a "pagan classic," Scroggs seeks to reemphasize the intentionality of the text itself. For a different listing of "approaches" to "methodologies used today" see the 1984 document of the Pontifical Biblical Commission, *Bible et christologie* (Paris: Cerf, 1984), trans. Joseph A. Fitzmyer, "The Biblical Commission and

Christology," *Theological Studies* 46 (1985) 407–79; *Scripture and Christology: A Statement of the Biblical Commission with Commentary* (New York: Paulist, 1986).

36. C. H. Dodd, *According to the Scripture: The Substructure of New Testament Theology* (London: Nisbet, 1952; New York: Charles Scribner's Sons, 1953). B. Lindars, *New Testament Apologetic: The Doctrinal Significance of Old Testament Quotations* (Philadelphia: Westminster, 1962). J. D. G. Dunn, *Unity and Diversity in the New Testament: An Inquiry into the Character of Earliest Christianity* (Philadelphia: Westminster, 1977; 2d ed. Philadelphia: Trinity Press International, 1990) 81–102.

37. G. W. H. Lampe and K. J. Woollcombe, *Essays on Typology,* Studies in Biblical Theology 22 (London: SCM, 1957). K. Froehlich, *Biblical Interpretation in the Early Church,* Sources of Early Christian Thought (Philadelphia: Fortress, 1984).

38. In addition to Lampe and Woollcombe, *Essays on Typology,* see von Rad, *Old Testament Theology* 2:364–74; L. Goppelt, *Typos: The Typological Interpretation of the Old Testament in the New* (Grand Rapids: Eerdmans, 1982).

39. R. E. Brown, "The History and Development of a Sensus Plenior," *Catholic Biblical Quarterly* 15 (1953) 141–62, and "The Sensus Plenior in the Last Ten Years," ibid. 25 (1963) 262–85; *The Jerome Biblical Commentary,* ed. R. E. Brown et al. (Englewood Cliffs, N.J.: Prentice-Hall, 1968) 71:56–70; *The New Jerome Biblical Commentary,* ed. R. E. Brown et al. (Englewood Cliffs, N.J.: Prentice-Hall, 1990) 71:49–51. Cf. J. M. Robinson, "Scripture and Theological Method: A Protestant Study in Sensus Plenior," *Catholic Biblical Quarterly* 27 (1965) 6–27.

40. The April 1977 issue of *Interpretation* (31, no. 2) provides a history of lectionaries (J. Reumann), their contextual use for interpretation (G. Sloyan), a critical assessment (L. R. Bailey), and resources for their use (E. Achtemeier).

41. The *Theologisches Wörterbuch zum Neuen Testament,* ed. G. Kittel and later G. Friedrich, trans. and ed. G. W. Bromiley, 10 vols. (Grand Rapids: Eerdmans, 1964–76). The *Theological Dictionary of the New Testament: Abridged in One Volume* by G. W. Bromiley appeared in 1985 (Grand Rapids: Eerdmans).

42. J. Barr, *The Semantics of Biblical Language* (New York: Oxford University Press, 1961).

43. *Theological Dictionary of the Old Testament,* ed. G. J. Botterweck and 'H. Ringgren (German 1970– ; Grand Rapids: Eerdmans, 1974– ). *New International Dictionary of New Testament Theology,* 3 vols., trans. and ed. C. Brown (Grand Rapids: Zondervan, 1975–78). *Exegetical Dictionary of the New Testament,* ed. H. Balz and G. Schneider, 3 vols. (Grand Rapids: Eerdmans, 1990– ).

44. Cf. Hayes and Prussner, *Old Testament Theology* 15–19.

45. Burrows, *Outline of Biblical Theology.*

46. Stauffer, *New Testament Theology.*

47. Dentan, *Design of the Scriptures;* McKenzie, *Theology of the Old Testament;* and Richardson, *Theology of the New Testament.* J. Bonsirven, *Theology of the New Testament* (Westminster, Md.: Newman, 1963).

48. For example, U. Mauser, *Christ in the Wilderness: The Wilderness Theme in the Second Gospel and Its Basis in the Biblical Tradition,* Studies in Biblical Theology 39 (London: SCM, 1963); G. W. Coats, *Rebellion in the Wilderness* (Nashville: Abingdon, 1968). A. M. Ramsey, *The Glory of God and the Transfiguration of Christ* (London: Longman, Green, 1948).

49. Hayes and Prussner, *Old Testament Theology* 126–36.

50. Von Rad, *Old Testament Theology;* Stevens, *Theology of the New Testament;* Bultmann, *Theology of the New Testament;* Conzelmann, *Outline.*

51. For this term, derived from the launching of rockets into space, see H. Koester and J. M. Robinson, *Trajectories through Early Christianity* (Philadelphia: Fortress, 1971) esp. 46, 56, 65–66, 113, 238, 266, 269–79. For objections to the term and a preference for "lines of development," see J. Reumann, "Exegetes, Honesty, and the Faith: Biblical Scholarship in Church School Theology," *Currents in Theology and Mission* 5 (1978) 23–25.

52. "The Form-Critical Problem of the Hexateuch" (German 1938), in von Rad's *The Problem of the Hexateuch and Other Essays,* trans. E. W. Trueman Dicken (New York: McGraw-Hill, 1966) 3–8.

53. M. Albertz, *Botschaft des Neuen Testament(e)s,* 4 vols. (Zollikon-Zürich: Evangelischer Verlag, 1947–57).

54. O. Cullmann, *The Christology of the New Testament,* trans. S. C. Guthrie and C. A. M. Hall (Philadelphia: Westminster, 1959; 2d ed., 1963). O. S. Barr, *From the Apostles' Faith to the Apostles' Creed* (New York: Oxford University Press, 1964). C. H. Thompson, *Theology of the Kerygma: A Study in Primitive Preaching* (Englewood Cliffs, N.J.: Prentice-Hall, 1962).

55. J. C. K. von Hofmann, *Interpreting the Bible* (Minneapolis: Augsburg, 1959). C. Preus, "The Contemporary Relevance of von Hofmann's Hermeneutical Principles," *Interpretation* 4 (1950) 311–21.

56. Cullmann, *Christ and Time* and *Salvation as History.*

57. See Childs, *Biblical Theology in Crisis, Old Testament Theology, Old Testament as Scripture,* and *New Testament as Canon.* For a discussion of Childs's work, see the review articles on his "Introduction to the Old Testament" in *Journal for the Study of the Old Testament* 16 (1980); James Barr, *Holy Scripture: Canon, Authority, Criticism* (Philadelphia: Westminster, 1983) chap. 4 and app. 2; J. Barton, *Reading the Old Testament: Method in Biblical Study* (London: Darton, Longman, and Todd, 1984) chaps. 6 and 7; Morgan and Barton, *Biblical Interpretation* 213–14; R. W. L. Moberly, "The Church's Use of the Bible: The Work of Brevard Childs," *Expository Times* 99 (1988) 104–8; and, for use of Childs's approach in a churchly, indeed "Catholic," direction, L. T. Johnson, *The Writings of the New Testament: An Interpretation* (Philadelphia: Fortress, 1986) 530–51, with support claimed from H. Frei (551).

58. See Macky, "The Coming Revolution," and chap. 7 below. For orientation to the immense body of literature in this area, several titles in the Guides to Biblical Scholarship series (Philadelphia: Fortress) are helpful, esp. N. Habel, *Literary Criticism of the Old Testament* (1971), W. A. Beardslee, *Literary Criticism*

*of the New Testament* (1970), N. R. Peterson, *Literary Criticism for New Testament Critics* (1978), and M. A. Powell, *What Is Narrative Criticism?* (1991). Also E. V. McKnight, *Meaning in Texts: The Historical Shaping of a Narrative Hermeneutics* (Philadelphia: Fortress, 1978) and *Post-Modern Use of the Bible: The Emergence of Reader-Oriented Criticism* (Nashville: Abingdon, 1988). *Why Narrative? Readings in Narrative Theology,* ed. S. Hauerwas and L. G. Jones (Grand Rapids: Eerdmans, 1989).

59. **Sociological approaches:** in Guides to Biblical Scholarship (Philadelphia: Fortress), R. R. Wilson, *Sociological Approaches to the Old Testament* (1984). D. J. Harrington, "Sociological Concepts and the Early Church: A Decade of Research," *Theological Studies* 41 (1980) 181–90, and "Second Testament Exegesis and the Social Sciences: A Bibliography," *Biblical Theology Bulletin* 18 (1988) 77–85. H. C. Kee, *Knowing the Truth: A Sociological Approach to New Testament Interpretation* (Philadelphia: Fortress, 1989). B. Malina, *The New Testament World: Insights from Cultural Anthropology* (Atlanta: John Knox, 1981). Bengt Holmberg, *Sociology and the New Testament: An Appraisal* (Minneapolis: Fortress, 1990).

**Religionsgeschichtliche approaches:** M. Smith, "The Common Theology of the Ancient Near East," *Journal of Biblical Literature* 71 (1952) 35–47. N. K. Gottwald, "Common Ancient Near Eastern Concepts of Divine Action in History," in *The Tribes of Yahweh: A Sociology of the Religion of Liberated Israel 1250–1050 B.C.E.* (Maryknoll, N.Y.: Orbis, 1979) chaps. 53–54, esp. 671–75. W. Brueggemann, "1: Structure Legitimation" 31–36: "the 'common theology' carries with it *a ground for social structure and moral coherence*" (36).

60. See, for example, Segundo, *Jesus of Nazareth,* and Sobrino, *Christology at the Crossroads;* Schüssler Fiorenza, *In Memory of Her,* and the literature in chap. 2, below.

61. Cf. titles in n. 60, above; Gottwald, *The Tribes of Yahweh,* and *The Hebrew Bible—A Socio-Literary Introduction* (Philadelphia: Fortress, 1985). F. Belo, *A Materialist Reading of the Gospel of Mark,* trans. M. J. O'Connell (Maryknoll, N.Y.: Orbis, 1981), exemplifies a Marxist approach.

62. In "Overtures to Biblical Theology" (Philadelphia: Fortress), vol. 2, *God and the Rhetoric of Sexuality* (1978), and vol. 13, *Texts of Terror* (1984).

63. So C. J. Pressler, "Feminism and Biblical Theology: A Creative Clash," *Koinonia* 1 (1989) 19–21, citing esp. Ruether's *Sexism and God-Talk* (Boston: Beacon Press, 1983).

64. *Koinonia: Princeton Theological Seminary Graduate Forum* 1 (Spring, 1989). See esp., for what follows, the article cited in n. 63 and that by S. L. Stell, "Feminist Biblical Hermeneutics: From Creative Clash to Perichoretic Construction" 36–54.

65. **Rhetorical approaches:** Donahue, "Changing Shape of New Testament Theology" 331. Cf. G. A. Kennedy, *New Testament Interpretation through Rhetorical Criticism* (Chapel Hill: University of North Carolina Press, 1984); B. L. Mack, *Rhetoric and the New Testament,* Guides to Biblical Scholarship (Minneapolis: Fortress, 1990); W. Wuellner, "Where Is Rhetorical Criticism Taking Us?" *Catholic*

*Biblical Quarterly* 49 (1987) 448–63; Wuellner, "Hermeneutics and Rhetorics: From 'Truth and Method' to 'Truth and Power,' " *Scriptura, Tydskrif vir Bybel en Teologie in Suider-Afrika, Journal of Bible and Theology in Southern Africa* 53 (1989) 1–54. T. O. Sloan and C. Perelman, "Rhetoric," *The New Encyclopaedia Britannica, Macropaedia* (Chicago: Encyclopaedia Britannia, 15th ed. 1975) 15:798–805.

66. Series include "Beiträge zur Geschichte der biblischen Exegese" and "Hermeneutische Untersuchungen zur Theologie" (Tübingen: Mohr-Siebeck); independent treatments, e.g., on Col. 1:24, J. Kramer, *Was an den Leiden Christi Noch Mangelt,* Bonner Biblische Beiträge (Bonn: Peter Hanstein Verlag, 1956). Sometimes an entire book may be treated, as in W. W. Gasque, *A History of the Interpretation of the Acts of the Apostles,* rev. ed. (Peabody Mass.: Hendrickson, 1989). A four-volume series, *Epochen der Bibelauslegung,* has begun to appear with vol. 1, *Vom Alten Testament bis Origenes,* by Henning Graf Reventlow (Munich: Beck, 1990). For essays on the history of exegesis and interpretative questions, see the papers for the 1990 Princeton symposium, "Viva Vox Scripturae," in honor of Karlfried Froehlich, *Biblical Hermeneutics in Historical Perspective,* ed. Mark S. Burrows and Paul Rorem (Grand Rapids: Eerdmans, 1991).

67. As in *The Book of Exodus: A Critical, Theological Commentary,* The Old Testament Library (Philadelphia: Westminster, 1974). Cf. also Childs, *New Testament as Canon* 547–56, "Selected Commentaries for Pastor and Teacher," and his *Old Testament Books for Pastor and Teacher* (Philadelphia: Westminster, 1977), all reflecting an interest in the history of exegesis.

68. G. Ebeling, *Kirchengeschichte als Geschichte der Auslegung der Heiligen Schriften* (Tübingen: Mohr-Siebeck, 1947); summary in Ebeling's *The Problem of Historicity in the Church and Its Proclamation* (Philadelphia: Fortress, 1967) 97–116; *The Word of God and Tradition* (Philadelphia: Fortress, 1968) 11–31.

69. Cited above, n. 14.

70. P. Perkins, "Crisis in Jerusalem? Narrative Criticism in New Testament Studies," *Theological Studies* 50 (1989) 312.

# 1 | THE PROMISE OF BIBLICAL THEOLOGY
## Some Current and New Perspectives

# 1 The Law in the Sermon on the Mount, and the Sermon on the Mount as Law

The Sermon on the Mount is a composed speech that the evangelist Matthew put together in chapters 5–7 of his work, using older bits of tradition. A considerable portion of the traditional material brought together here goes back to the Q source, as it is widely recognized in the field of New Testament research. Yet the Q source is not to be schematically presupposed. Q was presumably available to its users, Matthew and Luke, in two differing copies; in the incorporation of the Q writing into the Gospels of Matthew and Luke, one must also reckon with the influence of the community's oral tradition.

The oldest layer in the Q source is traced back to the proclamation of Jesus, even if there is still some question concerning the means with which, as well as the extent to which, the words of Jesus can be reconstructed. At this point I would like to refer to my commentary on the Sermon on the Mount,[1] in which I call attention to the "growth criterion," which makes the following assertion: in the course of being passed down, the sayings of the historical Jesus were, by means of later additions, adapted to conditions in the Christian communities, until such growth came to an end for the time being at the level of the redaction by the evangelist Matthew. On this basis we may presume that various kinds of sayings belong to the oldest layers of the Q source and thus to the proclamation of the historical Jesus—for example, three beatitudes (5:3-4, 6), three antitheses (5:21-22a, 27-28, 33-34a), the Lord's Prayer (6:9-13), and other logia of separate origin (e.g., 7:1).

The concept of *nomos* ("law") occurs only three times in the Sermon on the Mount (5:17, 18; 7:12), and two of these are in conjunction with *hoi prophētai* ("the prophets": 5:17; 7:12). None of these terms can be attributed to the proclamation of Jesus. This does not mean, however, that the theme of the "law" is to be ruled out for the historical Jesus. Even if one disregards the other synoptic texts,[2] the antitheses of the Sermon on the Mount offer an important lesson in the relationship of Jesus to the Mosaic law and to the understanding of the law in contemporary Judaism. When Jesus sets a "but I say to you" against the tradition of the "men of old," he is only outwardly comparable to a Jewish rabbi who confronts his scribal colleagues with his learned view. Jesus is not standing in the midst of an established rabbinism, which begins at the earliest with the School of Jamnia after the destruction of the second temple in the year 70. Hence, he is in disagreement not with a proto-rabbinic,[3] but with a prerabbinic Judaism, characteristic of which is the opposition of Sadducees and Pharisees.

Admittedly, efforts to obtain a clear picture of Judaism in Jesus' time have not yet come to an end.[4] Nevertheless, the lack of a concept of the law in the parts of the Sermon on the Mount that are claimed to belong to Jesus' proclamation point to the fact that Jesus addressed the Torah of Moses not fundamentally, but with an openness appropriate to each situation.[5] Moreover, the antitheses show that Jesus' understanding of the Torah is embedded in his eschatological message, in his call to repentance, which is based on the imminent reign of God and demonstrated by Jesus' behavior, especially his devotion to tax collectors and sinners.

## JESUS

Of the six antitheses in the Sermon on the Mount, presumably the first, second, and fourth go back to Jesus. This is also true of the antithetical framework ("You have heard . . . but I say to you . . . "), which (contrary to M. J. Suggs) comes not from the redactor Matthew but, like the content of the remaining antitheses, was a component of the Q source (cf. Luke 6:27-36; 16:18).

To the extent that the first antithesis is to be derived from the proclamation of Jesus, it has the following wording:

> You have heard that it was said to those of ancient times, "You shall not murder"; and "whoever murders shall be liable to judgment." But I say to you that if you are angry with a brother or sister, you will be liable to judgment. (5:21-22a)

For Jesus it is not a matter of a theoretical disagreement with the authority of Moses; rather, he takes aim at the tradition in which his listeners live.

They rely upon the "men of old," whose prohibition, to be sure, goes back to the Mosaic Torah. Word for word, a commandment of the Decalogue is cited (Exod. 20:13; Deut. 5:17).

Against this tradition Jesus places his view, which radicalizes the Mosaic law: not just murder, but even anger will be requited with judicial punishment. Jesus still, however, has not gone beyond the realm of Judaism, for anger is also reprehensible according to the testimony of Jewish scribes.[6] Thus, to begin with, the first antithesis is only a demonstration of the fact that Jesus is a representative of his people and moves, in his teaching, within the realm of the Jewish concept of the law. He seems to come on the scene as a Jewish teacher of wisdom who instructs his listeners in the deeper meaning of the Mosaic Torah.

Nonetheless, the interpreter cannot ignore the essential context of Jesus' proclamation. Matthew still had this context in view—a context that fundamentally defines the proclamation of Jesus—when he placed before the first antithesis an introductory condition according to which the righteousness of Jesus' followers must "exceed" if they want to enter the kingdom of heaven (5:20). Jesus announces the imminent reign of God. With his exhortation to repent and prepare for the coming reign of God, he resembles the wilderness prophet John. In the face of the impending arrival of the Judge of the world, John called the people streaming to him to repentance, induced them to confess their sins, and baptized them in the Jordan. If Jesus, like John, is a prophet who, faced with the impending end, summons the people to repentance, then the first antithesis is to be understood not only as a wisdom saying, but also as a prophetic exhortation that makes clear to its hearers the unconditional nature of the law's demand.

The sharpening of the Torah serves Jesus' critique of the Torah believers: they are called out of their self-assuredness. If even anger is forbidden and places one under judgment, then there is nothing left to do but confess one's guilt before God. The radical claim of the law is revealed. In the language of Luther's dogmatics, Jesus uses the law in the first antithesis not in the sense of a *usus civilis,* a "civil usage," but in a *usus theologicus* or *elenchticus legis,* a "theological usage."

Jesus' sharpening of the Torah leads us to the edge of our existence as human beings. Through the message of Jesus, the annihilating power of the law is experienced. Thus it corresponds to Jesus' call to repentance as it is expressed, for example, in regard to the unrepentant cities (11:20) or in comparison with the prophet Jonah (12:41). Jesus not only represents the love of God in his behavior toward tax collectors and sinners: in his proclamation he also makes present the judgment of God.

The second antithesis also gives expression to Jesus' call to repentance. Cited first here is the Decalogue's prohibition of adultery (Exod. 20:14; Deut. 5:18): "You have heard that it was said, 'You shall not commit adultery'" (5:27). Then Jesus' assertion is set against it: "But I say to you that every one who looks at a woman lustfully has already committed adultery with her" (5:28). Again, Jesus' counterthesis is set against the recognized Jewish tradition of his time and thereby ultimately against the law of Moses, and for this statement of Jesus, one also finds parallels in the rabbinic literature.[7] If one ignores the fact that these parallels are relatively late, Jesus in this passage has also not broken out of the realm of Jewish thought. Instead, he has sharpened the law in his Torah interpretation: not just the legal offense of adultery, but even the lustful look makes one guilty. As a matter of course, Jesus refers to the law that was given to the people Israel and is known to them.[8] Yet in this text the sovereignty of the prophet from Nazareth expresses itself in a way that raises the question whether the authority of Moses is not actually surpassed. Jesus makes God's will so immediately present to the listeners he addresses, the Torah of Moses can no longer offer an alternative and, vis-à-vis the call to repentance, cannot save them from the necessity of deciding "here and now."

In its original composition, which can be traced back to Jesus, the fourth antithesis has the following wording:

> Again, you have heard that it was said to those of ancient times, "You shall not swear falsely, but carry out the vows you have made to the Lord." But I say to you, Do not swear at all. (5:33-34a)

It is true that in this instance there is no direct confrontation with the law of Moses, but rather with the tradition that was said to "those of ancient times." Nonetheless, Jesus' claim at this point obviously implies not only a radicalization but also a revision of the Torah. A direct prohibition of swearing falsely is, to be sure, not attested in the Old Testament. We may presume that the sequence of the Decalogue is to be followed and that the basis for this antithesis is provided by Exod. 20:16 (or Deut. 5:20: "You shall not bear false witness against your neighbor").

Against this is set Jesus' counterthesis. It was expanded in later tradition with the addition of examples from Jewish and pagan practice, which show how oaths could be taken while avoiding the use of God's name. In contrast to this, Jesus' counterthesis is absolute; it denies every variation. Vis-à-vis Old Testament and Jewish practice, Jesus formulates a prohibition that is to be obligatory for him and his followers. It is not even limited by a positive instruction, for example, by the counsel always to tell the truth. Rather, it places one before the unconditional demand of the will of God, which brushes aside all promissory as well as assertoric swearing of oaths. Here repentance is demanded: whoever is open to the will of God needs no oath, even if this is allowed in the law of Moses and in the Jewish tradition.

The third antithesis deals with divorce:

> It was also said, "Whoever divorces his wife, let him give her a certificate of divorce." But I say to you that anyone who divorces his wife . . . causes her to commit adultery. (5:31-32a)

As a comparison with Luke 16:18 will make clear, this tradition can be traced back to the Q source. Paul and Mark have traditions that likewise attest a prohibition of divorce by Jesus (1 Cor. 7:10-11; Mark 10:2-9, 10-12). By comparing these various traditions, we may conclude with high probability that Jesus himself expressed an absolute prohibition of divorce, even if not in antithetical form. This prohibition (as well as that against oaths) is to be included among the ethical radicalisms that are based on the announcement of the coming reign of God. Jesus does not intend to set up a timeless norm for the communal life of humanity, especially since he did not deal with the duration of human history; rather, this instruction confronts one with the unconditional claim of the eschaton and, in the face of the imminent end of the world, calls to repentance. According to the presentation in Mark 10, Jesus expressly placed the prohibition of divorce against Moses' concession and based the indissolubility of marriage on the will of God in creation. Such an opposition between the order of creation and the Torah of Moses belongs to a later, more theoretical stage of tradition. Yet in it we can perceive that the proclamation of Jesus not only criticized the Mosaic allowance for divorce in accordance with Deuteronomy 24, but also declared it null and void.[9]

The commandment to love one's enemy in the sixth antithesis also belongs to the ethical radicalisms of Jesus: "You have heard that it was said, 'You shall love your neighbor and hate your enemy.' But I say to you, Love your enemies" (5:43-44a). The antithetical framework comes from the evangelist Matthew; he placed the demand of Jesus over against the Old Testament commandment to love one's neighbor (Lev. 19:18). In the Q tradition, the demand to love one's enemy was linked with the commandment of nonviolence and the prohibition of retaliation (Matt. 5:38-42 par.). Luke clarifies it with a presumably pre-Lukan admonition: "Bless those who curse you, pray for those who abuse you" (Luke 6:28). Jesus' demand to love one's enemies goes far beyond analogous Old

Testament-Jewish directives. It applies not only to the fellow members of one's own race (as is presupposed in the commandment to love one's neighbor in Lev. 19:18); nor is it restricted to the idea that one should give aid to one's personal enemy in a situation of special need (Exod. 23:4-5). Jesus' commandment is absolute. Nothing is to come between God's demand and the individual. The commandment of love of enemy is also not motivated by rational considerations or missionary goals. It is based only on the coming reign of God, which has its beginning in the appearance of Jesus.

Hearing this call, Jesus' listeners must admit that they have not fulfilled such an unconditional demand. Thus, the commandment to love one's enemy, like the other ethical radicalisms of Jesus, is a concrete call to repentance, a challenge to turn from the wrong way and open oneself to the coming reign of God. Jesus' commandment is not a general, timeless rule of behavior, nor does it represent a pacifist position; it is, rather, an exhortation to confess oneself as a member of the communion of sinners before a judging and pardoning God.

If a sketch of Jesus' understanding of the law is to be complete, it would have to be extended beyond the Sermon on the Mount. A critical stance vis-à-vis the Torah is revealed in the synoptic texts that deal with Jesus' relationship to the law of purity (Mark 7:1-23 par.) and describe Jesus' behavior on the Sabbath (e.g., Mark 2:23-27; 3:1-6). Yet Jesus also stands in the Old Testament-Jewish wisdom tradition, as is made clear by the double commandment of love (Mark 12:28-34 par.) and, not least of all, by various other kinds of sayings in the Sermon on the Mount (sayings on wealth, 6:19-24; on the overcoming of anxiety, 6:25-34; on the answering of prayer, 7:7-11; perhaps also the Golden Rule, 7:12 par.). Since it is essentially a question of individual, originally isolated sayings, it is not astonishing that they do not appear in connection with the announcement of the imminent reign of God.

For the overall picture we must presuppose that apocalyptic and wisdom sayings, prophetic and ethical sayings are bound together as a single whole in Jesus' preaching. The attitude demanded in the face of the eschaton includes concrete ways of behaving. The will of God brought to expression in Jesus' interpretation of the Torah is to be realized in the everyday life of the individual.

It is initially surprising that Jesus' critical attitude vis-à-vis the law left no recognizable traces in the early church in Jerusalem. Even the so-called circle of Stephen, that is, the Hellenistic part of the early church, did not maintain a law-critical—specifically a temple-critical—position until Luke's Acts of the Apostles. Here Luke uses the synoptic tradition of Jesus' words regarding the temple (Acts 6:11-14; cf. Mark 14:56-61 par.).[10] In truth, the group of Hellenists may have fit in with the Jewish-Christian position of the Jerusalem core congregation. Only with the Gentile-Christian church is a fundamental freedom from the law to be found (as it was worked out, for example, in the late phase of Paul's theology as the doctrine of justification). Thus it parallels the gradual separation of church and synagogue. Here there is no appeal to the words of Jesus, but rather a quest for one's own theological substantiations, which have as their presupposition the kerygma of the cross and resurrection of Jesus Christ. The fact that Jesus' critique of the Torah played scarcely any role in the following years can be considered confirmation of the thesis that Jesus' understanding of the law was articulated not in connection with an abstract theory, but as a situation-related call to repentance.

## AFTER EASTER

There was no unified understanding of the law in the post-Easter church. This is clear in the tradition of the Sermon on the Mount. In 5:18 Matthew passes on a saying that probably comes from the Q source, as comparison with Luke 16:17 demonstrates. It was originally composed in Aramaic or Hebrew and expresses the unconditional validity of the law in each of its component parts: "Until heaven and earth pass away, not one letter, not one stroke of a letter, will pass from the law." Not even a yod, the smallest letter in the Hebrew alphabet, not even a tittle, a minute stroke of the pen that distinguishes one letter from another or is added as embellishment, not even the tiniest part of the law is to be set aside. Without exception, the Torah is permanent. The question whether the historical Jesus expressed himself in this way may—with reservation—be answered negatively. Indeed, Jesus' specific authority appears precisely in his critique of the Torah. This kind of unbroken profession of the entirety of the law is hardly to be traced back to the proclamation of Jesus. It is more probable that this saying originated in a Jewish-Christian congregation in Palestine when an effort was made to preserve faithfulness to the Old Testament-Jewish law, in order, thereby, to maintain good relations with the Jewish synagogue.

Also a part of the pre-Matthean level of tradition is the community rule of 5:23-24, in which the admonition to reconciliation is placed before the cultic commandment of making an offering:

> So when you are offering your gift at the altar, if you remember that your brother or sister has something against you, leave your gift there before the altar and go; first be reconciled to your brother or sister, and then come and offer your gift.

Parallels to this rule occur in rabbinic literature.[11] The rule presupposes the existence of the second temple and makes clear that at this time the early Christian church in Jerusalem still had an unbroken relationship with the cultic law.

Nevertheless, this relationship changed in the course of the history of the early church. Also, depending on church structure, the relationship with the Jewish law became more flexible. An example is provided by the pre-Matthean Sermon-on-the-Mount tradition in the saying of 5:19, which belongs to the special material of Matthew's Gospel:

> Whoever breaks one of the least of these commandments, and teaches others to do the same, will be called least in the kingdom of heaven; but whoever does them and teaches them will be called great in the kingdom of heaven.

In form, this is a casuistic legal statement that Ernst Käsemann included among the statements of "holy law." As a reason for its origin, one may presume Jewish-Christian debates in which the relationship of Christians to the Torah was discussed. A distinction is made between small commandments, which, if need be, can be left out of consideration, and great commandments, which are absolutely binding. The small commandments may be identical with the rules of the ceremonial law as they are known from the Old Testament-Jewish tradition. The congregation that created this saying stands on the threshold between Jewish Christianity and gentile Christianity. They acquiesce when gentile Christians set aside the ceremonial commandments and conform only to the ethical directives, but they allow their gentile-Christian brothers and sisters only a small place in the kingdom of heaven. They themselves feel obliged to keep even the small commandments. Thus this congregation still stands firmly on the foundation of a Jewish Christianity that is loyal to the law, without shutting itself off from the necessities of the emerging gentile-Christian church.[12]

## MATTHEW

As previously noted, Matthew shaped the Sermon on the Mount in its present form. It is the first of five speech complexes that the evangelist composed and intentionally positioned in his work. Of the various traditions that appear together in the Sermon on the Mount, only one portion of them goes back to the written source Q, while another presumably comes from the oral tradition of Matthew's church. Redaction-historical analysis (also called redaction criticism) must ask what common thread in the Matthean conception binds together the various sayings-units and their divergent assertions. Matthew did not live in the age of the second temple. Therefore, he also could not fulfill the saying of 5:23-24 in the literal sense. Not the law of sacrifice, but the obligation to reconciliation is, no doubt, the ongoing demand that he derives from the tradition. In 5:19 also, Matthew could not have adopted the literal meaning. After the cult of sacrifice was abolished in Jerusalem, it was no longer possible to observe each individual demand of the law. Apparently, what is at stake for Matthew is the general assertion that the law remains valid in its fundamental meaning, as it is interpreted by the teaching of Jesus.

It is characteristic of the Matthean tendency toward fundamental truth that he hands down global formulas such as "the law or the prophets" (5:17) and "the law and the prophets" (7:12; 22:40). According to 5:17 the Matthean Jesus does not intend to abolish law or prophets; he has come, rather, to "fulfill"—that is, to bring to full measure—the law and the prophets as the essential components of the Old Testament. And so it happens through the teaching of Jesus: he brings no new law that is supposed to replace the Old Testament law, but rather fulfills and realizes the will of God expressed in the Old Testament.

One essential component of Jesus' teaching of the law in the Sermon on the Mount is the "righteousness" that is supposed to be more comprehensive than that of the Pharisees and scribes (5:20). The attitude demanded of Jesus' followers is measured antitypically against that of the Pharisees and scribes. They represent a casuistic interpretation of the law, propagate the external forms of the ceremonial law, and, in Matthew's view, are characterized by hypocrisy and lovelessness. They are seeking honor from the people, as their practices in prayer and fasting indicate. By contrast, Jesus admonishes his disciples to direct their attention not toward people, but toward God. In terms of content, this means striving for "perfection" (5:48), practicing unconditional "love" (5:44) and "mercy" (5:7), and giving, praying, and fasting in the right way (6:1-18). Ethical principles are also contained in the admonitions to trust in God (6:25-33) and to judge properly (7:1-6). All of this is subsumed under the demand for "righteousness" as the theme of the Sermon on the Mount (5:20) and flows into the concluding "Golden Rule" (7:12, "In everything do to others as you would have them do to you; for this is the law and the prophets"). This summary of the Sermon on the Mount brings to a climax everything previously said; only the closing admonitions, the closing parables, and the epilogue (7:13-29) follow.

Thus, in accordance with the Matthean intention, the Sermon on the Mount is thoroughly defined by a monitory-ethical orientation. It conveys the binding directives of the earthly, now resurrected Son of God for all who follow him. It is, in short, the law of the *Kyrios,* the law of the Lord. This is true already in the introduction: the beatitudes (5:3-12) urge the realization of Christlike humility and meekness; they demand the practice of righteousness and mercy, of peacemaking and endurance under persecution. The salutation *makarioi* is oriented toward the future, for example, "Blessed are the peacemakers, for they *will be* called children of God" (5:9). This echoes Jesus' expectation of the kingdom of God, according to which human life will reach its goal in a future meeting with God. When Jesus in Matthew's presentation proclaims the Sermon on the Mount as binding instruction for the church, is he a "new Moses"? Are the five speeches by Jesus in Matthew's Gospel an emulation of the five books of the Pentateuch? Probably not, because, as we have seen, Jesus' critique of the Torah suggests that he locates himself not equal to, but above Moses. And the "mount" on which Jesus gives his talk is hardly to be identified with Sinai, notwithstanding previous attempts to do so. Rather, *oros* ("mountain") in Matthew's Gospel is used as a typifying concept; it marks a place of revelation where an epiphanic event occurs. Thus on a hill Jesus heals the people who come to him sick (15:29-30), and according to 28:16 the resurrected One appears to his disciples on a mountain in Galilee. When Jesus sits down on the mountain in order to teach, he appears as superior teacher, one for whom, in the Matthean interpretation, high-ranking christological titles such as Son of God, Lord, and Son of man are appropriate.

With this foundation we can also look at the often discussed problem of "Jewish Christianity." The authority of the *Kyrios* Jesus not only stands above that of the lawgiver of the old covenant, but also has a prominent, universal significance for the future, since the First Gospel is written for the church of Jews *and* Gentiles. When the resurrected One at the close of this Gospel lifts up the demand, "[Teach] them to obey everything that I have commanded you" (28:20), this means the law of the *Kyrios,* understood—not least of all in the Sermon on the Mount—as ethical demand.

The Matthean Jesus, however, did not require observation of the Jewish ceremonial law (the purity regulations or the Sabbath rest). Hellenistic Judaism, vis-à-vis its gentile environment, had emphasized the ethical content of the Mosaic law and thereby prepared the way for the distinction between moral and ceremonial law. Matthew is writing in the context of the gentile-Christian church and its Greek-language tradition, as the use of the Septuagint indicates.[13] Even with the adoption of Jewish-Christian traditions, Matthew strengthened the ethical lines of interpretation of the Old Testament-Jewish law. Thus was it understood by the church fathers, who when quoting the Gospels preferred to quote Matthew's. The idea that the Matthean Jesus wanted to abolish the precepts of the ceremonial law from case to case, but not fundamentally,[14] is foreign to them. It also contradicts the Matthean assertion in 15:20: "To eat with unwashed hands does not defile." With this, Matthew closes the debate on purity regulations with a fundamental clarification that leaves no room for ambiguity.

If we continue on the level of historical reconstruction, we must also note that no less significance has been given in recent scholarly discussion to the problem of the theological evaluation of the Sermon on the Mount. Within Protestant interpretation, even into the present time, the Reformation distinction between "law and gospel" has been applied to the Sermon on the Mount.[15] Now it has been widely recognized, of course, that there is no corresponding terminology in the Gospel of Matthew, and that Matthew did not adopt the Pauline distinction between the indicative of the salvation event and the imperative of the ethical obligation.

Nevertheless, there have been attempts to carry out a corresponding distinction in this Gospel, since more than a few indicative statements are to be found. One such example is naming the Son of God Emmanuel, "God with us," in the infancy narrative (1:23).[16] Another is that the beatitudes at the beginning of the Sermon on the Mount are understood not only as promise, but also and especially as words of comfort full of salvation.[17] Another is that the Gospel of Matthew presupposes the indicative baptismal event; that is, it is to be understood as "postbaptismal doctrine of baptism."[18] Also, attention is called to the fact that the proclamation of God's will is embedded in a basic narrative structure in the total work of Matthew, which in its own way replaces the Pauline conceptual distinction between law and grace.[19] Yet there persists here the danger of introducing into Matthew's theology a distinction that is foreign to Matthew himself.

Matthew took the units of christological tradition handed down to him, consciously presented them in the form of a "life of Jesus," and thereby historicized them.[20] He did so not in order to relativize the Jesus tradition, but to assure the faith of his readers in the present and coming

Christ by pointing to the past Christ event. In this the ethical demand is not just an "implication of the Christology."[21] Rather, Christology and ecclesiology are also filled with the ethical demand. Thus it is seen in the Matthean validation of the sacraments,[22] as well as in the Matthean "church order" (18:1ff.), and above all in the redactional tendency to present Jesus as a model, since, according to the Matthean conception, the Son of God, through his life and death, realized his own demand in a way that is binding for the following generations.[23]

Accordingly, the Sermon on the Mount must be understood in the Matthean sense in the narrow context of Christology and ethics: the one who authoritatively brings to expression the will of God for his followers in every age is the same one who at the end of days, as the Son of man/Judge of the world, will pass judgment according to this very demand (25:1ff.). In this, his claim no longer has the character of *usus theologicus* or *elenchticus legis,* which can be traced in the proclamation of Jesus; it is, rather, the directive of the Son of God, which is to be practiced by every Christian and is also basically practicable. It is a directive that calls the communion of the "sons of God," constituted by the Son of God, away from prevailing social, national, and religious ties; it shows the right way and will lead to the final condition of election and divine perfection.[24]

The question that remains is whether such a Christianity that is oriented not toward the concept of law, but toward the ethical demand of righteousness, means a reversion to nomism, when considered in the Pauline perspective. Without doubt, in the scope of the New Testament canon, the Gospel of Matthew stands closer to the theology of the Letter of James than to the theology of Paul; for the demand for righteousness in the Sermon on the Mount agrees in content with the monitory intention of the Letter of James, according to which the royal law of liberty requires deeds of mercy (Jas. 2:8, 12-13). Matthew, like the author of the Letter of James, is not familiar with the problem of works-righteousness and the fallenness of humanity under the power of sin.[25]

In this singular orientation toward the ethical demand, Matthew can connect not only with early Christian ideas (5:18-19), but also with pagan concepts: not least of all, Stoic philosophy understands human beings as creatures who can reach the meaning of their existence only in harmony with the laws of the world, that is, with the reason that defines the cosmos.[26] It is presumably this agreement with the ethical thought of antiquity in general that allowed the Gospel of Matthew to become the Gospel writing most cited by the church fathers.[27]

The Sermon on the Mount contains basic assertions that, if they do not exclude the danger of nomism, still keep it in check: thus in Matthew's redaction we can still recognize Jesus' call to repentance, which reveals the dubious nature of any observation of the law, and (on Matthew's level) the equation of the demand of righteousness with the demand of love. This means that the proper ethical behavior of the Christian cannot ultimately be oriented toward a legal norm, but must be open without reservation to one's neighbor and even to one's enemy.

Only in the multivoiced choir of New Testament writers—only in connection with all of the assertions of the New Testament canon—not least of all next to the voices of Paul and John, can the contribution of the evangelist Matthew also release its full sound.

## NOTES

1. G. Strecker, *Die Bergpredigt: Ein exegetischer Kommentar* (Göttingen: Vandenhoeck & Ruprecht, 1984; 2d ed. 1985); *The Sermon on the Mount: An Exegetical Commentary*, trans. O. C. Dean, Jr. (Nashville: Abingdon, 1988).

2. See below.

3. So P. Sigal, *The Emergence of Contemporary Judaism*, 3 vols., vol. 1 in two parts as Pittsburgh Theological Monograph Series 29 and 29a (Pittsburgh: Pickwick, 1980, 1977, 1985); on Paul and James see 1:338. Further, Sigal's *The Halakah of Jesus of Nazareth according to the Gospel of Matthew* (Lanham, Md.: University Press of America, 1986); J. Amir, "Gesetz, 2. Judentum," *Theologische Realenzyklopädie* 13 (1984) 52–58.

4. Cf. K. Müller, "Gesetz und Gesetzeserfüllung im Frühjudentum," in *Gesetz im Neuen Testament*, ed. K. Kertelge, Quaestiones Disputatae 108 (Freiburg-Basel-Vienna: Herder, 1986) 11–28, and Müller's *Das Judentum in der religionsgeschichtlichen Arbeit am Neuen Testament: Eine kritische Rückschau auf die Entwicklung einer Methodik bis zu den Qumranfunden*, Judentum und Umwelt 6 (Frankfurt-Bern: P. Lang, 1983); R. Riesner, *Jesus als Lehrer: Eine Untersuchung zum Ursprung der Evangelien-Überlieferung*, Wissenschaftliche Untersuchungen zum Neuen Testament 2, no. 7 (Tübingen: Mohr-Siebeck, 1981). Additional literature in G. Dautzenberg, "Gesetzeskritik und Gesetzesgehorsam in der Jesustradition," in Kertelge, ed., *Gesetz* 67 n. 65.

5. Cf. J. Maier, "Jesus von Nazareth und sein Verhältnis zum Judentum: Aus der Sicht eines Judaisten," in *Jesu Jude-Sein als Zugang zum Judentum*, ed. W. P. Eckert and H. Henrix (Aachen: Einhard Verlag, 1980) 69–113, esp. 95–101.

6. See H. L. Strack and P. Billerbeck, *Kommentar zum Neuen Testament aus Talmud und Midrasch 1: Das Evangelium nach Matthäus* (Munich: Beck, 1926; 9th ed. 1986) 276–78.

7. Ibid. 299–300.

8. Cf. D. Lührmann, "Womit er alle Speisen für rein erklärte (Mk 7, 19)," *Wort und Dienst* 16 (1981) 84.

9. Further, D. Zeller, "Jesus als vollmächtiger Lehrer (Mt 5–7) und der hellenistische Gesetzgeber," in *Studien zum Matthäusevangelium: Festschrift für Wilhelm Pesch,* ed. L. Schenke, Stuttgarter Bibelstudien (Stuttgart: Katholisches Bibelwerk, 1988) 301ff.

10. Contra A. Weiser, "Zur Gesetzes- und Tempelkritik der 'Hellenisten,'" in Kertelge, ed., *Gesetz* 162, who presumes for the "Stephen circle" a criticism of the temple motivated "in part through Jesus' word and conduct."

11. Strack and Billerbeck, *Kommentar zum Neuen Testament* 1:287.

12. Cf. here also the characteristic understanding of the law in Philo of Alexandria, who through his consistent allegorizing comes de facto to a relativizing of the binding nature of the ceremonial law ("On the Confusion of Tongues" 190, trans. F. H. Colson and G. H. Whitaker, *Philo,* Loeb Classical Library, vol. 4 (London: Heinemann, and Cambridge: Harvard University Press, 1932) 112–15; "On Sobriety" 33, *Philo,* vol. 3 (1930) 460–61, among other references).

13. Contra U. Luz, *Matthew 1–7: A Commentary,* trans. W. C. Linss (Minneapolis: Augsburg, 1989) 79–82.

14. So, on Matt. 15:1-20, R. Hummel, *Die Auseinandersetzung zwischen Kirche und Judentum im Matthäusevangelium,* Beiträge zur evangelischen Theologie 33 (Munich: Kaiser, 1963) 49; I. Broer, "Anmerkungen zum Gesetzesverständnis des Matthäus," in Kertelge, ed., *Gesetz* 142.

15. Compare U. Luz, "Die Erfüllung des Gesetzes bei Matthäus (Mt 5, 17-20)," *Zeitschrift für Theologie und Kirche* 75 (1978) 433, 435; *Matthew 1–7* 86–87.

16. See H. Frankemölle, *Jahwebund und Kirche Christi: Studien zur Form- und Traditionsgeschichte des "Evangeliums" nach Matthäus,* Neutestamentliche Abhandlungen NF 10 (Münster: Aschendorff, 1974) 12–21.

17. Cf. I. Broer, *Die Seligpreisen der Bergpredigt: Studien zu ihrer Überlieferung und Interpretation,* Bonner biblische Beiträge 61 (Königstein/Ts and Bonn: Peter Hanstein, 1986) 46ff.; see on this treatment, G. Strecker, *Theologische Literaturzeitung* 112 (1987) cols. 187–88.

18. So W. Schmithals, "Evangelien, Synoptische," *Theologische Realenzyklopädie* 10 (1982) 616–17.

19. See U. Luz, "Erfüllung" 433; cf. his "Die Wundergeschichten von Mt 8-9," in *Tradition and Interpretation in the New Testament: Essays in Honor of E. Earle Ellis for His 60th Birthday,* ed. G. Hawthorne and O. Betz (Grand Rapids: Eerdmans and Tübingen: Mohr-Siebeck, 1987).

20. Cf. Charles H. Talbert, *What Is a Gospel? The Genre of the Canonical Gospels* (Philadelphia: Fortress, 1977) 16–17; D. Dormeyer and H. Frankemölle, "Evangelium als literarische Gattung und als theologischer Begriff," *Aufstieg und Niedergang der Römischen Welt. . . . Teil II: Principat,* 25.2 (Berlin and New York: de Gruyter, 1984) 1543–1704.

21. P. Vielhauer, *Geschichte der urchristlichen Literatur: Einleitung in das Neue Testament, die Apokryphen und die Apostolischen Väter* (Berlin and New York: de Gruyter, 1975) 364.

22. 3:15; 26:26-27; 28:16-20; cf. G. Strecker, *Der Weg der Gerechtigkeit: Untersuchungen zur Theologie des Matthäus*, 3d ed. Forschungen zur Religion und Literatur des Alten und Neuen Testaments 82 (Göttingen: Vandenhoeck & Ruprecht, 1971) 178ff., 216.

23. Strecker, *Weg* 177-78; *Bergpredigt* 99, *Sermon on the Mount* 95.

24. An interpretative consequence implies in this connection the thesis that the Lord's Prayer is to be seen as the "center of the Sermon on the Mount"; so G. Bornkamm, "Der Aufbau der Bergpredigt," *New Testament Studies* 24 (1978) 419-32; against this view, rightly, see J. Lambrecht, *Ich aber sage euch. Die Bergpredigt als programmatische Rede Jesu (Mt 5-7, Lk 6, 20-49)* (Stuttgart: Katholisches Bibelwerk, 1984) esp. 146-54; cf. Lambrecht's *The Sermon on the Mount: Proclamation and Exhortation*, Good News Studies 14 (Wilmington, Del.: Michael Glazier, 1985) 155-64.

25. G. Bornkamm, G. Barth, and H. J. Held, *Überlieferung und Auslegung im Matthäusevangelium*, 7th ed., Wissenschaftliche Monographien zum Alten und Neuen Testament 1 (Neukirchen-Vluyn: Neukirchener Verlag, 1975) 46 Anm. 3; *Tradition and Interpretation in Matthew*, trans. Percy Scott (London: SCM, 1963) 50 n. 2. Bornkamm here agrees with H.-J. Schoeps, *Theologie und Geschichte des Judenchristentums* (Tübingen: Mohr-Siebeck, 1949) 64-65, 343ff., where Matthew is distinguished from "heretical Ebionitism" but admittedly this is found only in the presentation of the church fathers (cf. the criticism of Walter Bauer on this point); in any case, James and Matthew are not to be ascribed to a nomistic Jewish Christianity.

26. See H. Koester, *Introduction to the New Testament* (Berlin and New York: de Gruyter, 1982) 1:148-49, and his article, "*physis*, etc.," *Theological Dictionary of the New Testament*, ed. G. Friedrich (Grand Rapids: Eerdmans, 1974) 9: 263-66.

27. Cf. on this point W.-D. Köhler, *Die Rezeption des Matthäusevangelium in der Zeit vor Irenäus*, Wissenschaftliche Untersuchungen zum Neuen Testament 2 n. 24 (Tübingen: Mohr, 1987).

PHYLLIS TRIBLE

# 2 Five Loaves and Two Fishes

## Feminist Hermeneutics and Biblical Theology

**A** half century ago feminist hermeneutics was an unrecognized subject. In the United States the first wave of feminism had passed: the voices of women were restrained. Emerging from the Depression, the nation hovered between two wars, without inclination to explore matters of gender. The theological enterprise reflected the culture. Now, near the close of the century, reflection continues in a different way as a second wave of feminism influences the North American scene.[1] This essay begins with an overview of feminism, proceeds with a sketch of biblical theology, and concludes by joining the subjects to consider offerings and make overtures.

### AN OVERVIEW OF FEMINISM

For the second wave of feminism, the date 1963 was pivotal. Betty Friedan voiced the voices of countless women with the publication of *The Feminine Mystique*.[2] This book reopened symbolically and substantively the question of female and male. Its contribution belonged to a tumultuous year. The assassination of John F. Kennedy marked a time since which "nothing has been the same."[3] The bombing of a black church in Birmingham, Alabama, killing four little girls, underscored the evils of a racist society. Upheaval characterized the nation. Within that context, feminism was hardly an isolated phenomenon.

An earlier version of this essay appeared in the fiftieth anniversary issue of *Theological Studies* 50 (1989) 279–95.

From 1963 on, many women and some men began to examine the *status quo,* pronounce judgment, and call for repentance. They espoused a prophetic message. *The Church and the Second Sex* by Mary Daly brought a distinctly religious voice to the movement.[4] This voice, like its secular counterpart, multiplied abundantly.[5] While feminism may have first appeared no more than a cloud the size of a woman's hand, in time it burst forth both as a storm of controversy and as spring rain reviving life. A brief overview of emphases, especially as they relate to theology, stages our discussion.

As a hermeneutic, feminism interprets existence. Although it is not monolithic in point of view, it focuses on gender and sex.[6] The word "gender" pertains to masculine and feminine roles as culturally perceived (rather than grammatical categories). More narrow in scope, the word "sex" denotes the biological distinction between male and female. While sex is given and for the most part unalterable, gender is constructed within particular societies and, theoretically at least, can be deconstructed. Historically, societies have used gender and sex to advocate male domination and female subordination. The term "sexism" denotes this ideology that fosters a system called patriarchy. Acquiring a definition beyond classical law, the word "patriarchy" describes the institutionalization of male dominance over women in home and society at large. Male authority does not necessarily imply that women have no power or that all women are victims. Patriarchy has assumed diverse forms. To name the many manifestations constitutes one task of feminism.

In talking about sexism and patriarchy, feminism not only describes but convicts. It opposes the paradigm of domination and subordination in all forms, most particularly male over female but also master over slave and humankind over the earth.[7] Sex, race, class, and ecology intertwine as issues. Theologically, the rule of male over female constitutes sin. This hierarchy violates the integrity of creation "in the image of God male and female" by denying full humanity to women and distorting the humanity of men. Consequently, both sexes suffer. Sexism as ideology and patriarchy as system must be exposed and rejected. In assuming this stance, feminism shows its prophetic base.

Prophecy calls for repentance. Beginning with a change of consciousness in individuals, it becomes a changing of society. Some feminists seek reform and others transformation.[8] However the issue develops, repentance bespeaks a future vision of wholeness and well-being for female and male. But feminists do not facilely claim this future. They know sexism is insidious and obstacles are numerous.

The designation "prophetic" engenders other observations. First, by definition prophetic movements advocate. This activity neither distinguishes nor demeans feminism but rather characterizes all theologies and methods.[9] For centuries church, synagogue, and academy have advocated patriarchy: the way things are and ought to be. In exposing their bias, feminism evokes a different hermeneutic. Second, as the generic term "prophecy" covers multiple perspectives, so the singular "feminism" embraces plurality and diversity. Time, place, culture, class, race, experience—these and other variables yield particular expressions of a shared cause. Though particularities induce conflict and contradiction, they serve a salutary purpose. It pertains to a third observation. Prophetic movements are not exempt from sin. Feminism struggles with this awareness. Jewish feminist theology, for example, detects anti-Jewish sentiments in some Christian formulations.[10] Third-world feminists criticize the privileged positions of class and race that afflict First-world feminism.[11] African-American women, claiming the identity "womanist," challenge white feminists.[12] On individual levels experiences of women differ, yielding diverse witnesses. Eternal vigilance is necessary. When announcing judgment on patriarchy and calling for repentance, feminism needs ever to be aware of its own sins.

This prophetic note concludes the overview of feminism; a sketch of biblical theology begins. The shift is jarring, as far as the east is from the west. Later, connections are forged.

## A SKETCH OF BIBLICAL THEOLOGY

Biblical theologians, though coming from a circumscribed community, have never agreed on the definition, method, organization, subject matter, point of view, or purpose of their enterprise. Drawing upon earlier studies, Johann Philipp Gabler (1787) formulated the discipline for the European world, particularly the German scene.[13] He deemed it a historical and descriptive undertaking distinguished from the didactic and interpretive pursuit of dogmatic theology. At the same time, he related the two fields by making biblical theology the foundation of dogmatics. For about a century afterward, the discipline flourished in disputation. Even the label "biblical theology" became suspect. Some scholars advocated the unity of Scripture; others separated the Testaments. The designation of "Old Testament theology" emerged to specify a Christian bias that not infrequently disparaged the Hebrew Scriptures.[14] Interpretive approaches began to contend with descriptive. Searches for unifying themes brought disunity. The concepts "universal" and "unique" vied for supremacy. Organizational differences furthered debate as chronologies of biblical content clashed with categories of systematic theology. Before the end of the nineteenth century, then, biblical theology had developed in myriad ways.

Thereupon followed forty years of wilderness wanderings (1880–1920). Emphasis on history of religions threatened the discipline by promoting environmental rather than theological perspectives. But over time, changes in the European climate, especially the impact of war and the rise of Barthian theology, revived interest. Two articles from the 1920s represented the discussion. Otto Eissfeldt argued for the legitimacy, yet discontinuity, of historical and theological approaches to the Old Testament.[15] By contrast, Walther Eichrodt maintained that an irreconcilable separation was neither possible nor desirable.[16] He rejected Eissfeldt's description of Old Testament theology as solely normative and interpretive. Like Gabler, he defined it as predominantly descriptive and historical, even while acknowledging a role for faith.

The year Germany came under National Socialist control (1933), Eichrodt produced in Basel the first volume of his theology, with the second and third in 1935 and 1939.[17] He himself made no explicit hermeneutical connections with the political scene. He described the discipline as giving "a complete picture of the Old Testament realm of belief." This picture formed the center panel of a triptych. On one side, religions of the ancient Near East showed comparatively the uniqueness of the Old Testament. On the other, the New Testament produced a theological union through the concept "the kingdom of God." Eichrodt denigrated Judaism. A "systematic synthesis" defined his method. Of the organizing categories—God and the people, God and the world, God and humankind (*Mensch*)—the first was basic. Covenant constituted its symbol. Though largely a product of nineteenth-century thought, this formulation dominated biblical theology into the latter half of the twentieth century.

Quite a different paradigm emerged in the work of Gerhard von Rad.[18] Volume 1 of his theology appeared just a little over a decade (1957) after the defeat of Germany in World War II; volume 2 followed three years later (1960). Like Eichrodt, von Rad made no explicit hermeneutical connections with the political scene. Form criticism and traditional history inspired his approach. Rather than positing a center (*Mitte*) for the theology or using systematic categories, he appealed to Israel's own testimonies about Yahweh's action in history. The first volume interpreted the Hexateuch, the Deuteronomistic History, and the

Chronicler's History, to conclude with Israel's response in the Psalter and the wisdom literature. The second volume investigated prophecy as God's "new thing" in the land. A brief look at apocalypticism led to the final section tracing the Old Testament into the New. Von Rad declared this movement the *sine qua non* of the enterprise. Without it, one has instead the "history of the religion of the Old Testament."

If Eichrodt be the *'aleph,* von Rad symbolized the *taw* of a prolific era in the history of biblical theology. During this time male German Protestant scholarship controlled the agenda. Its demise came through factors intrinsic and extrinsic to the discipline. Brevard S. Childs has chronicled these matters as they pertain to the North American scene.[19] Suffice it to note Childs's date for the end of this extraordinary period: 1963. From the perspective of this article, the timing is uncanny. That same year Betty Friedan wrote *The Feminine Mystique.*

In the last twenty-five years (1963–88) no major Old Testament theologies have dominated the field.[20] Yet the subject has grown through experimentation. It includes conversation between sociology and theology,[21] discussion of canon,[22] and development of bipolar categories for encompassing scriptural diversity.[23] More broadly, biblical theology has begun to converse with the world.[24] To pursue this expansion in reference to feminism requires first a few summary observations about the discipline throughout its two-hundred-year history.

First, biblical theology (more often Old Testament theology) has sought identity, but with no resolution. Over time the discussion has acquired the status of *déjà dit;* proposals and counterproposals only repeat themselves.[25] Second, guardians of the discipline have fit a standard profile. They have been white Christian males of European or North American extraction, educated in seminaries, divinity schools, or theological faculties. Third, overall, their interpretations have skewed or neglected matters not congenial to a patriarchal point of view. Fourth, they have fashioned the discipline in a past separated from the present. Biblical theology has been kept apart from biblical hermeneutics.[26]

Challenges to this stance now come from the many directions. Liberation theologies foster redefinition and application.[27] Issues such as ecology, medical ethics, creationism, and spirituality press for dialogue. Racial, religious, and sexual perspectives also enter the discussion. African-Americans, Asians, and Jews, for instance, shape the discipline differently from traditional proponents.[28] In short, biblical theology by whatever definition, method, or point of view must grapple with contemporary hermeneutics. This recognition leads to connections between feminism and biblical studies.

## FEMINIST HERMENEUTICS AND BIBLICAL STUDIES

### Perspectives and Methods

Joining biblical studies in the early 1970s, feminism has brought gender to the foreground of discussion.[29] It has exposed the androcentric bias of Scripture and scholarship. Different conclusions result.[30] Some feminists denounce Scripture as hopelessly misogynous, a woman-hating document beyond redemption. Some reprehensibly use patriarchal data to support anti-Jewish sentiments. They maintain that ascendancy of the male god Yahweh demolished an era of good-goddess worship. A Christian version holds that whereas the "Old" Testament falters badly, the "New" brings improved revelation. Some individuals consider the Bible to be a historical document devoid of continuing authority and hence worthy of dismissal. In contrast, other feminists despair about the ever-present male power that the Bible and commentators promote. And still others, unwilling to let the case against women be the determining word, insist that text and interpreters provide more excellent ways. Thereby they seek to redeem the past (an ancient document) and the present (its continuing use) from the confines of patriarchy.

Whatever their conclusions, feminist biblical scholars utilize conventional methods in studying the text. Historical criticism, form criticism, tradition history, literary criticism, sociology, anthropology, archeology, history of religions, and linguistics—all these and others illuminate the document, contributing variously to theological formulations. Though traditionally tied to patriarchal interpretation, the methods produce different results when feminist hermeneutics appropriates them. A few samplings indicate the terrain.

Working as a historical critic, Phyllis Bird has called for "a new reconstruction of the history of Israelite religion, not a new chapter on women."[31] A first step seeks to recover "the hidden history of women." She has contributed to this immense task in several articles examining women in ancient Israel and in the Israelite cult.[32]

Similarly, Jo Ann Hackett locates her rescarch in "the new women's history."[33] It attempts to recover the stories of females in their own right rather than measuring them by the norms of male history. In an examination of Judges 3–16, for instance, Hackett explores the leadership roles of women during a period of decentralized power. Paucity of evidence, difficulty of analysis, and resistance from established scholarship lead her to a pessimistic assessment about the impact of such work on so-called mainline scholarship.[34]

More sanguine about the possibilities, Carol Meyers has recently prepared the first book-length study of Israelite women.[35] Using the tools of social-scientific analysis combined with the new archeology, she seeks "to discover the place of women in the biblical world apart from the place of women in the biblical text."[36] She argues that "the decentralized and difficult village life of premonarchic Israel provided a context for gender mutuality and interdependence, and of concomitant female power."[37] And she sharply questions the validity of the description "patriarchal" for ancient Israel society. Yet to be tested, this revisionist thesis enlarges options within feminist biblical scholarship.

Literary analyses also show the diversity. In considering the mother figure, Esther Fuchs avers that the Bible is riddled with "patriarchal determinants."[38] It "uses literary strategies in order to foster and perpetuate its patriarchal ideology."[39] By contrast, in a close reading of the Exodus traditions, J. Cheryl Exum detects "positive portrayals of women."[40] Examining mothers of Israel, she finds "strong countercurrents of affirmations of women" within the "admittedly patriarchal context of the biblical literature."[41] Thus she calls for "reassessment of our traditional assumptions about women's roles in the biblical story."[42] A similar view governs the work of Toni Craven.[43] She compares Ruth, Esther, and Judith, recognizing the social dominance of the male in these stories but nevertheless asserting that "within this patriarchal milieu, the three women emerge as independent, making their own decisions and initiating actions in unconventional ways." These and other literary readings, whatever the persuasion, provide an exegetical base for theological reflection.

Feminist scholars who specialize in wisdom literature and in Israelite law also provide data for the theologian. With a multidisciplinary approach, Claudia V. Camp has explored female wisdom in Proverbs.[44] Viewing "woman Wisdom" as metaphor, she has isolated roles and activities within Israelite culture that influenced this personification. They include the figures of wife, lover, harlot, foreigner, prophet, and wise woman. Tikva Frymer-Kensky has studied specific legal cases regarding women, such as the trial of the suspected adulteress in Num. 5:11-31.[45] She has also tackled the large issue of how sex is viewed in biblical law, to argue that appreciation and anxiety vie without a way to channel the latter productively. "The result is a core emptiness in the Bible's discussion of sex."[46]

These samplings, focused on the Hebrew Scriptures, conclude with three books that differ widely in interest, approach, and purpose but share a common grounding. Particular experiences motivated their authors.

Unlike traditional male scholars, feminists often spell out hermeneutical connections between life and work. Citing an episode within her Jewish heritage as pertinent to her study, Athalya Brenner probes the familiar thesis that, as a class, women in Scripture are a second sex, always subordinate and sometimes maligned.[47] Her approach covers social roles and literary paradigms. Writing as a womanist, Renita J. Weems "attempts to combine the best of the fruits of feminist biblical criticism with its passion for reclaiming and reconstructing the stories of biblical women, along with the best of the Afro-American oral tradition, with its gift for story-telling and its love of drama."[48] Recounting unpleasant experiences within Roman Catholicism, Alice L. Laffey has prepared a "complement" to standard introductions of the Old Testament.[49] She approaches texts, for weal or woe, with the principle "that women are equal to men." However scholarly judgments measure these works, the experiences that prompted their authors and the methods they employ show yet again the diverse terrain of feminist biblical studies.

The samplings viewed above only hint at perspectives and methods. Studying Scripture from the viewpoint of gender, feminism explores ideas and advances theses shunned in traditional interpretations. Conventional methods produce unconventional results. Not all of them will endure. Yet the ferment can be salutary, for the storehouse of faith has treasures new as well as old. They necessitate the perennial rethinking of biblical theology.

### Overtures for a Feminist Biblical Theology

As a student of Scripture, I read biblical theology from duty and sometimes delight. As a student of feminism, I read feminist biblical scholarship from duty and sometimes delight. And then I ask: Can feminism and biblical theology meet? The question seems to echo Tertullian, "What has Athens to do with Jerusalem?" After all, feminists do not move in the world of Gabler, Eichrodt, von Rad, and their heirs, but those feminists who love the Bible insist that the text and its interpreters provide more excellent ways. So I ponder ingredients of a feminist biblical theology. Though not yet the season to write one, the time has come to make overtures.

At the beginning, feminist biblical theology might locate itself in reference to the classical discipline. Assertion without argumentation suffices here. First, the undertaking is not just descriptive and historical but primarily constructive and hermeneutical. It views the Bible as pilgrim, wandering through history, engaging in new settings, and ever refusing to be locked in the past. Distance and difference engage proximity and familiarity.[50] Second, the discipline belongs to diverse communities, including the academy, the synagogue, the church, and the world. It is neither essentially nor necessarily Christian. Third, formulations vary. No single method, organization, or exposition harnesses the subject: an articulation of faith as disclosed in Scripture. From these points of reference, feminism takes its first step.

*1. Exegesis.*    Mindful of the androcentricity in Scripture and traditional biblical theology, feminist interpretation begins with exegesis. It concentrates on highlighting neglected texts and reinterpreting familiar ones. The approach does not guarantee the outcome. Exegesis may show how much more patriarchal or how much less is a text.

Among the less patriarchal, and prominent among neglected passages, are female depictions of deity.[51] Hebrew poetry describes God as midwife and mother (Ps. 22:9-10, Deut. 32:18, Isa. 66:13). The Hebrew root *rḥm,* meaning "womb" in the singular and "compassion" in the plural, provides an exclusively female metaphor for the divine that runs throughout the canon. Supporting contexts strengthen this meaning. Thus Jer. 31:15-22 constitutes a poem replete with female imagery. It moves from the mother Rachel weeping for her lost children to the mother Yahweh promising to show mercy (*rḥm*) upon the virgin daughter Israel.

Among familiar passages, depictions of deity may require reinterpretation. Hosea 11 illustrates the point. Verses 3-4 describe God the parent teaching Ephraim the child to walk, picking him up, and feeding him. Patriarchal hermeneutics has long designated this imagery paternal even though in ancient Israel mothers performed these tasks.[52] Reclaiming the maternal imagery affects yet another verse (11:9). After announcing judgment upon wayward Ephraim, the Deity returns in compassion. A poignant outburst begins, "How can I give you up, O Ephraim!" It concludes, "I will not execute my fierce anger . . . , for I am *'ēl* and not *'îš,* the Holy One in your midst." Traditionally, translators have understood the words *'ēl* and *'îš* to contrast the divine and the human. Though correct, the interpretation misses the nuance. Rather than using the generic *'ādām* for humanity, the poet employs the gender-specific *'îš,* male. Thus the line avows: "I am God and not a male."

This translation makes explicit a basic affirmation needed in ancient Israel and the contemporary world. By repeatedly using male language for God, Israel risked theological misunderstanding. God is not male, and the male is not god. That a patriarchal culture employed such images for

God is hardly surprising. That it also countenanced female images *is*, however, surprising. If they be deemed remnants of polytheism, the fact remains that nowhere does Scripture prohibit them.

Shifting from depictions of deity to the human scene, feminist hermeneutics highlights neglected texts about women. The Exodus narratives provide several instances. So eager have been traditional interpreters to get Moses born that they pass quickly over the stories leading to his advent (Exod. 1:8—2:10). Two midwives, a Hebrew mother, a sister, the daughter of Pharaoh, and her maidens fill these passages. The midwives, given the names Shiphrah and Puah, defy the mighty Pharaoh who has no name. The mother and sister work together to save their baby son and brother. The daughter of Pharaoh identifies with them rather than her father. This portrait breaks filial allegiance, crosses class lines, and transcends racial and political differences. A collage of women unites for salvation; with them the Exodus originates. But existing biblical theologies fail to tell the tale.

Likewise, these theologies neglect the distaff conclusion of the Exodus story (14:1-21). The figure Miriam provides continuity between beginning and end. First appearing discreetly at the Nile River, later she reappears boldly at the Reed Sea. With other women she leads Israel in a triumphal song. Though biblical redactors would rob Miriam of her full voice by attributing the Song of the Sea to Moses (Exod. 14:1-18) and only a stanza to her (Exod. 15:20-21), historical criticism has recovered the entire Song for Miriam.[53] Feminist hermeneutics utilizes this work to show a conflict of gender embedded in the text. Miriam counters Moses. In time she questions his right to be the exclusive speaker for God (Numbers 11). Though the establishment censures her, fragments in Scripture yield another view. Unlike their leaders, the people support Miriam (Num. 12:15). At her death nature mourns; the wells in the desert dry up (Num. 20:1-2). Centuries later Micah proclaims her a leader equal to Moses and Aaron (Mic. 6:4). And Jeremiah alludes to her prominence in his eschatological vision of restoration (Jer. 31:4). Ramifications for biblical theology run deep when neglected Miriamic traditions emerge to challenge the dominant Mosaic bias.[54] Small things undermine patriarchal faith.

Even as it recovers neglected texts about women, feminist interpretation reexamines familiar ones. Genesis 2-3 is a prime example. Contrary to conventional understanding, this narrative does not proclaim male domination and female subordination as the will of God. Attention to vocabulary, syntax, and literary structure demonstrates no ordering of the sexes in creation. At the beginning, "Yahweh God formed the human from the humus" (Gen. 2:4b). Sexual identification does not obtain. At the end, this creature becomes female and male in the sexually explicit vocabulary *'iššâ* and *'îš* (Gen. 2:21-24). They are bone of bones and flesh of flesh, the language of mutuality and equality.[55] No concept of complementarity sets roles for them. The troublesome word *'ēzer,* usually translated "helper" and applied to the woman as subordinate, actually connotes superiority. The phrase "corresponding to" or "fit for" tempers this connotation to signal equality.

But with disobedience the mutuality of the sexes shatters. In answering the serpent the woman shows theological and hermeneutical astuteness. She interprets the divine command faithfully and ponders the benefits of the fruit. By contrast, the man is mindless and mute. Opposing portraits yield, however, the same decision. Each disobeys. The judgments that follow disobedience describe not prescribe the consequences. Of particular interest is the description, "Your desire is for your man, but he rules over you" (Gen. 3:15). This condition violates mutuality. Thus it judges patriarchy as sin, a judgment that Scripture and interpreters have failed to heed.

Despite the passages cited thus far, feminist exegesis does not hold that all neglected and reinterpreted texts turn out to be less patriarchal than usually perceived. (Indeed, some feminists would disavow altogether the hermeneutics pursued here to argue that patriarchy controls all biblical literature.) Exegesis also shows how much more patriarchal are many texts. The sacrifice of the daughter of Jephthah, the dismemberment of an unnamed woman, the rape of Princess Tamar, and the abuse of the slave Hagar constitute but a few narrative illustrations.[56] In prophetic literature the use of "objectified female sexuality as a symbol of evil" forms another set of passages.[57] Hosea employed female harlotry to denounce wayward Israel in contrast to the male fidelity of Yahweh (Hosea 1–3). Ezekiel exploited the female with demeaning sexual images (Ezekiel 23; 36:17). Zechariah continued the process by identifying woman with wickedness and envisioning her removal from the restored land (Zech. 5:7-11). Legal stipulations also evince an overwhelming patriarchal bias.[58] Addressed only to men, the law viewed women as property with concomitant results (Exod. 20:17; Deut. 5:21). While not excluded altogether from cultic functions, females were deemed inferior participants, obeying rules formulated by males. Not a few feminist exegetes find it sufficient to expose and denounce all such texts, asserting that they determine the biblical view of woman. Others recount them on behalf of their victims, thus establishing memorials in the midst of misery. However they are treated, such passages pose the question of authority—a central issue for all biblical theologies.

2. *Contours and Context.* Beyond exegesis the next step envisions the contours and content of a feminist biblical theology. Following neither the systematic-covenant model of Eichrodt nor the tradition-historical model of von Rad, it would focus upon the phenomenon of gender and sex in the articulation of faith. The following proposals, though tentative and lacking in thoroughness, come to mind.

First, a feminist theology would begin, as does the Bible, with Genesis 1–3. Recognizing the multivalency of language, interpretation exploits the phrase "image of God male and female," relating it positively to Genesis 2 and negatively to Genesis 3.[59] Allusions to these creation texts, such as Hos. 2:16-20, would also come into play. This passage envisions a future covenant between God and Israel that disavows the hierarchical ordering of husband and wife. To base understandings of gender in mythical rather than historical beginnings contrasts what female and male are and are meant to be with what they have become. Creation theology undercuts patriarchy.

Second, from a grounding in creation, feminist interpretation would explore the presence and absence of the female in Scripture, also taking into account relevant literature of the ancient Near East. Organization of this material remains unsettled. Narratives, poetry, and legal formulations need to be compared; minor voices, hidden stories, and forgotten perspectives unearthed; categories of relationships investigated. They include kinship ties of daughter, sister, wife, aunt, niece, and grandmother; social and political roles of slave, mistress, princess, queen mother, prostitute, judge, prophet, musician, adulterer, foreigner, and wise woman; and religious functions in cult, theophany, and psalmody.

Third, although it awaits sustained research, Israelite folk religion would become a subject for theological reflection. Denied full participation in the cult, some women and men probably forged an alternative Yahwism. What, for example, is the meaning of worship of the Queen of Heaven (Jer. 7:16-20; 44:15-28), of inscriptions that link Yahweh and Asherah,[60] and of female figurines at Israelite and Judean sites? What effect does folk religion have upon the character of faith, particularly debate about "the unique" versus "the typical"? Probing differences between the orthodoxy of the establishment and the religion of the people might bring the female story into sharper focus.[61]

Fourth, feminist theology would be truly biblical in exposing idolatry. Under this rubric it investigates language for God. Juxtaposing verbal images, animate and inanimate, shows that Scripture guards against a single definition. Further, passages such as the sacrifice of Isaac (Genesis 22), Elijah on Mt. Horeb (1 Kings 19), and selected prophetic oracles (e.g., Isa. 43:18-19; Jer. 31:22) demonstrate that no particular statement of faith is final. Without rewriting the text to remove offensive language, feminism opposes, from within Scripture, efforts to absolutize imagery. The enterprise uses the witness of the Bible to subvert androcentric idolatry.

Fifth, similarly, the pursuit would recognize that, although the text cannot mean everything, or anything, it can mean more and other than tradition has allowed.[62] Warrant for altering words and meanings runs throughout the history of interpretation and translation. No small example lies at the heart of Scripture and faith—the name of the Holy One. When Judaism substituted *Adonai* for the Tetragrammatron YHWH, it altered the text. "Thus it is written; but you read." Christianity accepted the change. The authority of believing communities superseded the authority of the written word.[63] *Mutatis mutandis*, feminist theology heeds the precedent in wrestling with patriarchal language. The verb "wrestle" is key. In the name of biblical integrity, interpretation must reject facile formulations; in the name of biblical diversity, it must reject dogmatic positions. And like Jacob (Gen. 32:22-32) feminism does not let go without a blessing.

Sixth, biblical theology would also wrestle with models and meanings for authority.[64] It recognizes that, despite the word, *authority* centers in readers. They accord the document power even as they promote the intentionality of authors. To explicate the authority of the Bible, a feminist stance might well appropriate a sermon from Deuteronomy (Deut. 30:15-20). The Bible sets before the reader life and good, death and evil, blessing and curse. Providing a panorama of life, the text holds the power of a mirror to reflect what is, thereby making choice possible. Like the ancient Israelites, modern believers are commanded to choose life over death. Within this dialectic movement, feminism might claim the entire Bible as authoritative, though not necessarily prescriptive. Such a definition differs from the traditional. In the interaction of text and reader, the changing of the second component alters the meaning and power of the first.

These tentative proposals only initiate a discussion that seeks to join feminist hermeneutics and biblical theology. The descriptive and historical task would explore the entire picture of gender and sex in all its diversity. Beyond that effort, the constructive and hermeneutical task would wrestle from the text a theology that subverts patriarchy. Looking at the enormity of the enterprise, critics of all persuasions might well ask, "Why bother?" After all, east is far from west; Athens has nothing to do with Jerusalem. At best, constructive interpretations offer no more than five loaves and two fishes. What are they among so many passages of patriarchy? The answer is scriptural (Matt. 14:13-21). When found, rightly blessed, and fed upon, these remnant traditions provide more than enough sustenance for life.

## NOTES

1. Note that the image of waves implies continuity between the periods. For background on feminism, see Alice S. Rossi, ed., *The Feminist Papers* (New York: Columbia University Press, 1973); Judith Hole and Ellen Levine, *Rebirth of Feminism* (New York: Quadrangle Books, Inc., 1971); Sheila M. Rothman, *Woman's Proper Place* (New York: Basic Books, Inc., 1978). For an example of recent and current attention to the topic of feminism and theology, see the articles published in *Theological Studies,* beginning with the issue subtitled "Woman: New Dimensions," *TS* 36 (1975) 575-765; also, Anne E. Carr, "Is a Christian Feminist Theology Possible?" *TS* 43 (1982) 279-97; J. H. Martin, "The Injustice of Not Ordaining Women: A Problem for Medieval Theologians," *TS* 48 (1987) 303-16; E. A. Johnson, "The Incomprehensibility of God and the Image of God Male and Female," *TS* 45 (1984) 441-65. More importantly, note the founding of the *Journal of Feminist Studies in Religion* in 1985, with publication continuing twice a year.

2. Betty Friedan, *The Feminine Mystique* (New York: W. W. Norton, 1963).

3. This sentiment has been uttered repeatedly by countless Americans, most recently during commemorations of the twenty-fifth anniversary of the assassination, Nov. 22, 1988.

4. Mary Daly, *The Church and the Second Sex* (New York: Harper & Row, 1968). In an autobiographical preface to the reprinting of this book (1975), Daly disowns it, charting her "change of consciousness from 'radical Catholic' to post-christian feminist."

5. For a sampling, a decade after Daly's work, see *Womanspirit Rising: A Feminist Reader in Religion,* ed. Carol P. Christ and Judith Plaskow (San Francisco: Harper & Row, 1979). Cf. also their recent collection, *Weaving the Visions: New Patterns in Feminist Spirituality* (San Francisco: Harper & Row, 1989).

6. See M. Gould and R. Kern-Daniels, "Towards a Sociological Theory of Gender and Sex," *American Sociologist* 12 (1977) 182-89. For a helpful exposition of these and other terms, see Gerda Lerner, *The Creation of Patriarchy* (New York: Oxford University Press, 1986) 231-43. Cf. Rosemary Radford Ruether, "Sexism as Ideology and Social System: Can Christianity Be Liberated from Pa-

triarchy?" *With Both Eyes Open: Seeing Beyond Gender,* ed. Patricia Altenbornd Johnson and Janet Kalven (New York: Pilgrim Press, 1988) 148–64.

7. For substantive statement of feminist theology, see Rosemary Radford Ruether, *Sexism and God-Talk: Toward a Feminist Theology* (Boston: Beacon Press, 1983); also Anne E. Carr, *Transforming Grace: Christian Tradition and Women's Experience* (San Francisco: Harper & Row, 1988).

8. This distinction resonates with the sociological categories of central and peripheral prophets. Cf. Robert R. Wilson, *Prophecy and Society in Ancient Israel* (Philadelphia: Fortress, 1980) 21–88.

9. At places in the current discussion, this point seems to be missed, with the word "advocacy" assigned to feminism as though it were, for better or worse, distinctive. Cf., e.g., the unsigned Editorial in *Interpretation* 42 (1988) 3–4; in these two pages some form of the word "advocacy" appears no fewer than seven times to describe feminism and its proponents, but not once to characterize its critics. Yet they too advocate!

10. Cf. Judith Plaskow, "Christian Feminism and Anti-Judaism," *Cross Currents* 28 (1978) 306–9. For a sampling of the diversity within Jewish feminism, see "Feminist Consciousness Today, Roundtable: The Women's Movement," *Tikkun* 2 (1987) 40–46; also Judith Plaskow, "Standing Again at Sinai: Jewish Memory from a Feminist Perspective," *Tikkun* 1 (1986) 28–34 and her recent book, *Standing Again at Sinai: Judaism from a Feminist Perspective* (San Francisco: Harper & Row, 1990).

11. See Letty M. Russell, Kwoh Pui-lan, Ada Maria Isasi-Diaz, and Katie Geneva Cannon, eds., *Inheriting Our Mothers' Gardens: Feminist Theology in Third World Perspective* (Philadelphia: Westminster, 1978).

12. The term womanist derives from Alice Walker, *In Search of Our Mothers' Gardens: Womanist Prose* (San Diego: Harcourt Brace Jovanovich, 1983) esp. xi–xii. See Delores S. Williams, "Womanist Theology," in Christ and Plaskow, eds., *Weaving the Visions* 179–86. Cf. Paula Giddings, *When and Where I Enter: The Impact of Black Women on Race and Sex in America* (New York: William Morrow, 1984).

13. See John Sandys-Wunsch and Laurence Eldredge, "J. P. Gabler and the Distinction Between Biblical and Dogmatic Theology: Translation, Commentary, and Discussion of His Originality," *Scottish Journal of Theology* 33 (1980) 133–58. For a history of the discipline, with ample bibliography, see John H. Hayes and Frederick C. Prussner, *Old Testament Theology: Its History and Development* (Atlanta: John Knox, 1985).

14. Nomenclature for the canon shared by Judaism and Christianity is currently a much-discussed issue weighted with theological import. This essay recognizes, though it does not solve, the problem. It intentionally refrains from using the designation "Old Testament" except where the description is proper to report views of others. For discussion see James A. Sanders, "First Testament and Second," *Biblical Theology Bulletin* 17 (1987) 47–49; Ernest S. Frerichs, "The

Torah Canon of Judaism and the Interpretation of Hebrew Scripture," *Horizons in Biblical Theology* 9 (1987) 13–25.

15. Otto Eissfeldt, "Israelitisch-jüdische Religionsgeschichte und alttestamentliche Theologie," *Zeitschrift für die alttestamentliche Wissenschaft* (*ZAW*) 44 (1926) 1–12.

16. Walther Eichrodt, "Hat die alttestamentliche Theologie noch selbstständige Bedeutung innerhalb der alttestamentlichen Wissenschaft?" *ZAW* 47 (1929) 83–91.

17. In English translation the three volumes became two. See Walther Eichrodt, *Theology of the Old Testament* (Philadelphia: Westminster, 1961; vol. 2, 1967).

18. For the English translations, see Gerhard von Rad, *Old Testament Theology,* vol. 1 (New York: Harper & Row, 1962); vol. 2 (1965).

19. Brevard S. Childs, *Biblical Theology in Crisis* (Philadelphia: Westminster, 1970).

20. But see, e.g., Ronald E. Clements, *Old Testament Theology: A Fresh Approach* (Atlanta: John Knox, 1978); for a theology spanning both Testaments, see Samuel Terrien, *The Elusive Presence: Toward a New Biblical Theology* (New York: Harper & Row, 1978).

21. See Norman K. Gottwald, *The Tribes of Yahweh* (Maryknoll, N.Y.: Orbis, 1979) 667–709.

22. Cf. Brevard S. Childs, *Old Testament Theology in a Canonical Context* (Philadelphia: Fortress, 1985), and James A. Sanders, *From Sacred Story to Sacred Text* (Philadelphia: Fortress, 1987).

23. See Walter Brueggemann, "A Shape for Old Testament Theology, 1: Structural Legitimation," *Catholic Biblical Quarterly* 47 (1985) 28–46; "A Shape for Old Testament Theology, 2: Embrace of Pain," *CBQ* 47 (1985) 395–415.

24. Numerous volumes in the series entitled "Overtures to Biblical Theology," published by Fortress (Philadelphia) from 1977 to the present, demonstrate the conversation. Overall, this series rejects the limitations of historical description to explore normative meanings. Distinctions between biblical theology and hermeneutics often collapse. Two recent titles illustrate the point: Sharon H. Ringe, *Jesus, Liberation, and the Biblical Jubilee: Images for Ethics and Christology* (1985), and J. Gordon Harris, *Biblical Perspectives on Aging: God and the Elderly* (1987).

25. See Henning Graf Reventlow, "Basic Problems in Old Testament Theology," *Journal for the Study of the Old Testament* 11 (1979) 2–22; cf. James Barr, "The Theological Case against Biblical Theology," *Canon, Theology, and Old Testament Interpretation,* ed. Gene M. Tucker, David L. Petersen, and Robert R. Wilson (Philadelphia: Fortress, 1988) 3–19.

26. For attention to the period since 1945, see George W. Coats, "Theology of the Hebrew Bible," in *The Hebrew Bible and Its Modern Interpreters,* ed. Douglas A. Knight and Gene M. Tucker (Philadelphia: Fortress, 1985) 239–62.

27. See, e.g., José Porfirio Miranda, *Marx and the Bible* (Maryknoll, N.Y.: Orbis, 1974); J. Severino Croatto, *Exodus: A Hermeneutics of Freedom* (Maryknoll, N.Y.: Orbis, 1981); Elsa Tamez, *Bible of the Oppressed* (Maryknoll, N.Y.: Orbis, 1982); Willy Schottroff and Wolfgang Stegemann, eds., *God of the Lowly: Socio-Historical Interpretations of the Bible* (Maryknoll, N.Y.: Orbis, 1984).

28. For the developing conversation between Judaism and biblical ("Old Testament") theology, see esp. Jon Levenson, "The Hebrew Bible, the Old Testament, and Historical Criticism," *The Future of Biblical Studies,* ed. Richard Elliott Friedman and H. G. M. Williamson (Atlanta: Scholars Press, 1987) 19–59; idem, "Why Jews Are Not Interested in Biblical Theology," *Judaic Perspectives on Ancient Israel,* ed. Jacob Neusner (Philadelphia: Fortress, 1989) 281–307; and most recently, his challenge to the use of the Exodus as a paradigm for liberation theology: idem, "Liberation Theology and the Exodus," *Midstream* (1989) 30–36. Cf. M. H. Goshen-Gottstein, "Tanakh Theology: The Religion of the Old Testament and the Place of Jewish Biblical Theology," *Ancient Israelite Religion,* ed. Patrick D. Miller, Jr., Paul D. Hanson, S. Dean McBride (Philadelphia: Fortress, 1987); also, cf. Rolf Rendtorff, "Must 'Biblical Theology' Be Christian Theology?" *Bible Review* 4 (1988) 40–43.

29. For a historical investigation, see Dorothy C. Bass, "Women's Studies and Biblical Studies: An Historical Perspective," *Journal for the Study of the Old Testament* 22 (1982) 6–12; cf. Ernest W. Saunders, *Searching the Scriptures: A History of the Society of Biblical Literature 1880–1980* (Chico, Calif.: Scholars Press, 1982). For an overview of some recent developments, see Katharine Doob Sakenfeld, "Feminist Perspectives on Bible and Theology," *Interpretation* 42 (1988) 5–18.

30. Recent collections exemplifying or discussing many of these conclusions include *The Bible and Feminist Hermeneutics,* ed. Mary Ann Tolbert, *Semeia* 28 (Chico, Calif.: Scholars Press, 1983); *Feminist Perspective on Biblical Scholarship,* ed. Adela Yarbro Collins (Chico, Calif.: Scholars Press, 1985); *Feminist Interpretation of the Bible,* ed. Letty M. Russell (Philadelphia: Westminster, 1985); *Reasoning with the Foxes: Female Wit in A World of Male Power,* ed. J. Cheryl Exum and Johanna W. H. Bos, *Semeia* 42 (Atlanta: Scholars Press, 1988); *"Ad feminam,"* ed. Alice Bach, *Union Seminary Quarterly Review* (1989), passim; *Interpretation for Liberation,* ed. Katie Geneva Cannon and Elisabeth Schüssler Fiorenza, *Semeia* 47 (Atlanta: Scholars Press, 1989), passim; and *Gender and Difference in Ancient Israel,* ed. Peggy L. Day (Minneapolis: Fortress, 1989), a volume that identifies itself as "primarily nontheological" (xiii).

31. Phyllis Bird, "The Place of Women in the Israelite Cultus," in Miller et al., eds., *Ancient Israelite Religion* 397–419.

32. The above note identifies one article; see also Bird, "Images of Women in the Old Testament," in *Religion and Sexism,* ed. Rosemary Radford Ruether (New York: Simon and Schuster, 1974) 41–88; " 'To Play the Harlot': An Inquiry into an Old Testament Metaphor," in Day, ed., *Gender and Difference in Ancient Israel* 75–94.

33. Jo Ann Hackett, "Women's Studies and the Hebrew Bible," in Friedman and Williamson, eds., *The Future of Biblical Studies* 141–64.

34. Cf. also Jo Ann Hackett, "Rehabilitating Hagar: Fragments of an Epic Pattern," in Day, ed., *Gender and Difference in Ancient Israel* 12–27.

35. Carol Meyers, *Discovering Eve: Ancient Israelite Women in Context* (New York: Oxford University Press, 1988).

36. Ibid. 23.

37. Ibid. 187.

38. Esther Fuchs, "The Literary Characterization of Mothers and Sexual Politics in the Hebrew Bible," in Yarbro Collins, ed., *Feminist Perspective on Biblical Scholarship* 117–36.

39. Esther Fuchs, "Who Is Hiding the Truth? Deceptive Women and Biblical Androcentrism," in ibid. 137–44.

40. J. Cheryl Exum, " 'You Shall Let Every Daughter Live': A Study of Exodus 1:8—2:10," Tolbert, ed., *The Bible and Feminist Hermeneutics, Semeia* 28: 63–82.

41. J. Cheryl Exum, " 'Mother in Israel': A Familiar Figure Reconsidered," in Russell, ed., *Feminist Interpretation of the Bible* 73–85.

42. Exum, " 'You Shall Let Every Daughter Live,' " in Tolbert, ed., *The Bible and Feminist Hermeneutics* 82. But in more recent work, Exum appears to adopt a harsher view toward the text itself, with ample use of the adjective "phallocentric"; see, e.g., "Murder They Wrote: Ideology and the Manipulation of Female Presence in Biblical Narrative," in Bach, ed., *"Ad Feminam"* 19–37.

43. Toni Craven, "Tradition and Convention in the Book of Judith," in Tolbert, ed., *The Bible and Feminist Hermeneutics, Semeia* 28: 49–61. See also Craven, "Women Who Lied for the Faith," in *Justice and the Holy: Essays in Honor of Walter Harrelson,* ed. Douglas A. Knight and Peter J. Paris (Atlanta: Scholars Press, 1989).

44. Claudia V. Camp, *Wisdom and the Feminine in the Book of Proverbs* (Sheffield: Almond, JSOT Press, 1985); also "Wise and Strange: An Interpretation of the Female Imagery in Proverbs in Light of Trickster Mythology," in *Reasoning with the Foxes,* ed. J. Cheryl Exum and Johanna W. H. Bos, *Semeia* 42 (Atlanta: Scholars Press, 1988) 14–36, and "Woman Wisdom as Root Metaphor: A Theological Consideration," in *The Listening Heart,* ed. Kenneth G. Hoglund et al. (Sheffield: JSOT Press, 1987) 45–76.

45. Tikva Frymer-Kensky, "The Strange Case of the Suspected Sotah (Numbers 5:11-31)," *Vetus Testamentum* 34 (1984) 11–26.

46. Tikva Frymer-Kensky, "Law and Philosophy: The Case of Sex in the Bible," *Thinking Biblical Law,* ed. Dale Patrick, *Semeia* 45 (Atlanta: Scholars Press, 1989) 89–102. The quotation comes from 99.

47. Athalya Brenner, *The Israelite Women* (Sheffield: JSOT Press, 1985).

48. Renita J. Weems, *Just a Sister Away* (San Diego, Calif.: LuraMedia, 1988). The combination proposed gives more weight to storytelling than to biblical criticism. Cf. also Weems, "Gomer: Victim of Violence or Victim of Metaphor,"

in *Interpretation for Liberation,* ed. Katie Geneva Cannon and Elisabeth Schüssler Fiorenza, *Semeia* 47 (Atlanta: Scholars Press, 1989) 87–104.

49. Alice L. Laffey, *An Introduction to the Old Testament: A Feminist Perspective* (Philadelphia: Fortress, 1988). Regrettably, factual errors mar this book.

50. See Elisabeth Schüssler Fiorenza, "The Ethics of Biblical Interpretation: Decentering Biblical Scholarship," *Journal of Biblical Literature* 107 (1988) 3–17.

51. See Phyllis Trible, *God and the Rhetoric of Sexuality* (Philadelphia: Fortress, 1978). Throughout the discussion, I draw upon this book.

52. Cf., e.g., "The Divine Father" in James Luther Mays, *Hosea* (Philadelphia: Westminster, 1969) 150–59; also Hans Walter Wolff, *Hosea,* Hermeneia (Philadelphia: Fortress, 1974) 197–203. For a recent attempt to hold fast to the paternal image, even while acknowledging the maternal, see Samuel Terrien, *Till the Heart Sings* (Philadelphia: Fortress, 1985) 56–57.

53. See esp. Frank M. Cross, Jr., and David Noel Freedman, "The Song of Miriam," *Journal of Near Eastern Studies* 14 (1955) 237–50.

54. See Phyllis Trible, "Bringing Miriam Out of the Shadows," *Bible Review* 5 (1989) 14–25, 34; "Subversive Justice: Tracing the Miriamic Traditions," in Knight and Paris, eds., *Justice and the Holy* 99–109.

55. See Walter Brueggemann, "Of the Same Flesh and Bone (Gen. 2, 23a)," *Catholic Biblical Quarterly* 32 (1970) 532–42.

56. See Phyllis Trible, *Texts of Terror* (Philadelphia: Fortress, 1984).

57. See T. Drorah Setel, "Prophets and Pornography: Female Sexual Imagery in Hosea," in Russell, ed., *Feminist Interpretation of the Bible* 86–95.

58. See Bird, "Images of Women in the Old Testament," in Ruether, ed., *Religion and Sexism* 48–57.

59. Contra Bird, " 'Male and Female He Created Them': Gen. 1:27b in the Context of the Priestly Account of Creation," *Harvard Theological Review* 74 (1981) 129–59, a study that assigns the text only one meaning and that a narrow one (procreation). The text imposes such restriction upon neither itself nor the reader.

60. See Z. Meshel and Carol Meyers, "The Name of God in the Wilderness of Zin," *Biblical Archaeology* 39 (1976) 11–17; William G. Dever, "Consort of Yahweh? New Evidence from Kuntillet 'Ajrud," *Bulletin of the American Schools of Oriental Research* 255 (1984) 21–37; Judith M. Hadley, "Some Drawings and Inscriptions on Two Pithoi from Kuntillet 'Ajrud," *Vetus Testamentum* 37 (1987) 180–213.

61. Cf. Patrick D. Miller, "Israelite Religion," in Knight and Tucker, eds., *The Hebrew Bible and Its Modern Interpreters* 201–37.

62. Cf. Alan Cooper, "On Reading the Bible Critically and Otherwise," in Friedman and Williamson, eds., *The Future of Biblical Studies* 61–79.

63. An appeal to canon as the prohibition to alteration is questionable because canonization is a fluid as well as stabilizing concept, subject to the continuing authority of believing communities, including the power of translators; *pace*

Phyllis A. Bird, "Translating Sexist Language as a Theological and Cultural Problem," *Union Seminary Quarterly Review* 42 (1988) 89–95.

64. See Letty M. Russell, *Household of Freedom: Authority in Feminist Theology* (Philadelphia: Westminster, 1987); Claudia V. Camp, "Female Voice, Written Word: Women and Authority in Hebrew Scripture," *Embodied Love*, ed. Paula M. Cooey, Sharon A. Farmer, and Mary Ellen Ross (San Francisco: Harper & Row, 1987) 97–113.

DANIEL J. HARRINGTON, S.J.

# 3  The Jewishness of Jesus as an Approach to Christology

## Biblical Theology and Christian-Jewish Relations

A major trend in recent biblical and theological discussion about Jesus has been the emphasis on his Jewishness.[1] This development is based in part on the renewed interest in the concrete humanity of Jesus. It is also rooted in the new, positive relationship between Jews and Christians since the end of World War II and the Second Vatican Council.[2] It is now possible to sketch a Christology that focuses on the Jewishness of Jesus—one that looks upon Judaism not as a rival but as a partner along the way to God, one that seeks to articulate the possibilities and problems that emerge when theologians take seriously the challenges of Christian-Jewish dialogue.[3]

There are good reasons for approaching Christology from the perspective of the Jewishness of Jesus. As Christians who profess faith in the incarnation, we affirm that Jesus of Nazareth was a Jew. The more we explore this fact, the better we can appreciate the divine economy. Moreover, we must respond to the new, positive relationship that has emerged between Christians and Jews since Vatican II. Christian theology should be done on the assumption that Jews are our brothers and sisters in the way to God, not our opponents. Finally, those who study Christology are or will be teachers or preachers. We have an obligation in justice to remedy the damage done by some Christian teachers and preachers in the past who have been (witting or unwitting) agents of anti-Jewish feelings.[4]

Christianity began within Judaism. For almost nineteen hundred years Christianity has usually found itself over against Judaism. The challenge of our new relationship is to be with one another. The aim of this paper is to see how the central figure of Christianity—Jesus of Nazareth—

71

looks from the perspective of our being with Jews on the path to God's kingdom.

First, focus will be placed on historical issues about Jesus and early Christian affirmations regarding him. Second, classic questions of Christology will be examined from the perspective of Jesus' Jewishness.

## FIRST-CENTURY JUDAISM AS JESUS' CONTEXT

From some presentations of Christology it is difficult to know that Jesus was Jewish at all. But the doctrine of the incarnation demands an appreciation of the land, people, and history in which the Word became flesh. A Christology focusing on the Jewishness of Jesus begins with an introduction to the physical geography of the land of Israel: its major regions in Jesus' time (Galilee, Samaria, Judea), the conflicts among them, and the importance of the Jerusalem temple. There should also be an overview of the major events in Jewish history of the Second Temple period: Alexander the Great's conquest of the Mediterranean world (323 B.C.E.), domination by the Ptolemies (300–200 B.C.E.) and the Seleucids (200 B.C.E.), the Maccabean revolt (165 B.C.E.) and Jewish independence, the intervention of Pompey (63 B.C.E.), the rule of Herod the Great (37–4 B.C.E.), the direct Roman control of Judea (C.E. 6–70), the Jewish War (C.E. 66–73), and the destruction of the Second Temple (C.E. 132–135).

Since the major resource for understanding Second Temple Judaism is the extant literature, there should be some introduction to Jewish writings: late Old Testament books, the Apocrypha and Pseudepigrapha, the Dead Sea Scrolls, Josephus and Philo, and the rabbinic writings. The findings of archeologists give an idea of the way people lived.[5]

Important dimensions of the world in which Jesus lived emerge from historical and literary research.[6] Jews were part of the Greco-Roman world; they were subject to Greek influence for some three hundred years before Jesus, both in Israel and the Diaspora. Even where there was resistance to Hellenism, there was a steady influence of Greek ways on Jews even in the case of the Maccabees. Jews in Israel found themselves frequently in conflict with foreign rulers (Seleucids, Romans) and used religion as a rallying point. Even in times of native leadership (Maccabees, Herod the Great) religion remained a sensitive area. The Jews' political situation has been described as a spiral of violence: oppression, resistance, repression, and revolt.[7] Jews of Jesus' time experienced great diversity among themselves. With the Jerusalem temple as the center of Jewish religious life and a minimal creedal unity (one God, land, covenant),

Jews divided themselves into Pharisees, Sadducees, Essenes, Samaritans, Zealots, and probably many other groups for which we have no extant evidence.

Posing a special problem is rabbinic Judaism, the Judaism shaped by the rabbis and the literature that preserved their teachings: Mishnah, Palestinian and Babylonian Talmuds, Targums, Midrashim, and so forth. Many Jews assume a historical continuity between pre-C.E. 70 Judaism, the Judaism of the rabbis, and at least some form of modern Judaism. But prominent Jewish scholars now raise questions about the relevance of rabbinic Judaism for understanding Jesus and early Christianity: How far back does rabbinic Judaism go? Does it represent the Pharisaic movement? How representative was rabbinic Judaism in its own time? How early and how widespread was its influence? How do modern Judaisms relate to rabbinic Judaism?[8]

Appreciation of the Jewish world in which the "Word became flesh" indicates some of the cultural constraints and possibilities of the incarnation. It also reveals that the problem of inculturation is always part of Christology—both with respect to the original Christ-event and to the ways in which that event has been expressed through the centuries and is understood today.

### Jesus as a Jewish Teacher

An initial step in coming to grips with Jesus as a Jewish teacher is a careful assessment of the four Gospels as sources. The most obvious fact about them is their diversity: the Gospels present the story of Jesus in different ways, with different purposes, for different communities, and with different theological emphases. They embody early sources: the sayings source Q, special Matthean and Lukan material, and (perhaps, in the case of the Fourth Gospel) a signs-source and revelation discourses. The infancy Gospels (Matthew 1–2, Luke 1–2) with their mixture of history, midrash, and theology pose special problems for historians. Even though the Gospels do not allow us to write a connected biography of Jesus, it is possible to know a good deal about the teaching of Jesus.[9]

The impossibility of a connected biography of Jesus should not blind us to those facts about Jesus' career and its consequences which are beyond reasonable doubt: There was surely a connection between the movements initiated by John the Baptist and Jesus. Jesus the Galilean preached and healed, called disciples (probably twelve), confined his activity to Israel, engaged in controversy about the Jerusalem temple, and was crucified outside Jerusalem by the Roman authorities. His followers continued as an identifiable movement after his death.[10]

It is generally conceded that Jesus spoke Aramaic in his teaching, though he may have used Hebrew and perhaps even Greek. The synoptic tradition presents Jesus' teachings in small packages: parables, controversies, proverbs, and short sayings. These teachings are generally concrete, picturesque, and somewhat elusive. As a Jewish teacher Jesus taught by word and deed. Those words and deeds were remembered to some extent by his disciples.

Besides exemplifying Jewish methods of communication, Jesus' teaching focused on typically Jewish topics. His central theme, the kingdom of God, grew out of the biblical doctrine of God's kingship. His Jewish predecessors, however, had given this doctrine an apocalyptic thrust (see Daniel; 1 Enoch 91:12-17; Testament of Moses 10:1-10). In this context God's kingdom refers to the time when God's reign over all creation will be recognized and acknowledged by all creatures. Jesus preached the coming of God's kingdom in future fullness much as his contemporaries did (see Matt. 13:31-50). Whereas some sayings indicate that God's kingdom will come soon (Mark 9:1; 13:30; Matt. 10:23), other sayings indicate that to some extent the kingdom is already present or at least inaugurated (Luke 11:20; 17:20-21; Matt. 11:12).

The kingdom of God provided the framework for the so-called ethical teaching of Jesus: his "ethical" teaching really was a response to the kingdom, penetrated various areas of life, and challenged his followers to live in accord with hope in God's reign and as witnesses of it. The inner group who received Jesus' teaching were disciples—primarily wandering charismatics who spread Jesus' message by going from place to place (see Matt. 10:1-42). The good news of Jesus and his followers was offered to all kinds of people but most readily accepted by the "poor"—persons who were suspect on the grounds of their religious or social status such as tax collectors, sinners, prostitutes, the sick, and the crippled.

Though thoroughly Jewish in methods and themes, Jesus the teacher surely represented some distinctive perspectives that brought about conflict with other Jews. His summary of the Torah as love of God and neighbor (see Matt. 22:34-40 parr.) is conventional enough, embodying two biblical precepts (Deut. 6:4; Lev. 19:18). He surely took a free attitude to the Jewish traditions surrounding the Torah on topics such as Sabbath observance and ritual purity (see Mark 2:1—3:6; 7:1-23), presumably on the grounds that they were human inventions (Mark 7:6-8). At several points—on the issue of divorce (see Mark 10:1-12; Luke 16:18; 1 Cor. 7:8; Matt. 5:32; 19:9) and in the antitheses (see Matt. 5:21-48)—

the New Testament pictures Jesus as abrogating points in the Torah itself. Do such cases indicate the special character of Jesus, or were they created by the early church in light of its faith and experience of the risen Lord?

Jesus' attitude toward the Jerusalem temple was mixed. While several sayings assume the smooth running of the temple (see Matt. 5:23-24; 23:16-22; Mark 1:44; 11:15-18), there also seems to be some threat against the temple and a contrast between it and one "not made by human hands" (see Mark 14:58; Matt. 26:61; John 2:19; Acts 6:14).

Most of the prominent christological titles (such as Messiah, Lord, Son of God, Son of David) are applied to Jesus by others. The title most consistently attributed to Jesus himself by himself is Son of man, which appears in three contexts: generic sayings, passion predictions, and future sayings. The Son of man sayings raise many questions: Do all three categories go back to Jesus? How does Jesus represent humankind? Did he really speak so plainly about his passion? Is Jesus the future Son of man? The authoritative "I" sayings (see Matt. 5:21-48; 10:16; Mark 9:25) indicate a special consciousness of mission and personal authority. Jesus' addressing God as "Father" (*Abba*) also suggests a special relation of intimacy with God (see Luke 10:21; 11:2; 23:34, 46; Matt. 26:42; Mark 14:36; John 11:41; 12:27-28; 17:1, 5, 11, 24-25) to which his followers are invited (see Gal. 4:6).

Jesus' friends were Jews. The Twelve as the inner circle of disciples surely had some symbolic significance with regard to Israel. Other friends included disciples sent forth to teach and heal, women who accompanied Jesus and his band (see Luke 8:1-3), and those who offered them hospitality (see Luke 10:38-42). His followers included other unlikely people such as tax collectors, prostitutes, and sinners, similar to those John the Baptist had attracted before Jesus (see Matt. 21:28-32). In general the rural Galileans would have been perceived to some extent as "outsiders" by their Judean cousins.

The Jewish opponents of Jesus are presented by the evangelists in an oversimplified manner as "scribes and Pharisees" (Synoptics) and "the Jews" (Fourth Gospel), most likely in the light of Christian-Jewish conflicts after C.E. 70. The sociological map of Jesus' own time was far more complicated. Jewish groups abounded: Sadducees, Pharisees, Essenes, Herodians, Zealots, Baptists, and Samaritans. The group with which Jesus surely had a positive relationship was that of John the Baptist. The group with which he is portrayed as entering into debate, and thus with whom he most often shared an agenda, is the Pharisees, though it is surely an exaggeration to call Jesus himself a Pharisee. The Roman officials such as Pilate and his non-Jewish mercenaries constituted

Jesus' non-Jewish opponents and were ultimately responsible for his death.

The miracles of Jesus also fit Jewish patterns to some extent.[11] They are not so much suspensions of the laws of nature as signs that God is at work. They point to the breaking in of God's kingdom (see Luke 7:18-23) and Jesus as its agent (see Matt. 14:32-33). They situate Jesus in a context of other Galilean miracle-workers such as Hanina ben Dosa and Honi the Circle-drawer. The dispute with Jesus' Jewish opponents did not concern the reality of his miracles but the power by which he performed them (see Mark 3:22). The distinctive elements of Jesus' miracles in comparison with those of his contemporaries include his ability to work by his own power (and not as merely a mediator with God) and the theological themes woven into the narratives (especially resurrection language).

### Jesus' Death

The Gospel stories of Jesus' passion were all written on this side of Easter and present Jesus from the perspective of faith. Each portrays Jesus in a distinctive way: suffering Messiah abandoned by his disciples (Mark), Son of God who fulfills God's will as expressed in the Old Testament (Matthew), the innocent martyr and good example (Luke), and the Man from Heaven taken back to God's glory (John). The Markan (and Matthean/ Lukan) and Johannine traditions differ on several points: the nature of the Last Supper (Passover meal or pre-Passover), the Jewish interrogation of Jesus (trial or preliminary hearing), and the day of Jesus' death (within or before the Passover celebration).

For all their theological distinctiveness and historical differences the passion narratives agree that Jesus was executed by a Roman punishment (crucifixion) on the charge that he was "King of the Jews" (see Mark 15:26; Matt. 27:37; Luke 23:38; John 19:19) under the authority of the Roman prefect Pontius Pilate. Jesus was perceived as another in a line of Jewish rebels who led uprisings against the political authorities in the land of Israel.[12]

The precise role of the Jewish leaders in Jesus' death is elusive.[13] There is, of course, no question of inherited guilt or the responsibility of all Jews in Jesus' time or even a large number of them. But there probably was some collaboration between Pilate and Jewish leaders. The Pharisees practically disappear from the passion narratives. The chief priests and elders may have been Sadducees, the conservative guardians of the temple and keepers of the peace with Rome. It is disputed even how active a role that they took in the proceedings (unwilling participants or active agents?).

The Markan "trial" scene (Mark 14:53-65) features two charges against Jesus: his threat to destroy and rebuild the temple (14:58), and blasphemy (14:64). The temple charge is probably based on Jesus' own saying, whatever he originally meant by it. The term blasphemy must be used in a nontechnical sense since Jesus' statement about the coming Son of man does not fulfill the definition expressed in Lev. 24:11, 16, and the punishment meted out to him (crucifixion) differs from the stoning specified in the biblical precept.

Despite all the complexities of the passion narratives, one fact shines forth: Jesus was executed by the Romans as "King of the Jews."

## Responses to the Resurrection

The earliest Christians proclaimed the resurrection of Jesus—a distinctively Jewish faith experience.[14] Neither resuscitation nor immortality of the soul, the Jewish doctrine of resurrection involves the whole person and looks to the complex of eschatological events (see Dan. 12:1-3). It was understood to be promoted especially by the Pharisees over against the Sadducees, and in this case Jesus sided with the Pharisees (see Mark 12:18-27 parr.). The striking claim made by the earliest Christians was that Jesus was raised as an individual before remaining eschatological events occurred.

The New Testament resurrection tradition divides into empty tomb stories (Mark 16:1-8 parr.; John 20:1-18) and appearance narratives (Matt. 28:16-20; Luke 24:13-49; John 20–21). Historical analysis of these texts shows, at most, that belief in Jesus' resurrection is compatible with the facts that Jesus' tomb seems to have been empty, that his followers said they saw him, and that his movement continued and spread.

The earliest complete New Testament writings that we possess are the Letters of Paul.[15] The focus of Paul's interest in Jesus was what he means for us and has done for us. Paul assumed the framework of Jewish eschatology: resurrection of the dead, last judgment, and fullness of God's kingdom. According to him and other early Christians, the resurrection of Jesus made it possible to anticipate the last judgment (justification) and to enjoy at least some benefits of the kingdom (life in the Spirit).

The pre-Pauline confessions (such as Rom. 1:3-4; 3:25-26; 1 Cor. 15:3-5) and hymns (such as Phil. 2:6-11) display a wide variety of approaches to Jesus between C.E. 30 and 55. Paul took them for granted and used them in his argument. Romans 5-8 is probably the richest source for understanding Paul's convictions about the consequences of Jesus' death and resurrection: freedom from sin, death, and the Law (chaps. 5-7), and freedom for life in the Spirit (chap. 8). The Christ-event has brought about justification, peace, access to God, the hope of glory, and so on. These traditional Jewish hopes are tied to Jesus the Jew of Nazareth.

Paul's alleged antipathy to the Torah flows from his conviction that Jesus Christ is the way to God, not the Torah.[16] This does not stop Paul from quoting the Torah as a theological authority or from asserting that the Law is holy (see Rom. 7:12). Paul's statements about the Torah have been called confused, reactive, or in the process of development. It is fair to say that Paul's statements about the Torah are difficult to hold together in a coherent package. Paul asserts that the Law was given because of transgression and served as a "pedagogue" (Galatians 3), and that it helped people to know sin and served as a stimulus to sin (Romans 7). He concludes that Christ is the "end" (telos) of the Law, though it is not clear whether Paul meant "end" as termination or goal. Paul's basic conviction was that through Christ the way to God has opened up. His problem with the Torah is that it is not Christ. His polemic comments about other Jews (see 1 Thess. 2:14-16; Phil. 3:2-3; 2 Cor. 3:7-18; Rom. 9:30-33) stem from his convictions that they walk on the wrong way, that is, on the way of Torah rather than on the way of Christ.

Another avenue toward understanding what early Christians believed about Jesus is through the christological titles (Messiah, Wisdom, Lord, Son of God, etc.), which express facets of Jesus' person and activity.[17] These titles have rich backgrounds in Judaism, and to understand them one must appreciate their Jewish roots. For example, the title "Messiah"[18] referred in preexilic times to kings, priests, and prophets, while in Second Temple times there arose various patterns of Messianism: the double priestly-royal messianism (Zech. 4:1-3, 14; Ezek. 40-48; Dead Sea Scrolls), as well as the hope for a Davidic ruler (Psalms of Solomon 17-18). The term Messiah (or Christ) was applied to Jesus without explanation by Paul, with some efforts at redefinition by Mark and John, and with easy confidence by Matthew and Luke. Another example is Wisdom understood as a personal figure (see Prov. 8:22-31) and interpreted with reference to Torah and temple (Sirach 24), the world-soul (Wisdom 7), and esoteric heavenly secrets (1 Enoch 42:1-3). The ideas and motifs connected with Wisdom were predicated of Jesus by early Christians in texts such as John 1:1-18; Col. 1:15-20; and Heb. 1:3.

Baptism and Eucharist were also early Christian ways of participating in Jesus' death and resurrection. These rituals had deep roots in Judaism.

From the biblical bathing rituals for priests (see Exod. 40:12-15; Lev. 16:4, 24), through the ritual purifications of the Qumran Essenes and the Pharisees, to the eschatological preparation proclaimed by John the Baptist, it is possible to trace a line to baptism "in the name of Jesus" (see Acts 2:38) that brings about participation in Jesus' death and resurrection (see Rom. 6:1-4).[19] Likewise, the Eucharist[20] should be viewed against the background of biblical covenantal meals with God (Exod. 24:11), sacrifices (Deut. 12:6-7; 14:22-26), the banquet of wisdom (Prov. 9:1-6), and the eschatological banquet (Isa. 25:6-8), as well as the Qumran community's meals (Mark 7:1-5). Jesus' meals with tax collectors and sinners (Matt. 11:18-19; Luke 7:33-34) reached their climax in his Last Supper with his disciples (Mark 14:22-25; Matt. 26:26-29; 1 Cor. 11:23-26; Luke 22:15-20; John 6:35-59) and in the appearance account meals (see Luke 24:13-49; John 21), and point forward to the heavenly banquet of the Lamb (Rev. 19:9, 17-18).

## SOME ISSUES IN CHRISTOLOGY

The first part of the article has sketched what it means to talk about the "Jewishness" of Jesus in a New Testament context. The world in which the Word became flesh was the Jewish world of what we call the first century C.E. The Word was a Jewish teacher—who spoke the language and used the methods of Jewish teachers, though surely in a distinctive manner. The ways in which the significance of his death was appropriated were thoroughly Jewish: resurrection, justification, honorific titles, and sacraments.

The second part will outline what an appreciation of Jesus' Jewishness might mean for the way in which we approach some classical christological issues in systematic theology: Where do we place Jesus in God's covenant with Israel? What happens when we do Christology "from above"? What happens when we do Christology "from below"? What theological questions does the Holocaust raise for Jews and Christians?

### Jesus and the Covenant(s)

Where do we place Jesus when we think about God's covenant(s) with Israel? The common Christian response is that Jesus brought about the new covenant, with the implication that the old covenant had been superseded. But there are other ways of looking at this issue when Christology is done from the perspective of Christian-Jewish dialogue.[21]

The many covenants (or renewals of covenants) in the Hebrew Scriptures (with such figures as Noah, Abraham, Moses, David) suggest the inadequacy of lumping all these under the rubric "old covenant." There are at least two kinds of covenants: unconditional (Abraham, David), and conditional (Sinai). God's ongoing covenantal relationship with Israel is expressed in different shapes and forms.

The New Testament writers agree that in Jesus God has done something of dramatic importance with regard to that covenantal relationship. The later writers tend to express the effects of the divine action in Christ in terms of replacement or supersession (see Eph. 2:15; 1 Pet. 2:9-10; Heb. 7:22; 8:13; 9:15; 12:24). But Paul traces the identity of God's people through Jesus the Messiah back to Abraham, thus providing a more organic model. His imagery of root-and-branches in Romans 11 envisions Jewish Christians as the principle of continuity, with gentile Christians grafted in and non-Christian Jews as temporarily cut off. Paul looks forward to the time (probably eschatological) when "all Israel will be saved" (Rom. 11:26a).

Paul's organic model of the history of the covenant tends to leave non-Christian Jews in a kind of spiritual "limbo" until God brings about their eschatological salvation. Some Christian theologians adapt the Pauline model by stressing the positive role of non-Christian Jews in the present economy of salvation. Others go further by suggesting that both Jews and Christians have a claim to be God's people and that there are separate ways for Jews and Christians to God.

Whatever its weaknesses and obscurities, the Pauline model has merits as a starting point for situating Jesus in God's covenantal relationship with Israel and for understanding Christian-Jewish relations today. From the Christian perspective Jesus holds a pivotal point in salvation history. But he is viewed as continuing God's covenantal relationship with Israel and opening it up to non-Jews. The eschatological dimension of Jesus' work is preserved, for the fullness of God's kingdom will not come until "all Israel will be saved." The organic model looks upon Israel as a special partner for Christians, not simply as another "world religion."

Christian theologians should also face up to some Jewish attitudes in these matters. Some Jews reject any Christian claim to be God's people and place Christians on the same level as pagans. Others raise serious questions about the fulfillment of the eschatological promises in Christ by pointing to the evil state of the world, especially as expressed in the Holocaust. The Jewish theologian, Irving Greenberg,[22] has an especially fresh and daring way of looking at these matters. He discerns three phases in God's relating with Israel, moving from most direct (biblical) to least direct (modern). He views Christianity as an extension of biblical (sacramental) Judaism and calls Christians to move toward a greater worldliness in their holiness. He interprets the state of Israel as a focal example of Jews taking responsibility for their fate and for the divine covenant with Jewry.

## Christology from Above

Christology "from above" takes God as the starting point, focuses on the divinity of Jesus, and speaks the language of philosophical theology. An articulate and influential representative of this approach to Christology was the late Karl Rahner.[23] Without providing a detailed summary of Rahner's Christology, we can say that, according to Rahner, Christology begins with the mysterious and transcendent God's willingness to open up the possibility of communication with humankind. Creation is the possibility for fuller communication on God's part and thus involves the possibility of the ultimate divine self-communication—the mystery of the incarnation. In fact, because it is in the movement of who God is for us, in a real sense the incarnation had to take place. There is a humanward movement in God and a Godward movement in humankind.

Jesus as the Logos is the real symbol of the Father: Everything that the Father wants to be for creation is expressed in the Logos. The humanity of Jesus is the perfect symbol of the Logos. Humankind searches for a symbol that expresses itself fully and for an original unity. That symbol is the person of Jesus, the Logos: in Jesus we recognize who we are and who God is.

How Jews might assess such a Christology from above can be seen from Eugene Borowitz's response to Rahner's Christology.[24] Borowitz admires Rahner for his positive attitude toward Judaism, the intellectual power of his thought, and his influence in Christian theology. He finds two key ideas in Rahner's Christology to be especially congenial to Judaism: that humankind is by its very nature oriented to God, and that there is a universal sense of messianic anticipation in the existential structure of humankind.

There are, however, several elements in Rahner's Christology "from above" which remain problematic for Judaism. The most obvious problem is that Christian beliefs about Jesus go far beyond Jewish ideas about the Messiah. With masterful understatement Borowitz says, "Jews find the idea of a man also being God fraught with difficulty." Along the same lines there is also an uneasiness for Jews in Rahner's approach to Jesus as the one who serves as a bridge between God and humankind.

In addition to his concerns about Christian claims for Jesus, Borowitz wonders whether Jesus is an appropriate Jewish Messiah. On the one hand, Jesus did not share the human experiences of love, parenthood, and social or political leadership. On the other hand, Jesus is not the only or even the best example of faithful Jewish suffering.

Finally, it is not clear whether Rahner's controversial concept of the "anonymous Christian" applies to Jews. That concept allows Rahner to hold together God's universal salvific will and the particularity of Jesus Christ and of faith in him. Non-Christians who do God's will as they perceive it have been drawn into God's action in Christ. Do Jews constitute a special category? Or are Jews on the same level as other non-Christians? The logic of Rahner's proposal would seem to place Jews alongside other non-Christians.

Borowitz's critique of Rahner's Christology "from above" can help Christians to get a sense of what their theology looks like to Jews and what points are most problematic: the claims about Jesus as Messiah, his role as the bridge between God and humankind, and the place of Jews in the divine economy of salvation in the present.

## Christology from Below

Christology "from below" takes human history as its starting point, focuses on the humanity of Jesus, and speaks the language of Scripture and (in some cases) politics. Latin American liberation theology is a good example of this approach.

Liberation theology concerns salvation or soteriology, as does classical Christian theology. Whereas classical approaches to soteriology emphasize liberation from sin, death, and ignorance, Latin American liberation theology takes a less individual and less spiritual approach. It talks about social sin, unjust social structures, and praxis. It looks toward and works for the end of false consciousness and the transformation of society. It relates Christology to a social theory of reality and demands that the truth about God be proved and tested in the present life of the church.

It is possible to discern two different approaches among liberation theologians. One approach, as represented by Gustavo Gutiérrez,[25] takes the Exodus tradition as the paradigm of liberation and reads the Scriptures from the perspective of the liberation of the oppressed. The "church militant" works for liberation and helps bring about God's kingdom. Another approach, that of Jon Sobrino,[26] stresses the identification of the historical Jesus with the oppressed, focuses on him as the Suffering Servant as a model for the church, and insists that the church be the church of the poor. Whereas Gutiérrez seems to encourage an activist stance, Sobrino appears to follow something like Gandhi's path. Yet in the final analysis such contrasts are unfair, since both theologians try to provide a balance of concerns.

Jewish reaction to Latin American liberation theology is generally negative, for various reasons. Liberation theologians frequently take up the Palestinian cause against the state of Israel. They often talk about Jews and Judaism in careless and negative ways; they appropriate the exodus for Christians and assume that Judaism is dead today. Jews look upon liberation theology as theologically naive and triumphalistic for its talk about building God's kingdom. They look upon it as philosophically and politically naive for its reliance on Marxist social analysis.

Despite the generally negative reactions among Jews to liberation theology, it is possible to discern the outlines of a more positive approach among Jewish theologians such as Dan Cohn-Sherbok[27] and Marc Ellis.[28] In fact, some themes in liberation theology are especially congenial to Jews. The first theme is Israel's exodus from Egypt as the paradigm of God's liberation of the oppressed and persecuted. The second theme is the role that humans play in making manifest God's kingdom and the conviction that the way of God's kingdom implies the building of a just society. The third theme is the place of the historical Jesus in the oppressive situation that prevailed in first-century Palestine. The fourth theme is the identification of Israel as God's Suffering Servant through the ages and the implications of that identity for solidarity with the poor.

Both negative and positive Jewish reactions to Latin American liberation theology are instructive for Christians. The negative reactions summarize the objections that are customarily made against this Christology from below but do so from the perspective of an "outsider" looking in. The positive reactions represent the beginnings of a new relationship that at least on theological grounds shows great promise.

## Christology and the Holocaust

While the sufferings of the Jewish people through the centuries have been enormous, the Holocaust, or mass murder of six million Jews in Europe during the 1940s, emerged as a horror beyond analogy. In fact, the analogies from Jewish history which Jews drew upon in the midst of the Holocaust were both inadequate and misleading.[29]

Christians today need a sense of how deeply Jews feel about the Holocaust. The main problem, of course, is the disproportion between Israel's "sins" and the murder of six million Jews. It is surely true that the Nazis murdered other groups besides Jews, but none so systematically or thoroughly.

Besides sharing Jewish feelings about the Holocaust and fighting against all tendencies to "de-Judaize" that event, Christians need also to understand the gigantic theological problem that the Holocaust poses for Jews. How could the God of Israel have allowed this monstrous event to happen? The most common response is something like that found in the Book of Job: evil is a reality, God's ways are unknowable, and the Holocaust is in the final analysis a mystery. There are, however, responses that go beyond the "mystery" approach. Some conclude from the Holocaust that God is dead (a Jewish variant of the "God-is-dead" movement in Christian theology). Some maintain that God has left Jews on their own (a Jewish variant of the secularization theology of the 1960s). Some believe that out of the evil of the Holocaust God has brought the good of the state of Israel (an application of the Suffering Servant motif). Some argue that the Holocaust shows that there are areas of creation over which God has no control.

Christians who take the cross as their central religious symbol should be able to enter into the mystery of the Holocaust on both emotional and theological levels. The Jesus whom we proclaim as Lord and Messiah was the victim of oppression and persecution in his native land. He died a cruel death on the cross as "King of the Jews." In some ways Jesus' death on the cross is similar to what happened to the Jewish people during the Holocaust. This fact makes Christian participation in and responsibility for the Holocaust all the more horrible and revolting.

The reality of the Holocaust also raises some very important questions for Christians who proclaim the crucified Jesus as Lord and Messiah. There are challenging theological questions that should not be avoided or pushed aside. What is the victory of the cross over death? Are there areas over which God has no control? What are we to make of the "once for all" character of Jesus' suffering in light of all the suffering in our world? Besides these christological issues, the Holocaust also raises questions about God whom we call the Father of Jesus Christ: Is this God immutable? Does God suffer along with his people? Was God powerless to stop the Holocaust?

It has been difficult for both Jews and Christians to speak about the Holocaust. One reason for this difficulty has been the very hard theological and philosophical questions that the Holocaust raises. To forget the Holocaust is to push away this set of hard questions. Neither Jews nor Christians can afford to do that.

The making of Christology began some two thousand years ago with the Jesus of Nazareth—a Jewish teacher and healer who was executed on a Roman cross. The making of Christology developed with the help of Jewish words and ideas, such as resurrection, justification, the christological titles, and the sacraments. In one sense Christology is always in the making, though the basic outline of development remains normative for Christians. Nevertheless, each age of Christians must discover Jesus anew. In this task Christians today have the help and criticisms of their Jewish brothers and sisters. As we Christians seek to appropriate Jesus as both a historical figure and a living reality today, we meet the Jewishness of Jesus. Focus on his Jewishness seems to constitute a way forward in Christology.

## NOTES

1. James H. Charlesworth, *Jesus Within Judaism* (Garden City, N.Y.: Doubleday, 1988), provides excellent bibliographic coverage of this development.

2. Eugene J. Fisher, A. James Rudin, and Marc H. Tanenbaum, eds., *Twenty Years of Jewish-Catholic Relations* (New York: Paulist, 1986).

3. Paul van Buren, *A Theology of the Jewish-Christian Reality,* Part 1: *Discerning the Way;* Part 2: *A Christian Theology of the People Israel;* Part 3: *Christ in Context* (San Francisco: Harper & Row, 1980–88).

4. Charles Glock and Rodney Stark, *Christian Beliefs and Anti-Semitism* (New York: Harper & Row, 1966).

5. For bibliographies on all these topics, see Daniel J. Harrington, *The New Testament: A Bibliography* (Wilmington, Del.: Glazier, 1985) 193–232.

6. For a good synthesis, see Shaye J. D. Cohen, *From the Maccabees to the Mishnah* (Philadelphia: Westminster, 1987).

7. Richard Horsley, *Jesus and the Spiral of Violence* (San Francisco: Harper & Row, 1987).

8. Jacob Neusner, *Judaism: The Evidence of the Mishnah,* rev. ed. (Atlanta: Scholars Press, 1988).

9. John P. Meier, "Jesus Among the Historians," *New York Times Book Review* 21 December (1986) 1, 16–19.

10. E. P. Sanders, *Jesus and Judaism* (Philadelphia: Fortress, 1985).

11. Geza Vermes, *Jesus the Jew: A Historian's Reading of the Gospels* (New York: Macmillan, 1974).

12. Jules Isaac, *The Teaching of Contempt: Christian Roots of Anti-Semitism* (New York–Chicago–San Francisco: Holt, Rinehart and Winston, 1964) 109–47.

13. John Pawlikowski, "The Trial and Death of Jesus: Reflections in Light of a New Understanding of Judaism," *Chicago Studies* 25, no. 1 (1986) 79–94.

14. Pinchas Lapide, *The Resurrection of Jesus: A Jewish Perspective* (Minneapolis: Augsburg, 1983).

15. Joseph A. Fitzmyer, *Paul and His Theology* (Englewood Cliffs, N.J.: Prentice-Hall, 1989).

16. Douglas Moo, "Paul and the Law in the Last Ten Years," *Scottish Journal of Theology* 40 (1987) 287–307.

17. James D. G. Dunn, *Christology in the Making* (Philadelphia: Westminster, 1980).

18. Jacob Neusner et al., eds., *Judaisms and their Messiahs* (New York: Cambridge University Press, 1988).

19. George R. Beasley-Murray, *Baptism in the New Testament* (New York: St. Martin's Press, 1962).

20. Jerome Kodell, *The Eucharist in the New Testament* (Wilmington, Del.: Glazier, 1988).

21. Michael B. McGarry, *Christology After Auschwitz* (New York–Ramsey, N.J.: Paulist, 1977) 62–107.

22. "The Relationship of Judaism and Christianity: Toward a New Organic Model," in Fisher et al., eds., *Twenty Years of Jewish-Catholic Relations* 191–211.

23. "On the Theology of the Incarnation," in *Theological Investigations* 4 (London: Darton, Longman & Todd, 1966) 105–20.

24. Eugene Borowitz, *Contemporary Christologies: A Jewish Response* (New York: Paulist, 1980) 71–98.

25. Gustavo Gutiérrez, *A Theology of Liberation* (Maryknoll, N.Y.: Orbis, 1973).

26. Jon Sobrino, *Christology at the Crossroads* (Maryknoll, N.Y.: Orbis, 1978).

27. Dan Cohn-Sherbok, "Jews, Christians and Liberation Theology," *Christian Jewish Relations* 17 (1984) 3–11; see the ensuing debate in *Christian Jewish Relations* 21 (1988) 3–60.

28. Marc Ellis, *Toward a Jewish Theology of Liberation* (Maryknoll, N.Y.: Orbis, 1987).

29. See Lucy Dawidowicz, *The War Against the Jews, 1933–1945* (New York: Holt, Rinehart and Winston, 1975); Martin Gilbert, *The Holocaust* (New York: Holt, Rinehart and Winston, 1986).

JAMES A. SANDERS

# 4 Canon as Shape and Function

The classical phrases that express the uses of the word "canon" as applied to the Bible are *norma normata* and *norma normans,* the first indicating canon as shape, the latter canon as function. I have tried over the past twenty years to contribute to both understandings.

## INTRODUCTION

I entered the field in 1968 with an attempt to understand the variant kinds of biblical literature recovered from Caves 4 and 11 at Qumran, not only the differing orders and contents evident in several scrolls of psalms from those two caves, but also the place of the Temple Scroll in whatever one should call the authoritative literature at Qumran.[1] It has become broadly accepted since that time that the canon was still open-ended, at least at Qumran, by the beginning of the first century C.E. While some, such as our late, beloved colleague, William Patrick Skehan, and Moshe Goshen-Gottstein view the variant scrolls of psalms as benign liturgical aberrations from an already accepted canon of the Psalter, others such as Rudolf Meyer and John Barton have taken the extant evidence to mean that no denomination in Early Judaism had a closed Psalter at the beginning of the first century of the common era.[2] In any case, it would appear that the Writings or *Ketuvîm,* the third section of the eventual Jewish tripartite canon, like the Psalter, was not yet closed but probably would be by the time of the Bar Kochba Revolt at the beginning of the second century C.E. The various codices of the Septuagint, preserved by the churches after the split of Christianity from Judaism, would further indicate that, while there was no Alexandrian canon over against the Palestinian, the churches went on using and copying Greek First Testaments without knowledge of, or without regard for, closure of the Jewish canon. My entry into the field of canon study was at first limited to such issues and questions.

But I had long had a second interest, which emerged four years later in *Torah and Canon*.[3] It catapulted me into canon studies in its other aspects as well. A recent report written at the request of the Pontifical Biblical Commission in Rome cites the call I sounded in the introduction to *Torah and Canon* for engagement by biblical scholarship in canonical criticism as the beginning point. In the report Dominique Barthélemy cites Brevard Childs's 1964 article, "Interpretation in Faith,"[4] as well as his 1970 volume, *Biblical Theology in Crisis*,[5] as antecedents and forerunners to what Childs calls reading the Bible in canonical context; he also cites my work with the Dead Sea Scrolls as antecedent to what I termed canonical criticism.[6] Barthélemy correctly notes that Childs has often objected to the term canonical criticism, one point among others that James Barr has failed to grasp.[7]

A realization I came to in 1972 as respondent to Brevard Childs's Sprunt Lectures at Union Seminary, Richmond, however, was that Childs and I, while using some of the same terms, were addressing the question of canon from quite different perspectives. That conference was quite enlightening to me not only in what I heard Childs coming to in the Sprunt Lectures but in the very lively discussions revolving around the lectures. Childs and I served together in those years on the advisory council of *Interpretation,* so that being together at Union Richmond was not a new experience; what was different was hearing in a systematic way what he understood by reading the Bible in canonical context.

While work on Early Jewish canons, or accepted collections of Scriptures, entails problems involved in *norma normata,* in *Torah and Canon* we were working in the areas of both *norma normata* and *norma normans.* We addressed the inverse of the question Gerhard von Rad had addressed in 1938 in his "Problem of the Hexateuch."[8] Von Rad had asked why in the early recitals or creeds in prophets, psalms, and histories in the Bible there is no mention of the stop at Sinai which is so central to the Pentateuch. I turned the question on its head and asked, since the entrance into the land is mentioned in nearly all the preexilic recitals of Israel's epic history, why is the Book of Joshua not in the Torah? I was asking a question about the shape of the Pentateuch or Torah, and in so doing, I was also asking about the function of Torah in believing communities.

The thesis we advanced was that one of the functions of Torah recited annually (or perhaps for a while triennially in antiquity) as canon was to give Jews their identity in ever-changing situations and circumstances in history, so that wherever they might be they would know who they were and not assimilate to the dominant culture of their time and place. We also suggested that since the largest Jewish community in the world from the sixth century B.C.E. to the Middle Ages was in Babylonia, it was important to note that both the Torah that Ezra brought with him to Jerusalem (Nehemiah 8) as well as the official Talmud of later Formative Judaism were both shaped in the very powerful Jewish communities in Babylonia.

## CANON AS FUNCTION: THE PROBLEMS

*Torah and Canon* thus dealt with canon both as *norma normata* and *norma normans*. From that point on until recently I dealt largely with canonical process, or canon as function. The principal reason was that I was very much impressed with how many so-called canons there had been in Judaism and Christianity and how much they varied in order, if not in both order and content. I agreed with Childs that canon as function had been largely set aside in biblical scholarship since the eighteenth century, precisely to accommodate the needs of biblical criticism in its task of working out the history of formation of the Bible, which Baruch Spinoza had so clearly called for in his *Tractatus* of 1670. But I could not go on with Childs to affirm "the final form of the text," which is essential to his system of thought. The reason was that my work with the Dead Sea Scrolls had taken me into First Testament text criticism which was being revolutionized precisely because of their discovery and assessment for determining the history of transmission of the Hebrew text of the Bible.

In 1969, five scholars from Europe and Britain and I embarked on the United Bible Societies' Hebrew Old Testament Text Project (HOTTP). We accepted the assignment because we not only believed in Eugene Nida's program in the Translations Department of the Bible Societies through observation of what the Greek New Testament committee had been doing, but also because we knew that First Testament text criticism needed radical overhauling. The recovery in 1948 of the famous Tiberian manuscript of the Bible called Aleppensis had inspired the founding of the Hebrew University Bible Project not long after the founding of the State of Israel and the discovery of the Dead Sea Scrolls. Their work as reported in the annual *Textus* and then in the *Sample Edition of Isaiah* in 1965, followed by Goshen-Gottstein's now famous 1967 article on Hebrew manuscripts, needed to be heeded and evaluated as much as possible in any such project as Nida had in mind.[9]

Moving into text criticism, as deeply and critically as required by work on such a project as the HOTTP, clearly meant that I could not follow Childs into his understanding of canonical context. Looking upon all the apparatus in BHK[1-3] (*Biblia hebraica*, ed. R. Kittel) and in BHS (*Biblia hebraica stuttgartensia*) with considerable suspicion, we found we had to do our own work on as many microfilms of ancient manuscripts as feasible. Beginning with Luther, and especially Morin and Cappellus, despite the strenuous objections by the Buxtorfs, father and son, Christian text criticism of the First Testament had moved decisively, by the end of the seventeenth century, into facilitating emendations and conjectures. While the field did not follow Luther's hermeneutic of *res et argumentum* (deciding problem readings in the light of the gospel), it definitely moved in the direction of making text-critical decisions based on higher-critical criteria. It also was striking to us how random had been the selection of manuscripts used in the great text critical compendia. Even Kennicott and de Rossi's collations did not solve the problem: they worked only on European manuscripts, and they largely disregarded the work of the Massoretes in so doing. Johann David Michaelis's criticisms of Kennicott's work are still pertinent; and yet Michaelis, probably the father of First Testament text criticism as it is largely practiced today, must take a great deal of the responsibility for the still prevalent method of text criticism in which a scholar decides contextually what Isaiah ought to have said and then emends the text in the light thereof.[10]

All this caused me in 1977 to leave the faculty of Union Seminary in New York to go to Claremont to help found the Ancient Biblical Manuscript Center so that scholars would no longer have to rely on the biases of interest and competence of earlier scholars who edited the so-called critical editions of crucial texts and versions of the Bible. In doing so and in investigating as many manuscripts as feasible, I have become more and more impressed with the lack of stability in order of books, even in the Jewish canon, after 2 Kings.[11] As Israel Yeivin rightly put it in his *Introduction to the Tiberian Masorah:* "The order of the Books in the Torah and the Former Prophets has been established from earliest times; however, the order of the books in the Latter Prophets and the Writings is not fixed."[12] A simple observation in this regard is that whereas the list in *Baba Bathra* 14b and the much later Second Rabbinic Bible of Jacob ben Hayyim place Chronicles at the end of the *Ketuvîm,* and hence of the Bible, both great Tiberian manuscripts, Aleppensis and

Leningradensis, place it first. Sometimes, however, Ruth is placed first. Whereas there is stability in the extant medieval manuscripts in placing the Books of the Three before the Book of the Twelve, and those before the Writings, it has now been established that the whole concept of the tripartite *Tanak* cannot be affirmed before the sixth century C.E., if then.[13]

This does not at all address the problem of the great variety in order of books after the Pentateuch in LXX MSS, the Bible of the Early Church until well after Jerome's work of *Hebraica Veritas* in the *Vulgata*. When one speaks of canonical context, one must do so very cautiously and with due regard to the facts. Then when one moves on to the Second Testament one must be equally cautious. No fewer than six different lists of the contents of the two testaments were officially received in the Greek church in the tenth century. Most eastern churches have always included 1 and 2 Clement. The Ethiopian Orthodox church has 35 books in its New Testament. According to the Alands in Münster, only 3 uncials and 56 minuscules contain the whole of the New Testament. And if one looks at their holdings, which are as complete as possible, while there are 2328 manuscripts of the Gospels, there are only 287 of the Book of Revelation.[14] As Bruce Metzger recently observed, "It is obvious that the conception of the canon of the New Testament was not essentially a dogmatic issue whereby all parts of the text were regarded as equally necessary."[15] Despite Athanasius's and Origen's lists of 27 New Testament books, both in the fourth century, it was not until 1546 that the Roman Church issued an absolute article of faith (the *De Canonicis Scripturis*), sealed by anathema, concerning the canon of the Christian Bible.[16] The various Reformed confessions at the end of the sixteenth and beginning of the seventeenth centuries list 27 books; and the sixth of the 39 Articles of Faith of the Church of England, issued in 1563, lists the 27. Apparently none of the Lutheran confessional statements includes such a list.

Whether one turns to lists or to actual manuscripts of either Testament, then, one has to be cautious and clear about the meaning of canonical context. This is also true when getting into text criticism of either Testament. In fact, one should probably not speak of a canonical text of either Testament, nor even some final form of the text. One can admire and appreciate the Massoretes and all their work, as I came to do in work on the Dead Sea Scrolls and on the United Bible Societies' HOTTP. Such appreciation, however, does not eliminate the need for sound method in text criticism, such as one can see in the two volumes so far published of *Critique textuelle de l'Ancient Testament*.[17]

## CANON AS FUNCTION: A PROPOSAL

Then what can be said about canon as shape, or *norma normata?* I suggest that, despite the uncertainty of order in the Jewish canon after 2 Kings, the considerable variety in order in the various Septuagint manuscripts also after 2 Kings (granting that Ruth is often placed after Judges), and despite the uncertainties about the content and order of the New Testament, there is a hermeneutical shape to the Jewish and Christian canons. The shape, however, is discernible largely in work on canon as function.[18] I even dare to suggest that what may truly be called canonical are the unrecorded hermeneutics that lie among all the pages of Scripture, and that this canonical hermeneutic derives from Scripture's basic, intertextual nature. Scripture is full of itself. Wherever one discerns an earlier tradition being recited or alluded to, one must ask what the ancient hermeneutics were by which the later tradent caused the earlier tradition to function. And there are very few passages of Scripture, outside the recording of ancient court and temple (civil and cultic) documents, which do not in some sense build on Scriptural traditions. And where Israel's authoritative traditions seem not to be called on, there is plenty of international wisdom alluded to and with which one may do the triangulation necessary to discern the hermeneutics by which the wisdom tradition, whether Israelite, foreign, Christian, or international, functions in the biblical setting.

I further dare to propose that the basic canonical hermeneutic—of whatever canon that has in actuality functioned in historically verifiable believing communities, Jewish and Christian—was "theocentric monotheizing pluralism." Clearly some of the literature monotheizes more thoroughly than others, and clearly some of so-called sectarian literature, whether at Qumran or at Nag Hammadi, tends to polytheize. And, indeed, some of the literature within some of the canons, including the current Protestant canon, does not seem to monotheize very well at all. The question becomes that of whether recognizing a hermeneutical shape permits the reader to read the parts in the light of the whole. I believe that it does.

Is it canonically fair to monotheize in reading a passage that does not exhibit authorial intentionality to monotheize? One must first grant that the first of the Ten Commandments does indeed reflect the basic hermeneutic thrust of what ended up in the canon. If one grants that, then one must still speak only of a theocentric monotheizing thrust that permits one to go back and read the apparently polytheizing and tribalizing passages in the light of the whole. I am satisfied that the canon as a whole, of whichever Jewish or Christian believing community, pursues ultimately the "Integrity of Reality," that is, the ontological and ethical oneness of God. I do not believe that the vast majority of people or their leaders in either ancient Israel or Judah managed to monotheize very well. The evidence is that they were as much polytheizers as modern Christians, and for that matter most ancient Christians. We are here concerned with the Bible as canon, not as a literature that accurately reflects the *vox populi*. On the contrary, if the number of laws against polytheizing and the number of prophetic indictments against it are any indication, most of the people were normal; they were polytheizers. But what got onto a tenure track toward canon, the literature that talked about God being the God of death as well as of life, of fallings as well as of risings, of defeats as well as victories, that was the literature, for the most part, that made it into the canon.

Again the question is not whether some of it tends to polytheize; some of it surely seems to do so. The question rather is whether it is canonically fair to read the parts hermeneutically in the light of the whole.

Another question I wish to address is that of whether, if a canon is read as paradigm, and not as a box of ancient jewels that are somehow still valuable and negotiable, there is warrant for us to do today what the canonical authors did in their time. That is, should we engage in active syncretism and adapt the wisdom of others, of nonbelievers?

First, is it canonically fair to monotheize while reading an apparently polytheizing or tribalizing passage? In Israel's monotheizing pilgrimage Israel at its best, while denying the existence of other gods, steadily added the attributes and job descriptions to Yahweh of most of the gods of the peoples they encountered. The names of the gods of the fathers, as Albrecht Alt and Martin Noth pointed out, became simply epithets of Yahweh. *El Elyon* and *El Shaddai,* as well as names of many other deities, became other names for Yahweh. There is a rabbinic tradition that God has seventy names. Hosea said that Israel did not know that Yahweh had given them the grain, the wine, and the oil (Hos. 2:10 [Eng. 2:8]). They had assumed that such a reputable and reliable agricultural deity as Baal had given them their flocks and crops. But now they were supposed to learn that one God, Yahweh, was not only their redeemer God from slavery in Egypt and their holy warrior God; Yahweh was also creator. Learning that God was creator as well as redeemer would bring the prophets to say that, even as holy warrior, Yahweh might be at the head of enemy troops invading Israel and Judah. This would cost them dearly, but they accepted the monotheizing thrust of the traditions they received and applied it to the life-and-death situation Israel and Judah faced.

There is a short pericope in Exod. 4:24-26 which puzzles many scholars. Scholarship generally agrees that it is a pericope. It can thus be excised without damage to the context in which it is presently found in Exodus 4. It clearly appears to be based on polytheizing thinking. A destroying deity threatens Moses' life, but Zipporah circumcises their son, touches Moses' own genitals with it, and thus saves Moses' life. But note, verse 24 clearly says that the destroying deity or demon (*'el mashhit*) was Yahweh! The editor or redactor Yahwized the story, and in effect monotheized it. It makes it all the more an embarrassment, or so some say. And yet, is not Yahweh the same *'el mashhit* when later God passes over Egypt and kills the Egyptian first-born, and again later causes the death and defeat of the Egyptian army at the Reed Sea? Why is it more embarrassing to have Yahweh attack our guy, Moses, than their guys? I suggest that if we take the clue given, we should ourselves monotheize in reading the whole of the book and see the theological validity of the three-verse snippet in Exod. 4:24-26. Otherwise, we too polytheize when we consciously or unconsciously think it all right for our God to kill their people for our sake.

What of the hardening of Pharaoh's heart? I recently suggested that it is our polytheizing hermeneutic in reading Exodus that causes us to translate the seven occurrences of the piel of *hazaq,* in which God affects Pharaoh's heart, as God hardening Pharaoh's heart. And that hermeneutic began with the LXX translators' using *sklērynō.* Everywhere else the same verb occurs with regard to God's somehow affecting Israel's heart, it is translated by such words as "encourage" and "hearten."[19] Anyway, why should Ramesses go soft-headed all of a sudden and abandon the responsibilities of his office to the Egyptian economy by letting all that cheap labor go free? Pharaoh had a lot of projects to complete. Have Christians who hold power in this country or in South Africa or anywhere else hastened to share their wealth and political power with blacks or other dispossessed folk? And what if Pharaoh had done so? There would have been no Exodus. There might have been a monument of stones set up outside Pithom, Raamses, and Goshen in gratitude to Pharaoh for Pharaoh's "emancipation proclamation," but there would have been no departing in haste, no eating of lamb by midnight, no miracle at the crossing of the waters. The Bible is a book of realism in whatever canon, Jewish or Christian, we know of. That means that it well reflects the ambiguity of reality in which humans live, but also witnesses to the impingement and intrusion of the Integrity of Reality at crucial junctures in our lives. And it means that God works with that ambiguity, with all its antagonists and protagonists, all the pros and cons, all the yins and yangs. The Integrity of Reality, Scripture insists, works with the ambiguity of reality to redeem it.

We Christians can say that the same God who chose one particular slave rebellion in the Late Bronze Age to make God's paradigm of liberation and redemption also chose one heir of the Abraham-Sarah family in the first century C.E. in whom to dwell fully and vulnerably. We do not know why God chose the one slave rebellion to make into God's gospel, any more than we know why God chose one particular Jew in whom to bring that gospel to its paradigmatic climax. Even christological statements of Christ's preexistence do not answer that question.

But if we Christians were to take seriously the canon's monotheizing thrust we would learn to read the New Testament a bit differently from the way we normally do. We would learn to read in the New Testament of God's Christ, not our Christ. We would learn to celebrate God's revelation of Christ in due season and in the fullness of time, and not celebrate how our Christ revealed God, or how our boy tamed the big, mean old God. We would learn to translate the verbs of resurrection in the theological passive, instead of in the middle voice: Christ "was raised," not Christ "arose," unless we clearly mean God's Christ. We would learn and teach that resurrection is a further act of Creation by the one, true God of all Creation. And even in those passages that seem to retribalize Christ, we would learn to reread in a monotheizing mode. John 14:6 would turn from an exclusivist's tribalizing dream into a prophetic indictment of how we have trivialized the concept of God's Christ into a Christian idol. It is true that no person comes to the parent God save through Christ; but it is not our precious idol, which we dearly clutch, who is the route to God, but rather God's Christ, always and ever far and near, always and ever strange and dear, always and ever *deus absconditus* as well as *deus revelatus*. How might Jeremiah or Luke's Jesus preach on such a Johannine passage, or even on the one in Acts 4:12 about there being "no other name"? Would not Our Lord himself challenge our assumptions that we have exhausted the meaning of God's Christ? Would he not challenge our tendency to think that our Christ domesticated God, that our Christ boxed God in for us? Would he not remind us that we are commanded to fear God as well as love God? Would he not teach us a fuller view of the incarnation than one that turns Christ into an idol, and God into a doting, avuncular figure?

## CONCLUSION

If the canon is viewed as paradigm of the monotheizing process, might it not provide us with clues as to how we should go on learning from others of God's children? And if we truly believe that God is the God of all creation, might we Christians not need to learn real humility and awe in speaking and thinking of God? Could we go on denying the work of God other than in our understanding of the gospel? To learn from others' wisdom and experience is to honor God. A true evangelism derived from a monotheizing reading of the Bible would result in the joy of living, speaking, dancing, and singing the gospel. It would issue in a healthy fear as to whether we might not be lost in our own tribalizing tendencies (our own corruption of consciousness) rather than in the self-serving fear that others are lost. And if God is ever more than we can think or imagine, is it not precisely that important to learn with respect and humility from others, as well as to share with enthusiasm and joy our ever-evolving and ever-renewing understanding of the gospel?

## NOTES

1. "Cave Eleven Surprises and the Question of Canon," *McCormick Quarterly* 21 (1968) 284–98, reprinted in D. Freedman and J. Greenfield, eds., *New Directions in Biblical Archaeology* (Garden City, N.Y.: Doubleday, 1969).

2. See John Barton, *Oracles of God* (Oxford: Oxford University Press, 1986) 86.

3. (Philadelphia: Fortress, 1972). Translated as *Identité de la Bible* (Paris: Cerf, 1975) and into Japanese (1984).

4. In *Interpretation* (1964) 432–49.

5. (Philadelphia: Westminster).

6. D. Barthélemy, O.P., "La critique canonique," unpublished paper requested by the Pontifical Biblical Commission in Rome, available from the author at the Institut biblique de l'Université de Fribourg en Suisse, or from the present writer.

7. *Critical Review of Books in Religion* 1 (1988) 137–41. By contrast see the perceptive articles by B. W. Anderson and S. Towner in *Religious Studies Review* 15:2 (1989) 97–103.

8. In *Das formgeschichtliche Problem des Hexateuchs* (Stuttgart: W. Kohlhammer, 1938). Trans. by E. W. Trueman Dicken, from von Rad's *Gesammelte Studien zum Alten Testament* (Munich: Kaiser, 1958), as *The Problem of the Hexateuch and Other Essays* (New York: McGraw-Hill, 1966) 1–78. See the very fine critique in historical perspective by Joseph W. Groves, *Actualization and Interpretation in the Old Testament* (Atlanta: Scholars Press, 1987), and the present writer's review of it in *Catholic Biblical Quarterly* 51 (1989) 329–31.

9. The annual, *Textus,* has been published irregularly by the HUBP since 1961; M. H. Goshen-Gottstein, *The Book of Isaiah: Sample Edition with Introduction* (Jerusalem: Magnes Press, 1965) 11–45; Goshen-Gottstein, "Hebrew Biblical Manuscripts: Their History and Their Place in the HUBP Edition," *Biblica* 48 (1967) 243–90.

10. For a cursory review of the hermeneutics of First Testament text criticism from the sixteenth to eighteenth centuries see the writer's "Hebrew Bible and Old Testament: Textual Criticism in Service of Biblical Studies," in *Hebrew Bible or Old Testament? Studying the Bible in Judaism and Christianity,* ed. Roger Brooks and John J. Collins, Christianity and Judaism in Antiquity 5 (Notre Dame: University of Notre Dame Press, 1990), 41–68.

11. Where the (hi)story line is continuous, that is, from Genesis to 2 Kings, there is stability in all Hebrew manuscripts as well as in lists in Jewish literature where available. Even before the widespread use of the codex, after the second century C.E., control of the order of Torah and Early Prophets scrolls was simple.

12. (Atlanta: Scholars Press, 1980) 38.

13. Georg Eicher, *Die Schrift in der Mischna* (1906) cited in Peter Pettit, "Comparative Study of Torah Citations and Other Scripture in the Mishnah." Unpublished major paper for Claremont Graduate School doctoral program in biblical studies.

14. Kurt and Barbara Aland, *The Text of the New Testament,* trans. E. Rhodes (Grand Rapids: Eerdmans; Leiden: Brill, 1987) 78–79.

15. B. Metzger, *The Canon of the New Testament: Its Origin, Development and Significance* (Oxford: Clarendon, 1987) 217.

16. See the writer's "Scripture, Canon of" forthcoming in *The Coptic Encyclopedia,* ed. Aziz Atiya.

17. D. Barthélemy, *Critique textuelle de l'Ancient Testament,* Orbis biblicus et orientalis 50, nos. 1 and 2 (Fribourg: Presses universitaires, 1982, 1986).

18. See the writer's entry "Deuteronomy" in B. W. Anderson, ed., *The Books of the Bible* (New York: Charles Scribner's Sons, 1989) 1:89–102.

19. See the writer's "The Strangeness of the Bible," *Union Seminary Quarterly Review* 42 (1988) 33–37, as well as "The Challenge of Fundamentalism: One God and World Peace," *Impact* 19 (1987) 12–30.

# 5 Historical Criticism

*Liberator or Foe
of Biblical Theology?*

In the history of theology in recent decades, "biblical theology" has had its up and downs. In this country during the 1950s, something like a biblical theology movement had emerged. Perhaps it is fair to say that the movement was spearheaded by G. Ernest Wright, who published in the early 1950s two modestly sized contributions that attracted wide interest and seemed suitable to serve as programmatic statements for a reorientation in biblical studies and a reassessment of their value for other theological disciplines.[1] Fully conversant with what appeared then to be reliable results of form-critical Old Testament studies, Wright projected biblical theology as a "recital" of "the mighty acts of God in history," which provided a structure and a summation of essential content common to both Old and New Testament. The recital of God's historical acts was not only perceived as the bond holding Old and New Testament together, but also as a rediscovery of the uniqueness of the biblical language of God whose contrast to religions of its environment Wright drew in very sharp lines of demarcation. For some years, this biblical theology movement produced considerable enthusiasm. It engendered confidence among biblical interpreters about the importance of their work, and it appeared to have enough power to invite other theological disciplines to a reevaluation of their basic assumptions.

Soon, however, the movement began to totter. After a few years, unable to take devastating critical blows, it went down for the count. The criticism came partly from the movement's own ranks, and partly from people who had never been sympathetic to its aims.[2] Biblical theology, at least in the United States, seemed defeated for good. There has, however, been resurgence of concern for biblical theology, especially in Germany but also in this country. Having been one of its advocates for many years, I venture to say that biblical theology has a chance again today. I do not know its future. But if it is to have a future, it will have to face squarely some of the criticisms that have been leveled against it. The list of criticisms raised against biblical theology is impressive, but for the purposes of this essay will not be collected and analyzed, let alone answered. But one single point of controversy over a long period of time has proven germane to the problem.

Modern biblical theology is indebted to Johann Philipp Gabler. In an inaugural address of 1787, entitled "Discourse on the Correct Distinction of Biblical and Dogmatic Theology and the Correct Definition of Their Goals," Gabler wanted to liberate biblical interpretation from the chains of a dogmatic and rationalist system that superimposed on biblical texts ready-made answers. He was convinced that biblical texts require for their correct interpretation a sensitivity for history so that the original meaning of those texts can be explained as products of a specific period of time. Biblical theology, therefore, requires historical research, the capacity to understand ancient documents as mirrors of their time. For Gabler, then, biblical theology called for historical investigation as its ally.[3] One hundred seventy years later, the proposal of a biblical theology offered by G. E. Wright received one of its most severe criticisms from historians, who objected that what Wright had called "the mighty acts of God in history" were in reality elements of Israel's faith whose grounding in "historical facts" was highly tenuous. Thus, historical research had turned into one of the strongest antagonists against a fundamental claim made by the biblical theology movement of the 1950s and 1960s.

This snapshot from the history of biblical interpretation marks our question: Is the domain of history, and the human urge to explore this domain, the liberator or the foe of biblical theology?

In order to approach the question, we should recall one of the most influential advocates of historical criticism of the Bible as well as of any other old document. Attempting to give historical research a sound methodological basis, Ernst Troeltsch formulated his famous three principles of historical research.[4] It is true that later critics have taken Troeltsch to task both for being too narrow in allowing for only three principles and for being too absolute in claiming for them virtual omnipotence.[5] In spite of such justified objections, I choose Troeltsch as paradigm because the issue emerges from his principles with the greatest clarity.

Troeltsch suggests that historical investigation has to involve the critical sifting of evidence in order to separate the wheat of what really happened from the chaff of errors, legends, and myths. To do that, the historian has to employ three operating principles, which Troeltsch calls the principles of criticism, analogy, and correlation. By criticism he means an attitude of reserve and detachment on the part of the historian, who initially will have to treat the documents with critical suspicion. By analogy he means the axiom that truth or falsity of events long past can only be established on the assumption that past events must have happened in analogy to present experience. And correlation, finally, stands for the thesis that there is an interconnection between the events in history (*Wechselwirkung*) so that every single point in time must be conditioned by its antecedents.

There is no question that historical investigation into the Old and New Testaments, guided or at least influenced by those principles, has produced a rich store of knowledge that has vastly improved our understanding of realities within which all biblical books were written. Respect for the Bible, the endeavor to be as accurate in its interpretation as possible, and the sixteenth-century Reformation's insistence on the literal meaning of Old and New Testament, demand a historical approach.[6] On the other hand, the harvest of a tremendous amount of historical research into the Bible has produced so many divergent and frequently contradictory hypotheses, leaving the student of Scripture bewildered by the fact that theories about origin, growth, use, and intention of biblical documents, theories that mean to illuminate what is *behind* the texts, are at least as full of riddles as the texts themselves.[7] So from time to time, one cannot escape the impression that seekers for historical truth in the Bible are encouraged to put on the full armor of historical research, gird their loins with the attitude of criticism, put on the breastplate of analogy, and have their feet shod with the idea of correlation, in order to set out for the conquest of the promised land of historical truth. During this campaign it happens on occasion that the biblical books and passages, instead of being cut loose from a chain of inaccuracies and superstitions, become victims of a new incarceration in the form of supposedly objective, historical reconstructions which are claimed to be indispensable presuppositions for their true understanding. Documents seem to be put on the rack of a historical methodology that is applied in the hope that, under painful investigation, they may finally confess the truth of a historical reality which they had successfully hidden under a camouflage of legends and myths.

A dilemma arises: Is the critical historian friend or foe of the biblical theologian? The dilemma seems related to two different perceptions of what constitutes human history, perceptions which are exemplified, on the one side, by a Greek approach and, on the other side, by an understanding of events in time as it emerges in some Old Testament traditions.

## THE WORD *HISTORIA* IN GREEK USAGE

The word first appears in Greek tradition in the Homeric epics. Twice in the *Iliad,* the word *histōr* (or *istōr*)[8] is used with the meaning of "umpire," "judge," or "arbitrator." Book 18 contains the famous description of the shield of Hephaestus, which is adorned with scenes from the life of gods and humans. One scene depicts the strife that arises between two men who argue about the blood price of a slain man. Since neither can win the argument before the throng in the marketplace, they both appeal the case to an experienced neutral arbitrator, "each was keen to win the issue on the word of a judge" (*histōr; Iliad* 18.501). In book 23 a dispute arises between Aias and Idomeneus about the claim of each to own the better horses. To settle the case, Idomeneus invokes the decision of Agamemnon who is to decide the issue as judge (*histōr; Iliad* 23.486). The Homeric *histōr* is a person who looks objectively at the facts, examines their merit, and then decides the issue. This involves both the activity of critical and impartial examination through inquiry and observation, and a judgment separating true from false claims. Hence, the basic meaning of *historeō* is not "to record history," but "to inquire, examine, critically observe," and the noun *historia* does not denote "history," but "inquiry, systematic and scientific observation."[9]

Among earlier Greek historians, this meaning of the words derived from the stem *histor* is not changed. Herodotus, often called the father of Greek history-writing, begins his work on the history of the Greek and Persian wars as follows: *Hērodotou Halikarnēsseos historiēs apodexis hēde* (1.1) which is not to be translated with "this is the account of the history composed by Herodotus of Halicarnassus," but rather by "what Herodotus of Halicarnassus has learned by inquiry is here set forth."[10] While numerous other examples of this usage of the word in Herodotus's work could be given, one further example may suffice. Herodotus tells us that in his travels in Egypt he met Egyptian priests who knew of stories concerning Helen of Troy. In order to find out more about this oral tradition, he asks the priests for more information. The priests' answer is introduced with the words, *elegon de moi hoi hirees historeonti,* "and the priests told me as I inquired of them" (2.113). Centuries later, in the Hellenistic age, historians writing in Greek still followed the same usage. Plutarch, for example, tells that Theseus was invited to a wedding, which gave him the occasion "to observe the country" (*kai tēn chōran historēsai, Theseus* 30), and that Cato the philosopher went up to Antioch "to inspect the city" (*historēsai tēn polin, Pompey* 40).

In Greek philosophy, the critical, scientific element in the word *historia* and its derivatives is even more pronounced. In philosophical language the adjective *historikos* means, therefore, not "historical,",but "exact, precise, scientific."[11] A smattering of examples from Plato and Aristotle can serve to illustrate this. Plato makes the distinction concerning the important concept of *mimēsis* between an imitation based purely on opinion, and one founded on knowledge, a scientifically supported imitation (*tēn de met' epistēmēs historikēn tina mimēsin, Sophist* 267c). In his *Phaedus* (96a) he calls scientific inquiry into nature *hē peri physeōs historia*, and Aristotle follows suit by writing about research on all forms of life as *hai peri tōn zōōn historiai* (*de Respiratione* 477a7).

It is true that the word *historia* could secondarily assume the meaning of "historical account," perhaps already in one instance in Herodotus (although this is contested) and certainly from Ephorus in the fourth century B.C.E. on. But even then the connotation of critical observation was retained. *Historia*, in this usage, means the account of events ascertained by research and objective judgment, as distinct from accounts of poets.[12]

*Historia* and *historeō* among Greek poets, historians, and philosophers, then, refer to the process of critical investigation, objective and detached examination and inquiry, aiming at the sifting of truth from error and at the establishment of reliable fact and information. Since modern historical research on which critical writing of history is built also has this aim, it is understandable and proper that Herodotus and Thucydides are each given the title "father of history." To this approach to history Ernst Troeltsch supplied his three criteria of historical criticism. We have no quarrel with this approach. We should also not allow ourselves, however, to be blinded to the fact that what happens from one human generation to another may also be perceived through a totally different set of eyes by a different people. With that in mind, we now turn our attention to the Bible and the outlook of its people.

## WORD AND WORKS OF GOD IN SOME OLD TESTAMENT TRADITIONS

There is no question that the Bible contains a great deal of narrative. About two-thirds of the New Testament have at least the appearance of historical works, and it is certain that a Jewish writer with Hellenistic education could, at the time when the New Testament was being written, refer to his own account of the Jewish heritage as a specimen of "history writing" (Josephus, *Jewish Antiquities* 1.1, *tas historias syngraphein*). It is, then, all the more striking that in the New Testament and in the Greek version of the Old Testament, words derived from the root *histor* are almost completely absent. None of the Gospels is called a *historia,* and even in Acts, written by an author with demonstrable erudition in Hellenistic culture, words of the *histor*-family are totally absent. Only once, in the New Testament, has a *histor*-word been used, but it has nothing to do with "history." In Gal. 1:18 Paul writes that he went up to Jerusalem in order to *historēsai Kēphan,* a phrase usually translated "to visit Cephas," which in the light of the previous discussion might also mean "to inquire of Cephas."[13] Whatever its precise meaning, Gal. 1:18 exhausts the use made in the entire New Testament of the word-family *histor,* and it has manifestly nothing to do with history writing. Whenever the New Testament coins words summarizing the content of its numerous stories into a single noun, it uses a different vocabulary. We find "gospel," "proclamation," "word," "witness," and corresponding verbal phrases, but never the word "history."

Nor is the matter different in the Greek translation of the Old Testament. Within the bounds of the Hebrew canon of Scripture, except for a single instance in the Book of Esther, the entire word family derived from the stem *histor* is completely missing in the Septuagint.[14] If one takes into account the Alexandrian Old Testament canon, the result becomes a little less lopsided. In what in Jewish and Protestant tradition is considered apocryphal Old Testament literature, the verb *historeō* appears three times, the noun *historia* five.[15] Five of these instances occur in 2 and 4 Maccabees, that is to say in books that exhibit an unusually high degree of Hellenistic influence. But it remains significant that the Greek translation of our canonical Old Testament books avoids the use of the word-family *histor* altogether, in spite of their being saturated with accounts that we would call history.

It is remarkable that neither the writers of the New Testament nor the translators of the Septuagint made use of the word-family *histor* to describe their work even if it consisted in large part in the chronicling of events. This omission may be coincidence, or it may signal a reluctance to use a word that was shaped by a mode of recording past events out of touch with the way they wished to appropriate the "history" with which they were concerned. The issue cannot be decided by the use or omission of a single word. But the omission of words from the family *histor* in the Bible may alert us to the possibility of looking further into alternative approaches to the recording of past events of which the Greek option is only one. In our search for a different option, we turn to an aspect of the Old Testament.

Biblical Hebrew has two words that approximate to some degree what we have in mind when we speak of history: *tôlēdôt* and *dābār*. In the interest of brevity, we concentrate entirely on the more important second word.

The Hebrew word *dābār* has an astonishingly wide range of meanings. Two of them are important to our purpose. The noun *dābār* can mean "the word," and the verb *dibber* means "to speak." Not infrequently, however, *dābār* denotes what we call an event, and the plural *dĕbārîm* a sequence of events, something close to our "history." In prophetic language, God is constantly said to speak, and what the prophet hears and communicates is the word of Yahweh. For the prophet it is impossible to pretend ignorance of the *dābār* from God: "the lion has roared, who will not fear? The Lord Yahweh has spoken, who can but prophesy?" (Amos 3:8). On the other hand, *dābār* and *dĕbārîm* often mean events and chains of events. Frequently in 1 Kings, the *dibrē hayyamîm* are not the "words of the day," but the "events of those days" (14:19, 29 among others); the *sēphēr dibrē Šĕlōmōh* is "the chronicle of the history of Solomon" (11:41). In Genesis the phrase *'aḥar haddĕbārîm ha'ēleh* (e.g., Gen. 15:1), meaning "after these events," occurs five times. Realities such as "event" and "word," which in our language and experience live in some rather critical distance from each other, are named in biblical Hebrew by one and the same word.

To get to the root of this baffling bifurcation of meaning, we propose four correlated theses drawn from that portion of Old Testament literature that provides for us the most illuminating stage of the tradition: the prophetic works of the eighth to the sixth centuries B.C.E., and the so-called Deuteronomistic history.[16]

1. The "word of God" that occurs to the prophet is the disclosure of Yahweh as personal will. This "word of God" does not reveal general and timeless information about divine qualities or attributes; it is in itself an event occurring in time and possessing time. In each "word of God" Yahweh is personally present, and the occurrence of this word remains unpredictably free. When Yahweh decides to speak, Yahweh speaks, and there is no law of history that could anticipate or categorize that event. In his *dābār*, Yahweh opens himself as known participant in the life of his people. In this *dābār*, Yahweh tells of his own involvement and participation in the decisions, acts, and thoughts of Israel. Thus the "word of God" announces what time it is for Israel in the eyes of God, and how God is affected and moved as participant of Israel's time. This

affect ranges from fury to the emotions of a lover. In his *dābār,* Yahweh can become Israel's contemporary as a mortal enemy whose situation is comparable to that of "someone [who] fled from a lion, and was met by a bear; or went into the house and rested a hand against the wall, and was bitten by a snake" (Amos 5:19), but Yahweh can also speak to Israel in cadences of patient love, as in Hos. 11:8-9: "How can I give you up, Ephraim? How can I hand you over, O Israel? . . . My heart recoils within me, my compassion grows warm and tender." In the event of Yahweh's *dābār,* then, Yahweh discloses himself as partner of Israel's time, in anguish and in anger, in compassion and in mercy, and this disclosure of God happens only when Yahweh wills to speak.

2. Yahweh's self-disclosure in his word holds within it, at the same time, the disclosure of the true character of human life in that moment of history when Yahweh speaks to Israel through the prophet. In this disclosure, the human opinion of what is real and decisive is frequently declared to be absurd from the vantage point of the divine governor of reality. A single example of this reversal of judgments, drawn from Isa. 7:1-9 and 8:5-8, must suffice.

The time is 733–732 B.C.E. (historical criticism has succeeded in pinning down those years!). An alliance of the Northern Kingdom of Israel, represented by its most important tribe Ephraim, and of the kingdom of Syria, headed by Rezin the son of Remaliah, is on the verge of invading Judah/Jerusalem. Jerusalem's King Ahaz, together with his aides and his population, are panic-stricken by what they can only perceive as mortal danger to their state. To them, the situation is desperate, calling for the desperate measure of appealing to Assyria for help, which is even now prepared to swallow up the entire Palestinian region. At this moment, Yahweh's *dābār* occurs to Isaiah and delivers an astoundingly different evaluation of the situation. Samaria and Damascus together are but two smoldering stumps of firebrands of whom one need not be afraid, but real apprehension is in order in view of Assyria, about which king and people are given to fantastic illusions because the presumed immediate danger blinds their eyes to the real menace farther north.

The picture presented by this flashback in history presents itself over and over again in prophetic texts. The event of the "word of God" yields an insight into the historical reality of Israel's life at the time, an insight that is diametrically opposed to the evaluation of those who are governed by what they can see as real life. The event of God's *dābār,* then, reveals the panorama of history which is hidden from everyday human understanding and discloses itself only when Yahweh utters his judgment of what is real.

3. But Yahweh's *dābār* is not only the unveiling of what is hidden within the stuff of history. It is also power that creates what is about to become historical reality. That which Yahweh discloses about himself, and that which he announces to be the God-envisioned truth of history, is no idle information. Yahweh's *dābār* is also Yahweh's will, which is certain to come to pass. Yahweh's *dābār* as word will invariably become Yahweh's *dābār* as historical reality. This is why in prophetic language and in the Deuteronomistic history the *dābār* of God is described as power that smashes every resistance and will assert itself contrary to all human judgments about historical realities and possibilities. This is why the prophets have experienced the "word of God" as the force that fashions events. Jeremiah can say, "Is not my word like fire, says the Lord, and like a hammer that breaks a rock in pieces?" (23:29). And Second Isaiah states, "As the rain and the snow come down from heaven, and do not return there until they have watered the earth, making it bring forth and sprout, giving seed to the sower and bread to the eater, so shall my word be that goes out from my mouth; it shall not return to me empty, but it shall accomplish that which I purpose, and succeed in the thing for which I sent it" (55:10-11).

4. The communication of the "word of God" by the prophet is itself a continuation and prolongation of the divine *dābār* to a degree that the prophet's own life becomes, in part and sometimes in much resistance, a fragmentary human form of Yahweh's powerful speaking. Since the *dĕbar Yhwh* is power that simultaneously illuminates as word and creates as event, the prophet who is the carrier of this *dābār* becomes subject in person to its formative strength. Thus in Hosea's marriage, in Jeremiah's and Ezekiel's prophetic sign-actions, the prophet himself becomes a human paradigm that carries in its flesh the "word of God." The prophet in person becomes a historical event that exhibits the creative history of Yahweh's *dābār.*

The New Testament presents the "history" of Jesus Christ guided by premises akin to the encounter with the word of Yahweh in early prophetic and Deuteronomistic groups in Israel. It completes and surpasses the lines traced in that part of the Old Testament tradition in all four points. Four aspects indicate the relationship.

1. The New Testament, in its account of the life of Jesus and its proclamation of the risen Lord, tells of a sequence of stories illuminated by speech which in their totality are honored and remembered as the complete and all-sufficient self-presentation of God in person.

2. The presentation of the words and acts of Jesus in the Gospels provides a vista of the reality of God in the world—the kingship of

God—which leaves the experts of "real life" with its history in amazement, presenting a "history" impregnated with "word of God" which no human eye had yet seen and of which no human ear had yet heard.

3. The "word of God" as power creating history achieves its unsurpassable apex in the resurrection of Jesus Christ from the dead in which a history of death is re-created through the power of God's verdict which fashions a new reality.

4. The prolongation and continuation of the event of God's *dābār* into the very life of the prophet is in the New Testament freed from all fragmentation and limitation in the assertion of the Gospel of John, "the Word became flesh," which is in its particular wording genuine only in the Fourth Gospel, but as a hermeneutical sign-post it is valid for the New Testament as a whole.


## SOME CONCLUDING OBSERVATIONS

The four premises guiding the writing of history in the New Testament are correlated to four characteristics of experiencing events in prophetic and Deuteronomistic writings in the Old Testament. This does not imply the view that specific early prophetic and Deuteronomistic ways of encountering and recording history were, consciously or subconsciously, received by New Testament writers as a deposit of normative traditions that were preserved intact and without modification over a period of some five hundred years. The Old Testament, before and after the emergence of early prophetic and Deuteronomistic concepts of worldly events as consequences of Yahweh's word, evidences a number of different approaches to the phenomena of history.[17] The correlation made between New Testament and prophetic-Deuteronomistic traditions intends to suggest that the early prophetic and Deuteronomistic body of writings reflects a way of seeing and of experiencing history completely dependent on the occurrence of a free act of self-communication by the God of Israel, an act that provides the ground upon which events are recorded. And this dependence on the happening of God's self-disclosure is also the premise that guides the manner in which the New Testament presents its history.

The centuries between 750 B.C.E. and the period in which the New Testament was written have provided, within early Judaism, new forms of seeing and perceiving history, and they have consequently also produced new possibilities of history writing. Some of them have influenced the New Testament very deeply and have added materially to its mode of writing history. The most important of these new understandings of history is its apocalyptic form, without which much New Testament recording of events cannot be properly understood. It may be said, however, that apocalyptic forms of presenting history, while being by no means a simple elongation of prophetic traditions, are in part intensifications of the four premises of seeing history in the prophetic-Deuteronomistic traditions. The revelational aspect of the word of God is intensified through the much more developed means of dreams, visions, and successive oral interpretations; the hiddenness of history's truth is further emphasized by the need for special disclosures of what had already previously been revealed (as in Dan. 9:1-2); the power of Yahweh's word to make history is elevated to the preordination of historical eras by divine decree; and the participation of the human agent in God's act on earth is given heightened expression in the form of mediator figures who enact God's will in their own life-story.[18]

This essay draws attention to a difference in premises beneath the accomplishment of writing history as they are exemplified by the Greek manner to tell *historia,* and some biblical traditions that view historical events as outcomes of God's word. The distance between these modes of perceiving events is very great. The one puts a premium on the critical evaluation of evidence, on the objectivity of judgment, and on the verifiability of data. The other tells a story as engaged participant, as passionate and intentional partisan of a position, and in the knowledge that the facticity of data and the perception of truth as seen in light of a divine disclosure of reality are far apart from each other. It is clear that the historical-critical method of interpreting the Bible owes a great deal to the Greek approach to writing history. In dealing with biblical texts it risks absolutizing its own presuppositions to the degree that it produces a method of investigation impervious to claims originating from altogether different assumptions about the essence of history. If that happens, historical-critical scholarship becomes blind to the essential features of events as biblical texts presented them, and then the task of interpreting texts in openness to and in the service of elucidating their own original intention is forfeited.

On the other hand, this essay is itself indebted to Greek methods of analysis, critical differentiation, and distancing objectivity. It does not purpose to put down Greek ways of observation and thought simply because they are Greek and not Hebrew.[19] It does not want to join the ranks of those who have decried the historical-critical method on principle.[20] After all, the presence of Luke in the New Testament may serve as a warning against drawing radically anti-Greek conclusions from the differences in viewing history among Greeks and some important biblical traditions. Both as evangelist and as chronicler of earliest Christian history, Luke was indebted to Greek ways of recording history. The prologue of his Gospel (1:1-4) does not just indicate his familiarity with technical terms of Greek writers of history, but it adopts their critical intention. The adoption of Greek traditions of recording history is undeniable in the speeches and narratives of Acts.[21] It is also necessary to emphasize that, both in his Gospel and in Acts, Luke remains the theologian who cares about historical truth in the service of a community that is founded by the word of Jesus and the apostles, a community that depends on the hearing and the realization of this word in its life, and that comes into being through faith in this word.[22]

The historical-critical approach to biblical interpretation is, therefore, neither the friend nor the foe of biblical theology. Renaissance and Reformation have jointly promoted the requirement in the Western tradition of the church to consider the original historical meaning of a passage of Scripture to be the primary sense of the Bible for the church, and its ever-new elucidation the primary exegetical task. There are philosophical questions regarding this basic requirement which demand answers, questions such as, "Is there a single original meaning in a given text?" or, "If a text is understood as a living power beyond its being first committed to paper, are not later conclusions from it part of its original depth?" But the thrust of the requirement to understand an ancient author on his or her terms remains fully valid. For the recovery of the intended meaning of biblical texts, the historical-critical method has supplied a storehouse of tools and data without which the modern interpreter cannot work and for whose application no apologies should be made. It does not invalidate the method that the roots of this approach lie in the Greek perception of history. Historical criticism is, therefore, no enemy to biblical theology.

The other side of the issue needs, however, equal emphasis. The reconstruction through historical-critical methods of original circumstances, historical conditions, and time-bound concepts does not by itself lead to the truth of history of which biblical texts speak. At least important traditions within Old and New Testament present themselves as apperceptions of history which are brought about by a divine judgment on the reality of historical life, apperceptions that do not arise from a human evaluation and that bind the entire existence of the recipient of this disclosure from God to the truth of the divine judgment. A critical distance to this truth is impossible because it would immediately involve the loss of this truth itself. A biblical theology that aims at restating, in our own words and concepts, this word of God must leave the possibilities of historical criticism behind to become a true echo of the self-communicating God whose verdict on history commits the inter-preter to its truth, is discontinuous with other forms of understanding history, and makes its arrival as a radically new possibility of perceiving, which is not the product of historical causes outside the power of this word itself. Therefore, historical criticism cannot simply be the friend of biblical theology. Historical-critical work on the Bible can remain a servant of biblical theology, a very valuable and indispensable servant, but it cannot displace or substitute for the indigenous power of biblical texts themselves in which human history and the history of the world at large are confronted with the lordship of the one God who, outside of the divine word, is unknown, distant, and therefore in the last analysis unhistorical.

## NOTES

1. G. Ernest Wright, *The Old Testament Against Its Environment,* Studies in Biblical Theology 2 (London: SCM, 1950); *God Who Acts: Biblical Theology as Recital,* Studies in Biblical Theology 8 (London: SCM, 1952).

2. Sympathetic to the aims of the movement was the highly influential book by Brevard S. Childs, *Biblical Theology in Crisis* (Philadelphia: Westminster, 1970); symptomatic for many attacks by writers who had not shared the movement's orientation was Langdon S. Gilkey, "Cosmology, Ontology, and the Travail of Biblical Language," *Journal of Religion* 41 (1961) 194–205.

3. This is true even though Gabler aimed in his concept of biblical theology at universal and abiding ideas that become the enduring elements of Christian doctrine. Historical investigation is necessary to sift the geographical, cultural, and temporal elements as dispensable from the stock of lasting universal notions. Therefore, historical investigation is an ally to biblical theology only in the sense that "it provides the grounds for its own transcendence," Ben C. Ollenburger, "Biblical Theology: Situating the Discipline," in *Understanding the Word: Essays in Honor of Bernhard W. Anderson,* ed. J. T. Butler et al., JSOT Supplementary Series 37 (Sheffield: JSOT Press, 1985) 46.

4. Ernst Troeltsch, "Über historische und dogmatische Methode in der Theologie," *Gesammelte Schriften 2. Zur religiösen Lage, Religionsphilosophie und Ethik* (Tübingen: Mohr-Siebeck, 1913) 729–53.

5. Van A. Harvey, *The Historian and the Believer: The Morality of Historical Knowledge and Christian Belief* (New York: Macmillan, 1966).

6. G. Ebeling, "Die Bedeutung der historisch-kritischen Methode für die protestantische Theologie und Kirche," *Wort und Glaube* (Tübingen: Mohr-Siebeck, 1967) 1:1–49; "The Significance of the Critical Historical Method for Church and Theology in Protestantism," in *Word and Faith,* trans. J. W. Leitch (Philadelphia: Fortress, 1963) 17–61.

7. P. Stuhlmacher, "Historische Kritik und theologische Schriftauslegung," *Schriftauslegung auf dem Wege zur biblischen Theologie* (Göttingen: Vandenhoeck & Ruprecht, 1975) 59–127. Stuhlmacher points out, through a synopsis of some conclusions arrived at by New Testament scholars in Germany during the early 1970s, that in several of the most crucial fields of study the rigorous application of historical criticism led to affirmations so much at variance with each other that the "conclusions" resemble more a "chain of contradictory theses and hypotheses" (my translation, 110) than a common ground. Such an occurrence is liable to produce a sense of skepticism with regard to the reliability of historical-critical methods (107–11).

8. The noun appears with and without aspirate, H. G. Liddell and R. Scott, *A Greek-English Lexicon* (Oxford: Clarendon Press, 1968) 842.

9. Ibid.

10. Such is the translation by A. D. Godley in the Loeb Classical Library, *Herodotus,* vol. 1 (Cambridge: Harvard University Press; London: Heinemann, 1946) 3.

11. Liddell-Scott, *Lexicon* 842.

12. F. Büchsel, "*historeō (historia),*" *Theological Dictionary of the New Testament,* ed. G. Kittel (Grand Rapids: Eerdmans) 3 (1965): 391–96, esp. 392–93.

13. G. D. Kilpatrick suggested the translation "to get information from Cephas"; "Galatians 1:18 *historēsai Kēphan,*" in *New Testament Essays: Studies in Memory of Thomas Walker Manson* (Manchester: Manchester University Press, 1959) 144–49. W. D. Davies preferred rabbinical usage amounting to the translation "inquire or seek after a tradition"; *The Setting of the Sermon on the Mount* (Cambridge: Cambridge University Press, 1964) 453–55.

14. The word *historia* is found in Esther 8:12g (LXX).

15. First Esdras (RSV Apocrypha) has *historeō* at 1:33 twice and at 1:42 (Greek 1:31, 40). Second Macc. 2:24, 30, 32; 4 Macc. 3:19; 17:7 use *historia.*

16. Compare to the summation in four points especially O. Grether, *Name und Wort Gottes im Alten Testament,* Beihefte zur Zeitschrift für die alttestamentliche Wissenschaft 64 (Giessen: Töpelmann, 1934) esp. 97–111.

17. An excellent brief discussion of the wide variety of historical traditions in the Old Testament, together with rich references to pertinent literature on the subject, can be found in R. Smend, "Tradition and History: A Complex Relation," *Tradition and Theology in the Old Testament,* ed. D. A. Knight (Philadelphia: Fortress, 1977) 49–68.

18. For the last point, see L. W. Hurtado, *One God, One Lord: Early Christian Devotion and Ancient Jewish Monotheism* (Philadelphia: Fortress, 1988).

19. T. Boman, *Hebrew Thought Compared with Greek* (Philadelphia: Westminster, 1960).

20. The historical-critical method is accused of destroying the appropriate understanding of biblical texts by G. Maier, *The End of the Historical-Critical Method* (St. Louis: Concordia, 1977), and by W. Wink, *The Bible in Human*

*Transformation: Toward a New Paradigm for Biblical Study* (Philadelphia: Fortress, 1973).

21. Following earlier works, M. Dibelius has treated the subject in several articles, most thoroughly in "The Speeches in Acts and Ancient Historiography," *Studies in the Acts of the Apostles* (London: SCM, 1956) 138–85.

22. F. Bovan, "Le salut dans les écrits de Luc. Essay," *Revue de théologie et de philosophie* 105 (1973) 296–307.

# II THE PRACTICE OF BIBLICAL THEOLOGY
## Biblical Theology as Practical Theology

# 6  Toward a Biblical Theology

Theology is what we say concerning God and, on the basis of that, what we say about ourselves, our world, and our neighbor. To speak of biblical theology means that what we say concerning these things—God, ourselves, our world, and our neighbor—is shaped and governed by the Bible. For the Christian the Bible is primarily the canonical books of the Old and New Testaments, sacred writings gathered and preserved by the believing community and regarded by the community as the word of God.

This situation raises serious and persistent problems for the biblical theologian, as the history of biblical theology clearly shows. To say, in the first place, that the Bible is the word of God raises the problem of revelation and history. How can the God who transcends history be revealed in a book of historical witnesses which is itself historically conditioned? To speak of the Bible as the word of God is also to assert its unity; and this is a second problem, for it is clear that within the Scriptures, even within each of the Testaments, there is great diversity. Again, to speak of the Bible as the word of God is to assume a confession of faith, but this may often be at odds with the biblical witness which is in itself a history of confessions of faith.

In the face of such problems it would appear that a theology of the whole Bible is not a possibility. The situation is not helped by the fact that for the most part the issues are dealt with primarily on an intellectual level. Unity is sought in common understandings and doctrines; revelation is seen primarily in terms of propositional truths. The result is twofold. Either one can only speak of diversity—theologies of the Bible—in a descriptive and objective way, avoiding the question of revelation and putting aside any confessional stance; or, going in the opposite direction, one can place the emphasis on the Scriptures as the *Verbum Dei,* denying their diversity, reinterpreting the history, and safeguarding it all by a doctrine of inspiration. In both cases the challenge to a biblical theology brought by the problems of unity and diversity, revelation and history, confession of faith and history of faith, is dealt with on an either-or basis, that is, by dissolving the tensions either in favor of history or in favor of faith.

The search, then, continues. Can we find some kind of unifying structure for a biblical theology? Is there a way to deal with the Scriptures as a whole without doing violence to the integrity of the faith of Israel or the faith of Christianity, to the unity and diversity within their ancient witnesses and confessions of faith, to the relevance of these historical witnesses for us? I think there is, and what follows is an attempt to suggest what it is by reflecting on the nature of biblical theology, especially in the light of the problems confronting it, as well as suggesting a structure for developing a biblical theology.

## THE RELIGIOUS QUESTION

The starting point is to be found in religion itself, in asking the basic religious questions that are asked by Israel, by the church, and by us. Religion deals with the basic questions of life. How do we live in our world? How do we live in relation to the things and forces and people and circumstances all around us? Every religion deals with these questions, even those that have no god as such. A theocentric religion asks the same questions, although in a more directed form: How do we live in our world in relation to God?

Religion is the attempt to find an answer to this question. Theology is reflection on the answer or answers to it. In this connection it is important to note that the answer to the basic religious question is not to be found in theology; the answer is to be found in living, living in our world in relation to God! It is not a matter of intellect, but of action and life. The answer is not given *in intellectu,* but *in actu.*

The religion of Israel, for example, is not a doctrine of God, nor a code of laws, nor a principle of justice, nor a vision of God's rule, nor a notion of God's holiness. All these things may be present, but the religion of Israel is a living, continuing encounter with Yahweh their God, and the Hebrew Scriptures are made up of fifteen hundred years of reflection and witnesses to this relationship. They are made in different ways by people of all kinds in all places, high and low. The answers vary, the points of view are different, the circumstances change and understandings are modified. Nevertheless, with all their variety, even tensions, they stand together in unity. This is possible because their unity is not to be found in an intellectual, logical system of thought, but in a common commitment to Yahweh, their living, demanding, loving God. The issue centers in a living relationship.

It is no accident, nor is it a shortcoming, that Judaism has no systematic theology. In Mishnah and Talmud, as well as in the midrashim, one constantly finds opposing, even contradictory views on theological matters. They simply stand together unresolved, but the unity of faith in God continues.

The basic question remains: How do I live in the world in relationship with God? Indeed, the faith, or religion, of Israel may be defined in just these terms, as a relationship between persons, Yahweh and Israel. The relationship is personal, not something static or purely contractual. The relationship is to be understood as "a living, continuing encounter" between God and Israel. Israel, too, is to be understood in personal terms, embracing both the community as a whole and the individuals within the community. To speak of Israel in this corporate fashion is not to set Israel as a collective, impersonal entity over against the individual and personal Israelite. This would be to misinterpret the notion of "corporate personality," which takes seriously the dynamic interplay and relation of individual and community. The faith of Israel is a living relationship between persons.

It is a relationship established and maintained by Yahweh's gracious and saving acts in history. It is a relationship in which the will of Yahweh is revealed and set forth as the means of living out the relationship. It is a relationship in which Israel comes into being as the people of Yahweh, created, chosen and continued by God's grace. It is a relationship through which the purpose of Yahweh will be achieved. The basic religious questions are all addressed: how the relationship is established, who are involved, how one lives in the relationship, and how this affects the world. To be sure, the understanding and reflections on these aspects of the relationship vary, not only from age to age, but within every age. Nevertheless the core remains; the relationship continues.

Such an approach as this provides a unifying structure within which to deal with the multiform witnesses of the Hebrew Scriptures, the varying ways of setting forth the same reality. While these varying reflections are products of their own times and so are time-bound, they are not necessarily bound to their times, nor caught in a continuum of tradition history.

Rather, they may speak now to this age and now to another, because the issues and dynamics of the relationship continue through all time.

This has profound significance for the Christian's understanding of the Hebrew Scriptures as the word of God. As Christians we deal with the same basic issues. What has been said of Israel is also true of Christianity. Christianity is a living, continuing encounter with God through Jesus Christ. The New Testament Scriptures are made up of a little less than a century of reflections and witnesses to this encounter. Like the Hebrew Scriptures there is a great diversity, but the unity stands, not in theological systems and doctrines, but in the common commitment to God who in Jesus Christ gives wholeness of life.

Israel and the church, Judaism and Christianity, both deal with the same basic questions. Their answers are different, but they have much in common. Indeed, the Hebrew Bible, the Scriptures of Judaism, are taken up by Christianity and combined with its own Scriptures, the New Testament. By this very term," New Testament," a close bond with the Hebrew Scriptures is affirmed, so that the Christian refers to them as the "Old Testament," and together, both the Hebrew and the Christian Scriptures are regarded as the word of God. The bond is so close that one often speaks of a Judeo-Christian tradition, and to a certain extent this is appropriate.

> The Hebrew Bible presents a testimony to God, a personal God who addresses Israel and through Israel all peoples. In brief, it testifies to the mighty God who acts, the holy God who comes, the righteous God who saves, the faithful God who forgives, the Lord of creation who makes known his will and purpose. Moreover, at the same time that God reveals himself, the true human situation is also revealed; and to this the Hebrew Bible also bears witness. Its testimony to God and to humanity's relationship to God speaks to all people in all ages.
>
> Ultimately in the witness of the Hebrew Scriptures all the problems of human existence recede before the primary and basic problem: our relationship to God....
>
> The testimony of the Hebrew Bible to God's revelation provides the primary categories for understanding God's act in Christ. Hence, the Hebrew Bible is not just a second book along with the New Testament, nor is it only an historical and cultural background to the New Testament; it is rather an inseparable part of the testimony to the gospel. The Hebrew Bible has the authority of the Word of God insofar as it testifies to the true, living God, insofar as it makes clear the situation of humanity and the world, and in view of this (the Christian says) insofar as it leads people to seek and long for Jesus Christ.[1]

It is, however, precisely at this point that one can no longer speak of a Judeo-Christian tradition. While Judaism and Christianity have much in common and deal with the same basic issues, they do not represent the same tradition. They are different. They may start from some common ground and share some common perspectives, but Israel and the church give two distinct and different answers to the same basic religious questions. The roots of Christianity may in large part be in the Hebrew Scriptures and Judaism, but its self-identity is not.

All this suggests again that a unifying structure for a theology of the Bible as a whole is not to be found in doctrines and answers, but in a common quest, that of seeking to come to terms with the basic religious questions that center in the dynamics of a living relationship with God now and in this world. Within such a framework one can deal meaningfully not only with the unity and diversity within the two Testaments, but also with the radical distinctiveness of each.

## THE BIBLICAL THEOLOGIAN

To approach the Bible in this way means that to engage in biblical theology is to be engaged in the quest itself. As *theologians* we are not simply observers, but participants. These are our questions, and they cannot be asked impassively or impersonally. As *biblical* theologians the quest centers in the Bible, where we are confronted both by historical confessions of faith and by the address of God.

The biblical theologian must deal with both. That the Bible is a document of history made up of many and different historical witnesses must be taken seriously. It is an essential part of the biblical theologian's task to understand the biblical texts on their own terms and in their own historical contexts, recognizing at the same time that, even employing the historical method in its best and most rigorous form, it is not possible to achieve such an objective, historical understanding. We must also take seriously that the Bible is not only a document of history, but is at the same the word of God. This, too, is part of the biblical theologian's task, recognizing at the same time that in carrying it out we inevitably reflect our own theological traditions and cultural milieus. Nevertheless, both tasks—despite their difficulties and risks—are essential to biblical theology. Skepticism about the historical method does not excuse us from the historical task, nor does the danger of reading our own theology into the texts permit us to withdraw from the theological quest.

Both must be done and done together. They are not two tasks that can be separated and done consecutively, as if to say that the concern for the historical witness is the task of the biblical scholar, while the concern for the word of God is the task of the systematic theologian. One may distinguish between the two tasks, but they are not to be separated.

This, however, is precisely what is done by what appears to be the prevailing approach to biblical theology in these days. The task of biblical theology is seen to be primarily if not solely "the descriptive task," to use the terminology of Krister Stendahl in a brilliant article in which he clearly sets forth this approach. A few brief excerpts will make clear what it is.

> It remains a fact that modern biblical theology would be quite inexplicable were it not for the fact that the *religionsgeschichtliche Schule* had drastically widened the hiatus between our time and that of the Bible, between West and East, between the questions self-evidently raised in modern minds and those presupposed, raised, and answered in the Scriptures. Thereby a radically new stage was set for biblical interpretation. The question of meaning was split up in two tenses: "What *did* it mean?" and "What *does* it mean?" These questions were now kept apart long enough for the descriptive task to be considered in its own right.
>
> From the point of view of method it is clear that our only concern is to find out what these words meant when uttered or written by the prophet, the priest, the evangelist, or the apostle—and regardless of their meaning in later stages of religious history, our own included. . . . Such a program is by and large a new feature in biblical studies, a mature fruit of the historical method. This descriptive task can be carried out by believer and agnostic alike. . . . Both can work side by side, since no other tools are called for than those of description in the terms indicated by the texts themselves. The meaning for the present—in which the two interpreters are different—is not involved.[2]

In this way the descriptive approach solves two major problems confronting the biblical theologian. The problem of revelation and history, expressed in the tension of the questions, "What it meant?" and "What it means?" is solved by dissolving it, by reducing biblical theology to historical description; and at the same time the danger of reading one's own theology into the text is avoided by putting the meaning for faith outside the concern of biblical theology.

What has happened, of course, is that the meaning of biblical theology has been radically reinterpreted. The biblical theologian is no longer a theologian, but has become a biblical historian, or better, a describer of theological witnesses in the Bible, and one, moreover, who brings no presuppositions of faith to the process, nor any concern for contemporary meaning. Not only does such an approach deprive biblical study of the theological task, but it assumes too much for the historical method. As carefully and deeply as it may be applied, we simply cannot by the historical method bridge the gap of time and culture. We cannot really say "what it meant." It is an optimistic view that in practice is unrealistic; we simply cannot put aside who we are and where and when we live.

Moreover, there is in this historical, descriptive approach an assumption that has clear theological implications, namely, that in interpreting the biblical text one can get to its meaning without assuming that it is the word of God. Indeed, in this view it is incumbent upon the biblical interpreter to assume that it is not the word of God. In this way, then, it is irrelevant whether the interpreter is Jewish, Christian, Moslem, or nothing religiously at all. The Bible is simply another book of history.

As biblical theologians, on the other hand, we do not see the Bible as simply another book of history. We bring to the study of the Bible the assumption that the Bible is indeed the word of God. It is not just a record of what others have said about God in the past, but these historical witnesses are the means through which God speaks. The Bible is the word of God, and so also it is a historical witness with authority for us. These are matters that clearly lie beyond the competence of the historical method, and this is readily affirmed by the historian, who then rightly limits biblical study to historical description. If the Bible, however, is the word of God, to limit its study to historical description is insufficient. The biblical theologian must be concerned with both.

But there is a difficulty here too. As biblical theologians we seek to understand not only the historical witness but also the word of God which it mediates. In trying to understand this revelation, however, we necessarily bring our own understandings. We cannot put aside our confession of faith when studying the Scriptures on whose witness our faith in God is based. This is not, however, a purely circular matter. It is not dogmatic exegesis by which we simply read back into the text our own faith and doctrines. Indeed, it is not a matter of doctrines at all. It is a creative dialogue with the biblical voices who with us are engaged in the religious quest. It is a creative dialogue in which we hear again and again the whole canonical witness, and so are forced again and again to reexamine what we understand about God, ourselves, our world, and our neighbor—and so how we are to live in relation to God, our world, and our neighbor.

The biblical theologian cannot be merely a descriptive historian; this would be to abdicate our role as theologians. The Bible, this historical document, is the word of God. With all the difficulties and risks, the biblical theologian must be involved both with the historical witnesses of the biblical writers and the contemporary address of God. The two may be distinguished, but they cannot be separated.

## THE BIBLE

In this undertaking, the task of the biblical theologian simply reflects the nature of the Bible itself. The Bible is a collection of writings made by the community of faith who heard and still hears in them the voice of God. None of these biblical writings was written to be "holy Scripture"; they are all very human in their origin and development. Yet they are normative for the community as the means through which God's revelation is vouchsafed. They are the word of God. They did not become this, however, by having imposed on them a dogma of inspiration by which the texts are inviolable and unchangeable. Such a dogma is not the beginning of the process, but the end of the process, a reflection on an accomplished reality.

There is always something else behind the Scriptures which leads the community to see them as God's word and so authoritative for the community. For ancient Judaism this "something" was Israel's living encounter with God, the experience of God's deliverance and providence. This was experienced and expressed in a variety of ways (not always compatible), interpreted and reshaped in succeeding ages; but it was always the continuing living encounter and experience that brought the community of faith to hear God's voice and to see these writings as revealing God's will and so normative. Similarly in the early church it was the living encounter with God through Christ and the experience of salvation that enabled believers to hear in these particular writings the address of God, and so led them to see these historical witnesses as normative. So also is it for us. It is the living encounter with God as we seek to live in relation to God and our world that brings us to hear the address of God in the Bible. It is not that the words of Scripture are by divine dictation. God did not speak these words, but through these words God speaks, and speaks to us now.

This is the tension within which the biblical theologian must work: the tension between the Scriptures in all their humanness, brilliant or faltering as it may be, and the revelation of God's will and purpose. The tension is not satisfactorily resolved by seeing these writings as divinely inspired, or by viewing them as nothing more than ancient texts. In the first case, history is not taken seriously; in the second case, revelation.

Indeed, the tension is to be maintained, for only in this way can both history and revelation be taken seriously. To take history seriously is to see that the Bible *is* a collection of ancient writings and like all literature has a history of its own. By maintaining the tension we also take revelation seriously, confessing that the God who transcends history speaks to us in our history where we live. Just as our Lord became incarnate, taking on our flesh, so in the Scriptures God still speaks through the faltering words and speech of our humanity.

It is the task of the biblical theologian to hear this speaking, and to bear witness to it. The task is one that is carried out within the community of faith, for the biblical writings are the Scriptures of the community, gathered by the community and acknowledged to be normative for it. Once again, however, there is a tension and it is twofold. It is first of all a tension between the authority of the Bible and the community that has shaped it and preserves it. Again, and closely related, it is tension between the authority of the Bible and the authority of the tradition which interprets and reinterprets the Bible as the life of the community continues to develop. These are tensions that will not be resolved by opting for one over the other. It is not a matter of removing the tension between Bible and tradition by giving precedence to one or the other. Bible and community, canon and tradition stand always in tension together. It is only when they are absolutized (historicized?) that the issue becomes either one or the other. The biblical theologian works within this tension, not by choosing one over the other, but by seeing that both stand under the living authority of the word of God which is spoken and heard in the continuing encounter with God in the give and take of the religious quest.

We have said that as theologians we are concerned with the basic religious question: How do we live in relation to God and to our world and to our neighbor? The question is not academic, but existential; and we are ourselves involved because it is also our question. As biblical theologians we seek an answer to this basic question in terms of the biblical witness. This we do because we are part of the community of faith which sees the Bible as both a human, historical record and the contemporary word of God. As part of this community of faith we share in its confession of faith and we are shaped by its tradition.

With all this we approach the task of biblical theology. We are consequently confronted by the issue of unity and diversity, the problem of faith and the history of faith, and the tension between revelation and history. These are problems that cannot be solved logically and intellectually. Indeed, they cannot be solved at all. They can, however, be dealt with; and this, not by an either/or dissolution of them, but by engaging in the basic religious quest, recognizing that, while these are problems inevitably raised whenever we speak of God in history, they are not the primary issues of biblical theology. In a sense they are only its by-products. This is not to say that these problems and tensions can be ignored. On the contrary, the biblical theologian must be fully familiar with them, because in fact they cannot be avoided. Yet they can be lived with because the task of biblical theology is directed not toward them, but toward the religious quest, the continuing encounter with God. It is a theological task in which the biblical theologian wrestles with the question of how we live in relation to God, the world, and our neighbor.

## TOWARD A STRUCTURE FOR
## A BIBLICAL THEOLOGY

This basic religious question provides a structure for a theology of the Bible as a whole. Religion is concerned with living in this world, with holding everything together with meaning. It begins with the question of God and one's relationship to God. On this basis it asks the further questions of relationships to the world and the people in it. These are our questions too. For us their answers are to be found in what God has done in Christ. To this action of God, we believe, the canonical Scriptures of the Old and New Testaments bear authoritative witness, and so our questions must always be asked in reference to them. It is not that they provide ready and easy answers; one must take seriously the problem of diversity and history. It is rather that with the people of God in past ages, we join in the quest.

These considerations form a necessary prolegomenon to a biblical theology. We must know what the religious questions are and what the Scriptures are. With these understandings the biblical theologian can take up the task of biblical theology itself, namely to participate in the quest: how to live in our world with our neighbor in relationship to God.

The starting point is our relationship to God, to understand its nature, how it is established and how it is maintained. What are the meanings and implications of grace, love, faith, and trust?

Reflections on how the relationship has come into being and how it is maintained raise the further question of what it means to be in relationship to God. This is essentially coming to terms with the meaning of salvation. In concrete terms, what does it mean to be saved? From what are we saved and to what? How are we to understand life and death, sin and forgiveness, grace and righteousness? What does life in relationship with God mean for the believer in the here and now?

Such questions naturally lead to a further consideration: How do we live in this relationship to God? The primary consideration here is the Spirit of God. What is life in the Spirit? What is meant by a new birth, a new heart, being a new creation? What is the role of law? How do we now regard ourselves and our world and culture? How by the Spirit of God are all things made new?

Such considerations, however, are not an individual matter. Living in relationship to God involves living in relationship to one another. In the first instance this means living in relation to those who share with us our relationship to God. Here we are concerned with the community of faith. What does it mean to be the people of God and to live together as a worshiping, ministering, and proclaiming community?

This leads in turn to the question of our relationship to those who are outside our community of faith in God. How do we regard them? How do we act toward them? What is our responsibility to them? In what way can we help them as they wrestle with the basic religious questions that we have in common? How do we engage in mission and evangelization? What is the meaning of ecumenism?

The question of our relationship to those outside our faith community raises the further question of our relationship to society and the affairs of the world. How do we as people of God participate in the life of the world? How do we share the burdens of our world? How do we respond to our neighbors in matters of race, gender, sexuality, life-styles, crime and punishment, war and peace?

Such, in outline form, is a biblical theology shaped in response to the basic religious questions. Briefly sketched as it is, it is clear that such a structure permits the biblical theologian to do theology. The issues are basic, dealing with the very meaning of life. The questions are real and the dialogue with the scriptural witnesses is not just academic; for we are not just dealing with voices of the past, but with the address of God. The questions are persistent and provide a way of cutting through the tensions of history and revelation, of unity and diversity, of faith and the history of faith, not by ignoring or dissolving them, but by seeking the God who speaks through them. In such an approach there are, of course, no pat answers, no ready-made theologies; there is only the excitement of the quest: seeking and being found by God who enables us to live with our neighbors in God's world.

## NOTES

1. Excerpted from "Old Testament Theology," a paper presented to the LaSalle University graduate faculty, Philadelphia, July 1979.

2. Krister Stendahl, "Biblical Theology, Contemporary," in *The Interpreter's Dictionary of the Bible,* ed. G. A. Buttrick et al. (Nashville: Abingdon, 1962) 1:418–32, excerpts from 419 and 422.

# 7 Narrative Theology and Biblical Theology

Scripture, Martin Luther remarked, is "through itself most certain, most easily accessible, comprehensible, interpreting itself, proving, judging, and illuminating all the words of all people."[1] No reformer would have quibbled. Scripture's authority stood outside theological debate, not high and lifted up, although it was that too, but at the base of theological reflection, its bedrock and origin. But if Scripture were the ground beneath theological reflection, and not part of that argument itself, then Scripture must be most certain, accessible, comprehensible, and self-interpreting. If it were not, if Scripture were itself in need of interpretation, then Scripture was hardly the bedrock of theological discourse, but itself rested on some still more fundamental authority, an interpretive office or foundational principles that guided interpretation. Only if Scripture were transparent could it serve as the fundament of the Christian life and authentic Christian discourse. Scripture's authority rested on its clarity and self-interpretation.

In actual exegetical practice self-interpreting hardly meant that Scripture presented no obscure passages. Rather, to be self-interpreting meant that the hermeneutical keys to Scripture were to be found within Scripture itself. Luther found two keys, the redemptive events of the death and resurrection of Christ narrated in the Gospels and, not clearly distinguished from this first key, the law/gospel dialectic derived from Paul's epistles. Reading with these keys opened the manifest meaning of the Bible, which everywhere spoke of Christ and him crucified. The hermeneutical keys that made Scripture's meaning manifest neither rested on interpretations of Scripture nor imposed external principles on the text. The keys lay in the text itself. Scripture, simply as a matter of fact, provided its own hermeneutical guides, it interpreted itself.

Theology grounded in this self-evident sense of Scripture was of its nature biblical theology. Biblical theology of this sort was a matter of intense practical interest to the whole Christian community, and not in the first instance an academic discipline. Theology was a matter of thinking along with Scripture as questions of faith and practice arose in the life of the Christian community and was in no sense speculative. By virtue of the consistency within Scripture and the consistency with which Scripture was applied to questions raised by the Christian life, biblical theology assumed a systematic character. But it was not systematic in the sense of a consistent articulation of propositions according to foundational principles discovered outside of Scripture. Scripture was itself foundational, its normative authority for the life of faith dependent on no external principles, demonstrations, or arguments but only on the clarity of its witness to God.[2]

Much has changed since the days of the reformers. But the Reformation's enduring legacy to Protestant tradition, at least, has been the steadfast insistence on the perspicuity of Scripture as a fundamental axiom of its proper function as foundation of the Christian life. Implicit in Scripture's perspicuity and its role as communal norm is the prescription that Scripture must be clear to all, not just to an elite group of interpreters. All who hear or read Scripture equally hear its message of grace, without the intervening mediation of external authorities. The priesthood in which all believers participate is access to God through the clear Word of God in Scripture. Obscurantism of any sort denies this access to God through the Word and therefore poses a mortal threat to the integrity of the community of faith.

We now live in an age of the greatest paradox in biblical studies. At no time in history have we known more about the ancient world, about the processes that produced the Bible, about the groups that shaped the biblical traditions and received the final texts. The contribution of critical scholarship to our fund of knowledge is enormous and certainly not to be lightly esteemed. Yet at few times has the Bible seemed so generally obscure. The great power of our research capabilities is nearly precisely matched by a practical confusion over the meaning and theological significance of the biblical texts. It is more than a harmless irony that much of the general obscurity surrounding the meaning of passages in the Bible may be traced to the sophistication of our methods of investigation. Biblical studies have become such a complex and technically demanding discipline that no layperson can be expected to comprehend the professional discussion of even a restricted stretch of Scripture. The specialized study represented by a Ph.D. in biblical studies represents a minimal requirement for addressing the biblical text. Much of lay interpretation of Scripture, or even the professional interpretation offered by trained pastors who are not able to devote the sort of continuous study required to keep up with even a small sector of biblical studies, must stand under the bad conscience of inadequate preparation. The problem seems to be more than a simple educational challenge, as if better means of popularizing and disseminating the results of the most recent scholarship would resolve the difficulty. The inverse proportion between the sophistication of our research methods and our ability to make their results practically intelligible stands as a systematic challenge to the theological usefulness of a rigorous program of historical research.

On another front the complexity of biblical study has led to a proliferation of methods, schools, and perspectives which have undermined consensus on the meaning of scriptural passages. Failure to reach consensus on interpretation, which now appears a perpetual condition of modern scholarship, winks at talk of Scripture's clarity or accessibility, and so also at the notion of Scripture as a common norm for the Christian life.

As the difficulties of biblical studies appear more intractable, especially to laypersons, the options narrow. Either the community of faith withdraws from Scripture as the fundamental norm of the Christian life or it becomes increasingly dependent on specialists who have the requisite knowledge to allow them to interpret texts for the church. Neither option is particularly attractive. Withdrawal from Scripture leaves the church bereft of an authoritative center for its common life. Reliance on specialists, important as their contribution may be, poses a mediator between the common life of the community of faith and the source of that common life in direct recourse to Scripture.

## THE PROPOSAL OF NARRATIVE THEOLOGY

A point to be argued here is that narrative theology represents a response to this crisis in the perspicuity of Scripture. Not all narrative theology, to be sure. Narrative theology is hardly monolithic. Different theologians grew from different ground and turned toward different questions. The point to be made here largely concerns the narrative theology associated most closely with the late Hans Frei of Yale, and a circle of theologians associated with him and largely sharing his views. Even in this more restricted quarter it would be overstating the case to suggest that Frei was only concerned with the perspicuity of Scripture. But it is true that among other aims Frei and the narrative theologians around him were concerned to return Scripture to its time-honored position as source, foundation, and norm of theological discourse. And no less than Luther and the reformers, they were certain that, for Scripture to stand as common norm of the Christian life, it must be clear, self-interpreting, and accessible.

For Scripture to be clear and accessible, one must possess the hermeneutical key to it. For Scripture to be self-interpreting, the hermeneutical key must be found within Scripture itself. Frei himself never claimed to have discovered a new hermeneutical key, either within Scripture or anywhere else. A claim to innovation would deny the self-evident quality of the hermeneutical key—why was it never seen before? Frei simply meant to restore attention to an obvious fact about Scripture which had served as a hermeneutical key in the past: much of Christian Scripture, including the central passages recounting the death and resurrection of Christ, was narrative of a particular type. To describe the literary type represented in the Bible, Frei borrowed the term "realistic narrative" from literary criticism, particularly the work of Erich Auerbach, but also coined a favored term, "history-like narrative."

"History-like" called attention to obvious similarities between the biblical narratives and history. Like history, biblical stories followed a nonreversible chronological sequence. Creation occurred but once, in the beginning, David did not precede his father Jesse, and Christ's resurrection did not anticipate his baptism. Ordinary temporal sequence prevailed and provided the ordering principle for the biblical accounts, just as chronological sequence ordered history. Again, events in the biblical accounts were unique, one-time occurrences, not interchangeable symbols. The same might be said for events in history. Moreover, events in the Bible's chronological sequence were contingent upon one another in precisely the causal ways familiar from history. A battle lost eventuated in the king's fall from power. Jealousy and hatred brought predictable results, the death of a leader, as well as less predictable results, the salvation of humanity. Normal causal relations prevailed in biblical stories, just as in history, with the exception that biblical stories entertained the reality of divine or miraculous causation. Here biblical narrative and modern historiography parted, although the difference was not sufficient to impugn the history-like character of biblical narrative. The pattern of causality in the biblical narratives, whether involving natural or supernatural agency, maintained the form of history.

The nature of characterization in the biblical accounts likewise supported the history-like aspect of the stories.[3] Most importantly, the characters were thoroughly entangled in contingent events. Characters took their identity from the role they played in determining the course of events. We know something, for instance, of Abraham's character from his actions. Faced with drought and threat of famine, he turned to Egypt and forfeited his wife, choices that both determine the immediate course of action in the story and enact Abraham's character. Concrete events of the narrative are the enacted intentions of the characters of the stories. In turn, events shape and mold character. As a result, characters in the biblical accounts have a roundness to them, a fullness that arises from their involvement in the full complexity of concrete events. There are no stick figures or cartoons nor yet mythic figures dissociated from the profound superficiality of unfolding events.

On one last and essential matter biblical narratives and history agreed: neither had a point, if by point was meant an abstract idea that the narrative simply embodied or illustrated. Although the Bible might contain parables, it was not itself one protracted parable or a series of morality tales meant to inculcate theological or ethical lessons that might more cogently be stated in other terms. Actions, characters, or events in these biblical accounts did not take their meaning from antecedent ideas or morals that they expressed. If they did, if the meaning of texts was nothing other than the ideas they embodied, then specific narratives might be displaced either by an abstract summary of their point, a precis of the ideas expressed in the narrative, or by a more forceful or in other areas more adequate narrative expressing the same idea in better fashion. Against the reduction of narratives to their ideas, both biblical narrative and history maintain that the meaning of an event is, in a sense, the next event that follows from it, then, more broadly, the role of that event in the sequence as a whole. For their part characters are not allegorical figures, Goodness in combat with Evil. They are agents enacting concrete events, their meaning or identity inseparable from those events in which they participate. Biblical narratives, like history, remain at the level of concrete realism, intractable facts resisting sublimation into ethereal ideas.

The realistic, history-like character of biblical narratives was, for Frei, an obvious fact about much of the Bible, a fact that could be observed in the Bible itself and appropriately described using terms drawn from literary criticism. But acknowledging the realistic narrative character of the Bible did not yet raise that observation to the status of hermeneutical key to reading the Bible. Other observable facts about the Bible might as well serve as hermeneutical keys. Choosing the realistic character of biblical narrative as the hermeneutical key seems to require an additional argument. It is at this point that Frei becomes wary. If one seeks to provide a theoretical justification for taking the narrative quality of the biblical texts as hermeneutically central, as Paul Ricoeur, for instance, has attempted through a sophisticated phenomenological analysis of human understanding,[4] then the hermeneutical key no longer rests within Scripture itself but is dependent on the cogency and foundational adequacy of the theoretical justification. Interpretation comes to be dominated by apologetic interests. Frei declines the apologetic task. The importance of realistic narrative to biblical interpretation within the church is not a hypothesis under adjudication as to the adequacy of its grounds. It is, simply, the historic practice of the church, the way the church has read its Scripture. The turn away from apologetics reflects confidence that in its traditional practice the church has indeed found the hermeneutical key to Scripture. At the same time the foundational character of Scripture is reaffirmed—it is dependent on no external argument—and biblical theology assumes the character once again of thinking along with Scripture, not justifying one's interpretation of Scripture.

If realistic reading of Scripture were to rest on anything more fundamental than the nature of the text and the practice of the church for Frei, it would certainly be the nature of the incarnation. Frei sees a profound fit between the incarnation of God in the concrete individual Jesus of Nazareth and the realistic form of the biblical narratives. More specifically, history-like narrative was the only medium adequate to recount the central salvific events of the death and resurrection of Christ. Like historical events, the death of Jesus was unique and nonrecurrent. Character was revealed through action, and actions were understood as the enacted intentions of the characters; crucially, Jesus' death and resurrection enacted Jesus' intentions to help humanity "against the power of chaos and death which oppresses him."[5] Most importantly, the meaning of these crucial events was not an idea separable from the events themselves. The meaning of the death and resurrection of Christ lay in the concrete character of Jesus as God Incarnate enacted in the events of his death and in the world-transforming effects that the events of Jesus' death and resurrection had on ensuing events. Only realistic narrative could adequately present Jesus' enacted character and the force of his death and resurrection on ensuing human experience.

Despite the descriptive facts that the central events of Jesus' death and resurrection were realistically depicted, that much of the rest of the Bible shared this history-like character, and that realistic narrative made a fit with Christian understanding of the incarnation of God in Christ, Frei was forced to speak of realistic reading of the Bible largely in the past tense, as, indeed, the natural and normative way of reading the Bible, but now one nearly moribund. Biblical narrative experienced an eclipse, in Frei's own term.[6] It is important to understand precisely how this happened.

In the period before the rise of critical study of the Bible the literal sense of a passage and its reference to actual events in the history of Israel or life of Jesus were felt to be identical. This natural identity was entirely unproblematic. The fact that a passage made literal sense was adequate to establish the reality of the reference. Literal meaning and real reference cohered. But beginning in the late seventeenth century and then increasingly through the eighteenth and nineteenth, the literal meaning of the biblical narratives and their reference came apart. Independent sources of information about the ancient world, a rising skepticism about miraculous events, a dominant rationalism, and a general critical attitude toward all claims about reality were among the forces that pulled apart the identity between the literal sense of the biblical accounts (what the passages themselves seemed to claim), and what actually happened in historical reality (the facts as they might be established through independent inquiry).

As the critical fissure between literal sense and reference widened, the locus of meaning shifted away from the concrete mutual implication of events and characters represented within the biblical narratives to either the real historical world to which the biblical narratives rather inadequately referred or to a separable realm of symbolic, mythical, or ideal meaning. In either instance the shift in meaning was driven by concerns for truth. If the meaning produced by a realistic reading of the biblical narratives did not agree with the reality to which it putatively referred, the meaning of the Bible was simply untrue. If this conclusion was unacceptable, and its acceptance meant no less than the demise of Christianity, then the true meaning of Scripture had to be located elsewhere. Driven by these apologetic concerns, the meaning of the biblical texts came to be identified with something other than their realistic sense. The historical situation to which the texts seemed to refer could be reconstructed using accepted historical methodology and substituted for the inaccurate biblical account, preserving so much of the biblical sense as could be defended. Or the theologically significant idea or teaching that the story was trying to get across could be distilled from the welter of accurate and inaccurate details and presented as the true meaning of the passage. In either case, the hermeneutical key within Scripture was lost, and with it the sense of the Bible as clear, accessible, and self-interpreting.

Frei's point in drawing attention to the eclipse of biblical narrative was not simply to document a development in the history of interpretation, a slightly different perspective on the movement from precritical to critical interpretation. The point was that the realistic character of the Bible was only eclipsed, not obliterated. The realistic character of the biblical narratives was as much a fact as it had ever been in precritical times. No one ever denied the realistic character of the biblical narratives. But the dark shadow thrown by questions of truth and accurate reference occluded the biblical narratives. Frei hoped to remove the shadow.

The shadow was not to be removed by one more round of apologetics. A simple return to precritical reading was not possible and mindless fundamentalism long a lost cause. The shadow could only be removed from realistic reading by denying that the apologetic questions of accurate reference and truth as formulated by critical scholarship eclipsed the narrative meaning by standing between the reader and the sense of the text. The proper relationship within the community of faith gave priority to the plain meaning of Scripture, that is, Scripture read according to the hermeneutical key contained within Scripture itself. Apologetic matters remained distinct from the question of the clear meaning of the Bible and, within the Christian community at least, secondary. For the community of faith the essential question was what the Bible meant, followed by the concomitant question, how to live faithfully on the basis of the biblical witness. Placing apologetic concerns in the forefront obscured the most obvious answer to the first question, that what the text meant was precisely what it said, at heart, a realistic account of the death and resurrection of Christ and then, more broadly, the narrative of events leading up to those central events, and the sequelae from them. Obscurity on the first question led to uncertainty on the second. Only the incarnate Christ whose life, death, and resurrection were fitly and uniquely narrated in the realistic narrative of the Bible could serve as the foundation of the life of faith.

To summarize before moving on, the narrative theology associated with Frei held that the Bible did, in fact, have a perspicuous, clear, indeed self-evident, meaning that, alas, had been obscured by apologetic concerns. Narrative theology sought to reassert the traditional priority of this self-evident sense of Scripture, to reclaim its traditional place as the foundation of both the life of faith and theological discourse. No compelling logical argument could be mounted for the preeminence of the realistic reading of the text because essaying an argument would imply that Scripture depended on some factor outside itself. In addition, offering an argument would again suggest the subordination of the normative meaning to apologetic concerns. All that could be done to establish the case was to describe the obvious realistic nature of Scripture, to appeal to the traditional practice of the church in using its Scriptures and elucidate the logic of that usage, and to point to the unique fit between the history-like nature of biblical narrative and the church's understanding of the nature of the incarnation.

## SIGNIFICANCE FOR BIBLICAL THEOLOGY

The narrative character of the hermeneutical key to Scripture carried implications for the form of biblical theology. Reduction of the biblical narratives to principles that might serve as premises for systematic elaboration violated the realistic character of biblical narrative. A narrative theology must take seriously the sheer, bold concreteness of events and characters and must refuse to detach meaning from the mutual implication of events and characters that constituted the narrated order. The theological center of the Bible was a narration of events and characters, a history-like story. To appropriate that story meant for the Christian church to see its own story in part as included in that biblical story, in part as a continuation of that same biblical narrative. For the church to be a continuation of that story meant recognizing that the events narrated in the Bible, and preeminently the death and resurrection of Christ, had changed the conditions of the world in which the church found itself. The redemption of the world was already accomplished and the church simply lived in anticipation of the final culmination of the story, a fit ending already announced in the biblical story itself. Until God brought the story to a close the church lived out its commission, which was also narrated in the Bible. There was no hiatus between biblical story and story of the church.

For the church to see its own story as included in the biblical narratives involved first a general recognition that the world depicted in the Bible was the same world in which the church found itself. There were not two separate realities, one biblical, one contemporary, but only the one world represented in a unified story. The church could therefore read the Bible as descriptive of the world in which it found itself. Indeed, the Bible stood as the normative description of that world. But the church could also find its story in the Bible in a more specific sense through an exercise in typology.[7] Because the biblical narratives and the story of

the church were a single story, events in the biblical account could stand
as types of events in the life of the church. In contrast, for instance, to
allegory, typology respected the concreteness of the narrated events in
the Bible, their history-like character, but still allowed the church to find
the specificity of its own concrete situation within the normative biblical
accounts. The storied world of the Bible and the contemporary world of
the church were united into a single narrative.

It might seem that the centrality of textual meaning to narrative theology would argue for a great deal of methodological reflection and
sophistication, in the first instance, to guide the exegesis that discovered
the narratives' meaning and, in the second instance, to serve as a guarantee or check against misunderstandings of the Bible. Indeed some schools
of narrative theologians have been nearly preoccupied with matters of
appropriate method. But Frei and those who followed him were once
again very wary of harnessing the realistic sense of the biblical narratives
to a single, theoretically elaborated methodology. In part the concern
was once again for the perspicuity of the text. If one must first learn an
appropriate methodology, can the text be said to be self-interpreting or
indeed clear in its own right? Would not the hermeneutic key lie outside
the text itself, either in the methodology or in the theoretical considerations that supported the interpretive method? And would not the text
itself cease to be the normative center of faith, since its proper interpretation would now depend on the validity of a method of interpretation
external to itself? If Scripture were to fulfill its normative role in the life
of the church, it could not depend on any external authorization. The
question of method was properly answered by asserting the perspicuity of
the text, its clarity when interpreted according to the hermeneutical key
contained within itself, and not by articulating a systematic discovery
technique.

This does not mean that narrative theology emerged in complete isolation from developments in theory of literature or practical criticism.
Frei was heavily influenced by the work of Erich Auerbach, particularly
his 1946 study *Mimesis*.[8] But, significantly, Auerbach's classic treatment
of realistic narrative which aided Frei in giving precision to his own
description of the history-like character of the biblical narratives was a
work of description and not of literary theory. Auerbach made no effort
to speculate on why realistic narrative developed, did not explore the
underlying structure of the human mind or the process of human understanding. Auerbach simply described the genre of realistic narrative, its
form and conventions. The description applied to the biblical narratives,
and Frei drew on it.

The emergence of narrative theology also bears a relationship to a major shift in particularly American literary criticism of the twentieth century. Rene Wellek and Austin Warren described the contrast between what they called extrinsic literary criticism and intrinsic criticism.[9] Extrinsic criticism referred the meaning of a text to factors that lay outside the text itself: events in the author's biography, social conditions at the time of composition, cultural movements, and so forth. The mode of explanation was largely causal. Some factor in the world outside the literary work conditioned the effect observed in the text, and therefore served as its adequate explanation. Intrinsic criticism focused on the work itself and not what lay outside it. Meaning was constituted by the pattern of literary elements that made up the plot, characterization, and setting established within the work itself. It was possible to talk about the intrinsic meaning of a literary work without a word of discussion of the author, the circumstances of composition, or the social or historical milieu at the time of writing. Explanation was relational—how one action fit with others to advance the plot, for instance—and completely within the work itself. The shift from extrinsic criticism of literary works to intrinsic criticism had been led in America by the New Critics, of whom Wellek and Warren were themselves leading figures. The New Critics had largely succeeded in directing critical attention to the text itself as a literary work and in defining meaning as a textual phenomenon internal to the literary work itself.

Clearly, the New Critics' recentering of the text itself as the focal point of critical interest was part of the intellectual climate within which narrative theology developed. Yet narrative theology never adopted New Criticism, let alone more formalistic critical methodologies, as its official theory or methodological guide. Although New Critical methods of analysis of literary works are often helpful in describing and discussing the biblical narratives, they are only appropriated on an ad hoc basis. The realistic reading of Scripture may employ any methodology that is consistent with its own hermeneutical key, but the realistic reading may never become dependent on the perceived validity of the method. Literary critical theories and methods are fleeting, as we see all too clearly in recent critical practice. The church's understanding of its Scriptures is not hitched to any literary critical star, whether ascending or descending.

The ad hoc nature of narrative theology's adoption of critical practice raises the issue of the place of traditional historical-critical methodologies within narrative interpretation. It should be quite clear that classical historical-critical methods were developed for a different task than articulating the realistic narrative sense of the biblical texts. There can therefore be no question of a wholesale appropriation of either the results of historical-critical research or the methods themselves into a narrative theology. Much of the information gained by historical-critical analysis will simply not fit into a narrative reading of the texts because it pertains to matters that lie outside of the text, extrinsic to the narrative in Wellek and Warren's sense. But other information gained through diligent historical research can, in fact, sharpen the history-like character of the biblical narratives by deepening the sense of concreteness and temporal fixity already present in the literary form of the narratives.

An example might be found in Ezekiel 8. God transported Ezekiel to Jerusalem to be a witness to the abominations of the city. Near the Temple gate he is shown "women weeping for Tammuz" (8:14). We know from its place in sequence with a number of other cultic sins that this weeping is sinful, probably a denial of proper worship to God. But what is the specific fault in weeping for some individual named Tammuz? Historical research can significantly sharpen our narrative understanding of the passage by identifying Tammuz with the minor Babylonian god Dumuzi, whose biography features an annual descent into the underworld during which he is mourned by his human adherents. Historical information of this order can in fact reinforce the history-like character of the biblical narratives, if it is brought into the reading as the narrative itself demands and is not regarded as a necessary precondition to making sense of the narrative. The narrative reading that proceeds along intrinsic lines must determine when external information is pertinent. By the same token the narrative sense cannot determine the course of historical research, which must follow the methods, rules of evidence, and canons of judgment appropriate to whichever historical discipline is employed.

A narrative reading of a text and historical research into the background of a text are two distinct enterprises. Their distinctive goals, methods, and standards of validation must be respected. Still, their results are not closed to one another. Borrowing occurs, however, strictly on an ad hoc basis.

This essay began with a discussion of the clarity, accessibility, and self-interpreting quality of Scripture. In the precritical period those qualities of the text could be unproblematically asserted. The text simply meant what it said when it was read as a realistic account of events in the history of Israel, the life of Jesus, and the experience of the church. That unproblematic, confidently held sense of the meaning of the text was eclipsed centuries ago. Many would say that the eclipse was necessary, even fortuitous. The precritical realistic reading could not be defended against its contradiction of newly acquired certainties about the nature of our world. Yet the loss of the realistic sense of the text that occurred when it went into eclipse has not been made good by some worthy successor. Who could make Luther's bold assertion today?

Narrative theology as I have described it is a restorative movement. It seeks to go behind the eclipse, to reassert the clear and self-interpreting sense of Scripture and give it back to the church. It seeks to make every member of the community of faith a competent biblical interpreter, not by schooling each Christian in the *arcanum* of new methods of biblical research, but by affirming that the sense of Scripture is accessible and intelligible to everyone. Read according to its own hermeneutical key, Scripture can, indeed, prove and judge all the words of all people.

## NOTES

1. Martin Luther, "Assertio omnium articulorum," *Werke*, vol. 7 (Weimar: Böhlaus, 1897) 97. This treatise, against the bull of Leo X in 1520, is not included in standard English translations. A closely related text from the same period (1521), Weimarer Ausgabe (WA) 7:308–57, states, "Holy Scripture must necessarily be clearer, simpler, and more reliable than any other writings"; "Defense and Explanation of All the Articles," *Luther's Works*, vol. 32, *Career of the Reformer 2*, ed. George W. Forell (Philadelphia: Muhlenberg Press, 1958) 11; WA 7:317.

2. See Karl Barth, "Die Schrift und die Kirche," *Theologische Studien* 22 (1947) 3–4. Barth argues that any discussion of the authority of Scripture for the church involves only analytic statements about the way that Scripture actually functions in the church. Arguments for scriptural authority are futile at best and more nearly misleading than edifying. Scripture does not require a foundation. It is itself the foundation of the Christian life.

3. Frei shared with Barth the conviction that the primary function of the biblical accounts was to present the central character of all history, Jesus the Christ. Compare Frei's *The Identity of Jesus Christ: The Hermeneutical Bases of Dogmatic Theology* (Philadelphia: Fortress, 1975) with Karl Barth, *Church Dogmatics* 4, no. 2 (Edinburgh: T. and T. Clark, 1936) 3–377. For a discussion of the relationship between Barth and Frei, see David Ford, "Barth's Interpretation of the Bible," in S. W. Sykes, ed. *Karl Barth: Studies in his Theological Method* (Oxford: Clarendon, 1979) 65–67.

4. Paul Ricoeur, *Time and Narrative*, vols. 1, 2, and 3, trans. Kathleen McLaughlin and David Pellauer (Chicago and London: University of Chicago, 1984, 1985, 1987).

5. The phrase is Barth's, *Church Dogmatics* 4, no. 2, 239.

6.  Frei chronicles the loss of narrative reading of the Bible in *The Eclipse of Biblical Narrative: A Study in Eighteenth and Nineteenth Century Hermeneutics* (New Haven and London: Yale University Press, 1974), from which the following discussion is largely taken.

7.  The discussion of typology by G. W. H. Lampe and K. J. Woollcombe, *Essays on Typology*, Studies in Biblical Theology 22 (London: SCM, 1957), is still a useful introduction to the theory and historical practice of typology.

8.  Erich Auerbach, *Mimesis: The Representation of Reality in Western Literature*, trans. Willard E. Trask (Princeton: Princeton University Press, 1953; Garden City, N.Y.: Doubleday Anchor Books, 1957).

9.  Rene Wellek and Austin Warren, *Theory of Literature*, 3d ed. (San Diego, New York, London: Harcourt, Brace, Jovanovich, 1977) 73–251.

# 8 Preaching as Biblical Theology

*A Proposal for a Homiletical Method*

I sit at my desk on a Monday morning, knowing that in six days I must again stand in the pulpit and dare to announce the gospel to a congregation. Before me are the three passages of Scripture assigned for reading next Sunday. As I search the texts, my mind leaps from them to the congregation I must face. Before long I feel torn, stretched in two different directions. First my mind moves toward the Scripture, and I feel the impulse simply to repeat its message—to say what I know about the text and its historical setting. But then I am reminded of the members of the congregation—I see the faces of this person and then that, each image conjuring up my knowledge of their lives, their problems, their sufferings. I wrestle with the tradition of the Christian community, on the one hand, as it is represented in the Scripture lessons. I struggle, on the other hand, with the contemporary situation of a specific community of Christians and their life together. My mind leaps repeatedly from one to the other and back to the first again.

This leaping process goes on until finally there seems to be a convergence of the two entities, the Scripture lessons and my images of the congregation. Sometimes the convergence is only a vague one, an obscure sense of relatedness. But my mind pursues it like a hungry wolf pursuing its prey, for I must have something to say that is both true to the lessons and true to the people to whom I have been called to minister.[1]

It is a common dilemma, one every preacher experiences again and again. The analysis of that delicate process of relating text and congregation—of finding that point of convergence—is a nearly impossible task. It is a process difficult to analyze for numerous reasons, not least of all because often it is a very personal and subjective one. Nonetheless we search for ways of better understanding how that convergence is discovered. What happens when the connection is seen (or made)? How is it that the text yields up its secret store of relevance when it is properly queried? We search for ways of helping that connection come more clearly and easier. How can I better understand this process, so that I might make my preaching on the text more faithful and relevant?[2]

I propose a way of understanding that convergence. It is one of the insights that results when we are informed by the discipline of biblical theology as well as the homiletic task. My proposal in brief is that the preacher is engaged in a task similar to that of the biblical writers. Like the authors of the Scripture texts we are attempting to relate a tradition to a contemporary situation.

To develop such a proposal requires that we journey through a series of steps. The first of those steps is a suggestion regarding the nature of biblical theology. The second involves a comparison of biblical theologizing and preaching. The last is an effort to demonstrate what is meant by the claim that preaching is a form of doing biblical theology, which will require an example of a biblical text and a concrete contemporary situation.


## BIBLICAL THEOLOGY AS COMMUNITY THEOLOGY

Biblical theology has been variously defined and understood since its emergence in the eighteenth century. Its precise nature has changed with the theological climate of each century.[3] But several things seem constitutive of the task of biblical theology today in the light of biblical studies in the last quarter of the twentieth century. It is clear, in the words of Otto Betz, that biblical theology attempts the "presentation of the witness to faith, and of the theological views, of the biblical writers, in the context of the covenanted people, Israel and the early church."[4] That is, biblical theology is the effort to describe the views of the biblical authors regarding matters of faith, specifically how they thought about God, Christ, the human situation, redemption, and other matters important to belief.

But most important for our project is the recognition that biblical theology avails itself of the literary, historical, and exegetical work of biblical scholars and pursues its goals on the basis of the findings of those methods.[5] So, for instance, the theology of the Lukan writings attempts to work with the theories proposed by the literary, exegetical, and historical studies of the Lukan texts. Biblical theology takes as its foundation the critical work of the whole of the biblical interpretative enterprise. In the light of the findings of that criticism biblical theology attempts to articulate the faith of the authors of the canonical texts.[6]

The process of isolating and articulating the faith of the biblical writers today entails understanding that each of the biblical documents was composed for specific, historical communities of faith. It has long been recognized that the biblical documents were not composed for general consumption. They are the products of efforts to address specific groups of people within their historicity. Hence, behind each of the biblical books there reside the first "intended" readers of the documents, communities wrestling with the concrete tasks of living their faith in that time and place.

Furthermore, the biblical authors in each case were recipients of traditions preserved in religious communities. The authors' task was to interpret their traditions in such a way as to address the immediate needs of their contemporary communities. In some cases, the traditions received by the biblical authors were written and in some cases they were still preserved in oral form. In either case, the traditions were most often rooted in an oral process of transmission. Whether the biblical author was for the first time translating the tradition into written form or revising an already written tradition, his or her task was to allow that tradition to speak its relevant word to the community or communities for which the writing was intended.

In some cases the relationship between the tradition and the biblical writer's redaction of that tradition is evident. Given the theory of the priority of Mark, it is evident in the Gospels of Matthew and Luke, for instance. We can see how the first and third evangelists each utilized the Markan tradition, supplementing it with other traditions (supposedly both with Q, as well as Matthew with Special M and Luke with Special L). Redaction criticism in the last quarter of the century has shown with considerable success, if not total consensus, how each evangelist employed traditions to shape a peculiar message for a particular audience. However, the separation of tradition and redaction is less clear in many other cases. It is difficult to isolate the precise tradition employed by Mark or John and hence difficult to discern how their traditions have been reshaped and interpreted for their first readers of those Gospels (such as the thorny problem of whether the passion narrative in Mark was already shaped by the time it was incorporated in Mark's Gospel or whether it is a Markan construction from fragments and bits of tradition).[7]

Nonetheless, contemporary biblical theology must work from the premise that the faith of the biblical authors was influenced and informed by the traditions that they received. It operates on the assumption that each of those authors then attempted to interpret their traditions for the sake of a historical community. Hence, contemporary biblical theology is "community theology"[8] in the sense that it is the articulation of the views of authors who were writing *out of a community* that had preserved a tradition and *for a community* that needed to hear that tradition interpreted for its needs. Contemporary biblical theology most often, then, takes seriously the importance of the traditions laying behind the written texts and the communities out of which those traditions came and for which the biblical authors have reinterpreted them.[9]

While this brief introduction to contemporary biblical theology as community theology is far from complete, it supplies us with a basic perspective from which we can view preaching.

## PREACHING AS BIBLICAL THEOLOGIZING

Our proposal is that the homiletical task becomes clearer to us when we understand how tradition and historical communities shaped the biblical message that lies before us. The preacher is mandated to accomplish essentially the same thing the biblical writers attempted. That is, as the biblical authors attempted to reinterpret the traditions of their communities in such a way as to address contemporary needs in their communities, so too do preachers reinterpret a tradition for the sake of its relevance to their communities.

The Bible is the tradition of our congregations. It is the tradition the church has preserved through the centuries. The canonical Scriptures are the creation of the church, maintained for the continued life of the community of faith. The church claims that in the tradition we call the Bible there is preserved the essential witness to God's actions on behalf of humanity. But like every tradition the biblical witness requires interpretation if its relevance for the present day is to be released. Except for perhaps only a few of the most radical conservatives, no one would deny that the authority of Scripture for the church does not preclude the necessity of interpretation. That such is the case is evident today, for instance, in the struggle to understand how one is to interpret the biblical view of sexuality in the light of contemporary homosexuality,[10] or in the necessity created by the women's liberation movement to seek a new understanding of the biblical tradition regarding the role and place of women and men.[11]

Week after week the preacher undertakes the task of reinterpreting, for the sake of the issues facing a historical Christian community, the tradition preserved in Scripture. For example, it is clear that the third evangelist was especially interested in matters concerning wealth and poverty.[12] Luke exploits the traditions at his disposal to teach the importance of sharing wealth with the needy and builds a consistent case for the dignity of the poor and their special place in the eyes of God.[13] Luke did so, we believe, because the issue of wealth and poverty was especially important in the community or communities addressed by the Third Gospel. It is not clear if the Lukan community was smitten with poverty and needed to hear the message of God's inclusive love of the poor, or whether the community was a wealthy one that had tended to lose sight of its obligation to the poor and needed to understand who the poor were. Most likely, perhaps, is the proposal that the Lukan community was one comprised of both extremes of economic welfare and that there was a division among them along economic lines, with the affluent using the power of their wealth to subjugate the poor. The contemporary preacher must deal with such texts (such as the parable of the Rich Fool, Luke 12:13-21) in the context of her or his congregation. The text will be interpreted differently by the preacher whose congregation is comprised of poverty-stricken inhabitants of the inner city than by the one who preaches to an affluent congregation in a wealthy suburb. The point is that the tradition preserved and interpreted by Luke is now reinterpreted in and for different contexts.

We might even dare to say that preaching is the primary means by which the biblical tradition receives its reinterpretation and the chief vehicle by which the tradition is made relevant to contemporary life. This is not to deny the importance of other forms of biblical interpretation but to acknowledge the fact that it is through sermons that the mass of Christians today come to learn the relevance of the biblical tradition for their lives.

The need to interpret the biblical tradition does not necessarily imply that the tradition is deficient or inadequate in and of itself. It simply recognizes that every tradition from the past was formed in the light of the pressing issues of its own day. As the tradition attempted to address those issues of its day with the word of God, so the interpretation of the tradition attempts to find in the tradition a word of God for another and new day. Every word of God arises within an historicity—a setting in time and space. There are no "eternal truths" in the tradition to be abstracted which will be applicable in every age and every place. But there is a sense in which the tradition yields up its word for another time and place when it is placed in a new setting and seen in the light of contemporary concerns. The interpretation of tradition is precisely that "recontextualizing" of the message of the tradition. It is holding up the tradition in a new context, allowing the light of the present situation to cast its beams on the text. When that happens the tradition in turns illuminates the present.[14]

The evangelists Luke and Matthew reinterpreted the tradition they found in the Gospel of Mark. They attempted to view the Markan tradition in the light of their context—their historicity. In exactly the same manner the preacher recontextualizes the biblical tradition in each and every sermon. The tradition is set in the context of a late twentieth century situation in this particular congregation. Thereby the preacher interprets the tradition anew, following the practice of the biblical authors themselves.

It is true, however, that there are some differences between the interpretation of tradition we find in the biblical authors and that which takes place in contemporary preaching. The preacher is dealing with a tradition that has become canon. That is, it has been set apart as normative for Christian life and faith. There is little evidence that the biblical writers understood the traditions they received as normative. Still, there is evidence that the traditions employed by the biblical writers were treated with respect and honored as embodying that which was essential to the Christian community. So, for instance, we find traditions preserved even when they were not always necessary to the biblical author's own point of view. It is curious, for instance, that we find preserved in John 9:1-7 a healing story that involves the practice of primitive medicine, the use of mud made from spittle to heal blindness. Every indication is that such traditions of Jesus' healings were repressed in favor of an emphasis on the sheer divine power in his acts (for example, compare Mark 7:31-37 with Matt. 15:29-31 and note that neither Matthew nor Luke recounts the narrative found in Mark 8:22-26; 5:41). Yet the fourth evangelist seems to respect the tradition enough to preserve this feature, whatever unfortunate inferences might be drawn from it.[15]

On the whole, however, it appears that the biblical writers felt free to reinterpret the traditions they received. Paul knows the tradition of Jesus' prohibition against divorce (1 Cor. 7:10), yet is bold enough to counsel divorce to Corinthian Christians who found themselves wedded to unbelievers who desired to be separated (1 Cor. 7:15). It is clear from this passage that even the words of Jesus were interpreted for different situations. We assume that Luke knew the tradition of the cry of dereliction from the cross (Mark 15:34; cf. Matt. 27:46), yet that evangelist chose not to place those words on the lips of the dying Jesus. The evidence is weighted toward the conclusion that there was a freedom in the biblical authors' handling of their traditions.

The preacher feels less free in the treatment of a canonical tradition. In that sense the tradition the preacher interprets for the congregation is set, less flexible, and established. Yet it is still a similar process the preacher undertakes, however limited may be the freedom with which it is done. Furthermore, a sampling of contemporary sermons suggests that there is an exercise of homiletical freedom in interpreting canonical materials that is not unlike the liberties we see in the biblical authors' handling of their traditions.

There is another sense in which the process of reinterpreting the tradition is different for the preacher than it was for the biblical authors. The biblical writers were translating oral tradition to the written word, or revising written tradition. Homiletics, on the other hand, demands the retranslation of the written word back into oral form. If the biblical traditions had their origins in nearly every case in oral word, the preacher returns the tradition to its oral mode. The tradition began in the power of orality—the power of personal presence in the speaker, the immediacy of the message embodied in flesh and blood. The written word, on the other hand, sets something between the proclaimer and the audience, namely the written page.[16] The written witness is less personal and more distant. But through preaching, the power of the tradition itself is enhanced through its reincarnation in orality. In this sense, the preacher restores to the tradition a personal power once sacrificed for the sake of preservation in written form.

Whatever the differences from the process evident in the biblical authors, when the preacher sets a bit of the biblical tradition within the context of a specific contemporary congregation with all of its needs and strengths, she or he does a bit of biblical theologizing. The tradition is reinterpreted in the light of a new situation. Its message is revitalized by being seen in a new context. There are differences. The tradition is now canon. The tradition is written and its interpretation oral. But still the process is essentially similar to the community theologizing done by the biblical writers as they handled their traditions.

Therefore, the homiletical task employs the method of the theologizing done by the biblical authors. Their procedure for doing theology for their day was to bring the tradition of the community to bear on the current situation. That theological method is what we have taken to be the heart of biblical theology in general. The preacher simply imitates that theological method. Theology is not done without recourse to tradition, but neither is it done without attention to the situation of a specific historical community of faith. Much emphasis is placed on the necessity in preaching of being true to the content of the biblical faith. I am suggesting that an equal emphasis needs to be placed on being true to the method of the biblical theologians.[17]

Seeing our task as doing biblical theology for our own day enables us better to understand the process of the convergence of the message of the tradition and the needs of the contemporary congregation. This perspective is a liberating one. It frees us to reinterpret the message of the Scriptures for our day, for we know that this process is the lifeblood of Scripture itself. It bestows a "homiletical license" to interpret the biblical tradition in fresh ways. This proposal also dictates the essential elements in the homiletical task. It facilitates our taking with equal seriousness the biblical tradition and the needs of the congregation. It frees us from both biblical bondage and the idolatrizing of the contemporary. It honors the procedure by which we set the text in a new context.

## AN EXAMPLE: 1 JOHN 3:18-24

But our proposal can only be tested in concrete terms. What does it mean to recontextualize a text in a manner similar to that of the biblical authors? An example will facilitate our understanding of this method, while at the same time testing our proposal for its usefulness in preaching.

The example I have chosen is the second lesson for the Fifth Sunday of Easter, Series B—1 John 3:18-24. In several ways this text lends itself to illustrating our proposal. Interpreters of 1 John are fairly confident of the situation this author is addressing, due in large part to the clues to that situation found in 1 John. But this is also a text in which the tradition the author employs is relatively clear, allowing us to see how that tradition has been interpreted for the situation being addressed. While the examples used above have appealed to the Gospels, this text is found among the Epistles. It is at the same time a text that does not immediately appear to be relevant to many Christian people today.

First John, we believe, was written to a community of Christians that had only recently experienced a traumatic schism within its ranks.[18] The author suggests that a segment of the community had withdrawn from the congregation (2:19), and the separatists are sharply attacked and criticized (for example, 2:9-11; 4:5-6, 20-21). The document seems designed to warn the first readers against the erroneous beliefs (4:2-3) and behavior (2:9-11) of the schismatics but also to reassure and strengthen the embattled parent group. The tone of the writing shifts from polemic to exhortation to reassurance. It seems that the purpose of 1 John is to strengthen a sundered community by instructing and reassuring them.

To accomplish this purpose the author has obviously drawn on the tradition the community treasures. We know that tradition as the Gospel of John. The similarities between the Gospel and 1 John are evident to even the casual reader and well documented by scholars. Many believe that the author of 1 John draws heavily on that tradition and interprets it to serve the purpose of the document.[19] However, the Gospel of John addressed a far different situation than that posed by the community or communities for which 1 John was intended. The fourth evangelist seems concerned to strengthen a community that had recently been expelled from their religious home in the synagogue and was now struggling to find its identity as an independent entity.[20] So the tradition that was shaped by the fourth evangelist to address a community orphaned by its spiritual parents is now interpreted by the author of 1 John to speak to one abandoned by some of its own spiritual siblings. In the Gospel of John the antagonists are the members of the synagogue; in 1 John they are former members of the Christian community itself. The author of 1 John freely adapts the tradition of the Fourth Gospel and reshapes it to address a different situation. The theology of the first of the Johannine epistles is a community theology, employing the heritage of the community to speak to its current needs.

First John 3:18-24 exhibits the characteristics we have just described. Verses 18-22 are designed to reassure those smitten with uncertainty and doubt—the self-doubt that arises when one's precious beliefs have been challenged by those with whom one once shared fellowship. The tone shifts in v. 23 to exhortation. It is an exhortation to believe and behave in a distinct way from those who were challenging the first readers and who had withdrawn from among them. The tone, however, shifts again in v. 24, this time back to reassurance.

The text is filled with the traditional language of the community, language of the Gospel of John. The use of the word "truth" in v. 19 is similar to that found in the Fourth Gospel. Verse 22 sounds like a rendering of John 14:13 and 15:16b. John 15:12 and passages like 14:21 are echoed in 1 John 3:23. The theme of "abiding" is a common one in the Gospel of John (15:4-10), as is the theme of the Spirit (14:17, 26; 15:26; 16:13). It is obvious that the author of 1 John has employed the tradition the community holds dear and authoritative to make the point of the passage.

But now I, the preacher, am asked to use this text to address the congregation I serve. That congregation has known none of the trauma of schism experienced by the community originally addressed by the text. It does not experience the self-doubt of having its beliefs and practices challenged by former brothers and sisters in the faith. The necessity of believing in Christ and loving one another is not being disputed within my Christian community. How shall I allow the tradition preserved and interpreted in 1 John 3:18-24 to speak through my words?

Attention shifts to the congregation for whom the sermon is intended. While the congregation does not know the experience of schism or any of its resultant agonies, members do know other kinds of self-doubt and uncertainties. They are a middle to upper-middle class congregation with not a few upwardly mobile younger members intent on success. They know the self-doubt that arises from the guilt and uncertainties of contemporary urban life. They feel the remorse of having to deny their children all of the pleasures of family life for the sake of the work ethic. They know that they have neglected important values in their heritage in order to have the finer things in life that come only with affluence. Women know the guilt of having departed from the values of their mothers in order to pursue their own careers while raising children at the same time. Men know the guilt of pressing ahead in their vocations even when it means stepping on the lives of others. All experience a certain uneasiness with their affluence, because they sense its incongruities with some old values they were taught.

There is then a kind of uncertainty in this congregation, albeit a different kind than that which the author of 1 John perceived in the Johannine congregation. "Our hearts condemn us," rightly or wrongly. We do not "have confidence before God."

The author of 1 John recontextualized the tradition arising from the Gospel of John to address the situation in the Johannine community of that day. I now recontextualize the tradition I find in 1 John by setting this text in the midst of the congregation I know and for which I bear some responsibility. I freely reinterpret the tradition, aiming it, as it were, at a different sort of uncertainty and self-doubt.

A digest of the sermon could be as follows. First, the doubts and uncertainties felt in the lives of so many of the people— the common experience of having our hearts condemn us before God—would be articulated. Second, the good news that "God is greater than our hearts," that God's condemnation is not necessarily signaled by the guilt we feel, since God's acceptance surpasses our self-acceptance would be proclaimed. But, third, shifting moods as the text does, the imperative that arises from the good news of the Gospel would be expressed. The imperative is that we trust the act of God in Christ and that we love one another. Our uneasiness with our lives may indeed be rooted in a justifiable guilt. Have we loved one another? Finally, a return to assurance and Gospel. We live in a relationship ("abide") with God that is founded in the divine faithfulness. That we can know this and live on the basis of this fact is the work of the Spirit in our lives.[21]

Our sermon digest suggests only the most general and preliminary outline of the sermon, but it is enough to indicate several features. The most important of those features is that the text has been interpreted in the light of a new situation, a new time and place. The original message of the text has been shifted to suit the needs of this congregation. The sermon holds promise of being true to the preacher's knowledge of the lives of the congregation. But it is also true to the text in the sense that it captures the themes of reassurance and exhortation found there. Like the moods of text, the moods of the sermon shift from reassurance to exhortation and back to reassurance.[22]

The theological method of the author of 1 John has been employed in this homiletic process. The free use of the Johannine tradition witnessed in the text has been repeated this time to address a twentieth-century, American, suburban community of faith. The sermon does biblical theology because it employs the motifs of an earlier Christian preacher in new ways. The sermon is biblical, community theology in the sense that it imitates the method of the biblical theologian witnessed in 1 John. The convergence of tradition and contemporary situation arises because the homiletician is sensitive to the nature of biblical theology as community theology and is thereby freed to reinterpret the biblical tradition.

## CONCLUSIONS

If this proposal is clear and worthy of reflection, it remains only to suggest two concluding points.

First, the proposal that preaching is a kind of biblical, community theologizing means that the preacher must be knowledgeable of the findings of contemporary biblical scholarship. Minimal, it seems to me, is the expectation that the preacher understand how scholars view the purpose and historical setting of the text. If we are to do our reinterpretations of the biblical tradition with consciousness and intentionality, we must know as best we can how the biblical writers were using tradition and to what purpose. Only then can we legitimately and fully understand our own reinterpretation of the text for our situation. The preacher is called, therefore, to basic research on the texts to be preached.

When we are conscious of the fact that we are reduplicating the method of the biblical writers, the convergence of text and specific, contemporary congregation occurs more readily and more clearly. That consciousness is absent when we fail to understand how it is that the biblical writer in the text before us was practicing the method I have called community theology. That self-consciousness depends on our taking seriously the task of reading the findings of biblical scholarship on any given passage. If preaching is to be biblical theology and if biblical theology is done on the basis of current literary, historical, and exegetical studies, then preaching must arise from some awareness of those studies.[23]

The second point is a corrective to the emphasis of this article. The method proposed here focuses on the historical setting of the biblical text. It assumes that we can go "behind" the text to see glimpses of its original purpose in a historical setting. This should not, however, preclude attention to the text itself. The text is more than a window to the history behind the text. The text has an authentic integrity of its own and is not merely a means to discover the past. Therefore, the proposal that preaching be understood as biblical, community theology requires attention to the form and content of the text as it stands before us. No historical knowledge gained from commentaries can substitute for the preacher's immersion in the text itself. The legitimate reinterpretation of the tradition in the text occurs only when that tradition is fully understood in itself.[24]

Preaching viewed as biblical theology heightens still further the awe and timidity of the preacher as she or he faces the homiletic task. That I am to do with the biblical text what the original authors did, that I am to imitate the method of the biblical authors, fills me with fear and humility. Yet any preacher knows that his or her task is an incredibly bold act. Our heightened sensitivity to the demands of the task can only accentuate our dependence upon the power of God to enable us to do that to which we have been called.

## NOTES

1. What I have described here is discussed in different terms by Reginald Fuller. He speaks about preachers' concern with "two poles—the text and the contemporary situation" and states that it is preachers' "task to build a bridge between these poles. To do this they need to know as much as they can about both poles." *The Use of the Bible in Preaching* (Philadelphia: Fortress, 1981) 41.

2. The various ways of conceiving of this "process of convergence" are discussed in Ernest Best, *From Text to Sermon* (Atlanta: John Knox, 1978) 54–96. William D. Thompson develops the process in terms of "correspondence" between the text and the contemporary world. *Preaching Biblically,* Abingdon Preacher's Library (Nashville: Abingdon, 1981) 50–54.

3. Cf. John Reumann, "Introduction: Whither Biblical Theology?" and Ulrich Mauser, "Historical Criticism," both in this volume, as well as Brevard S. Childs, *Biblical Theology in Crisis* (Philadelphia: Westminster, 1970) 13–87. For New Testament theology in particular Hendrikus Boers offers a helpful discussion in *What Is New Testament Theology?*, Guides to Biblical Scholarship, New Testament Series (Philadelphia: Fortress, 1979).

4. Otto Betz, "Biblical Theology," in *The Interpreter's Dictionary of the Bible,* ed. George Arthur Buttrick (Nashville: Abingdon, 1962) 1:432.

5. Ibid. 418.

6. This is illustrated in Rudolf Bultmann's discussion of the theology of the Gospel of John in his *Theology of the New Testament* (New York: Charles Scribner's Sons) 2 (1955): 3–69, published in German in 1948. There he consistently makes references to the exegetical work in his commentary, *The Gospel of John* (Philadelphia: Westminster, 1971), the first German edition of which appeared in 1941.

7. Cf., for instance, the discussion of the issue by John R. Donahue in *The Passion in Mark,* ed. Werner H. Kelber (Philadelphia: Fortress, 1976) 8–16.

8. Cf. Ulrich Müller, *Die Geschichte der Christologie in der johanneischen Gemeinde,* Stuttgarter Bibelstudien 77 (Stuttgart: Katholisches Bibelwerk, 1975), esp. 69–72.

9. However, see the important work of Brevard S. Childs, e.g., *Introduction to the Old Testament as Scripture* (Philadelphia: Fortress, 1979), *Old Testament Theology in a Canonical Context* (Philadelphia: Fortress, 1986), and *The New Testament as Canon* (Philadelphia: Fortress, 1985). Cf. Gene M. Tucker, David L. Petersen, and Robert R. Wilson, eds., *Canon, Theology and Old Testament Interpretation* (Philadelphia: Fortress, 1988).

10. Several important examples include Robin Scroggs, *The New Testament and Homosexuality* (Philadelphia: Fortress, 1983), and the "Background Papers" on Old and New Testament passages relating to homosexuality in *A Study of Issues Concerning Homosexuality: Report of the Advisory Committee of Issues Relating to Homosexuality, Lutheran Church in America* (New York: Division for Mission in North America, Lutheran Church in America, 1986).

11. See for example the influential works of Phyllis Trible represented by her article in this volume and her books, *God and the Rhetoric of Sexuality,* Overtures to Biblical Theology 2 (Philadelphia: Fortress, 1978) and *Texts of Terror,* Overtures to Biblical Theology 13 (Philadelphia: Fortress, 1984), as well as Elisabeth Schüssler Fiorenza, *In Memory of Her: A Feminist Theological Reconstruction of Christian Origins* (New York: Crossroad, 1983).

12. Cf. the excellent work of Walter E. Pilgrim, *Good News to the Poor: Wealth and Poverty in Luke-Acts* (Minneapolis: Augsburg, 1981), and Halvor Moxnes, *The Economy of the Kingdom: Social Conflict and Economic Relations in Luke's Gospel,* Overtures to Biblical Theology 23 (Philadelphia: Fortress, 1988).

13. Cf. for instance the provocative suggestion of Raymond E. Brown concerning the source of the canticles in the Lukan birth narratives, *The Birth of the Messiah* (Garden City, N.Y.: Doubleday, 1977) 350–55.

14. Darrell H. Jodock speaks of recontextualization as the means by which we are to understand the authority of the Bible today. *The Church's Bible: Its Contemporary Authority* (Minneapolis: Augsburg Fortress, 1989) esp. 129–43.

15. Raymond E. Brown, *The Gospel According to John,* Anchor Bible 29 (Garden City, N.Y.: Doubleday, 1966) 372, and Robert Kysar, *John,* Augsburg Commentary on the New Testament (Minneapolis: Augsburg, 1986) 149–50.

16. On this subject see Werner H. Kelber, *The Oral and the Written Gospel* (Philadelphia: Fortress, 1983). On the role of orality in preaching see Sheldon A. Tostengard, *The Spoken Word,* Fortress Resources for Preaching (Minneapolis: Augsburg Fortress, 1989).

17. In this sense the theology of the biblical authors provides us with a paradigm for doing theology as well as preaching, although I understand the paradigmatic role of canon differently than does James A. Sanders in his article, "Canon as Shape and Function" included in this volume.

18. For the discussion of 1 John that follows, cf. Robert Kysar, *1, 2, 3 John,* Augsburg Commentary on the New Testament (Minneapolis: Augsburg, 1986).

19. Cf. Raymond E. Brown, *The Epistles of John,* Anchor Bible 30 (Garden City, N.Y.: Doubleday, 1982) 122–29.

20. Cf. Kysar, *John* 11–15.

21. I suggest that the sermon digest includes those elements Herman G. Stuempfle has so well described in his book, *Preaching Law and Gospel* (Philadelphia: Fortress, 1978), namely, law, gospel, and "the call to obedience."

22. The importance of the literary form of the text in preaching is described in Thomas G. Long, *Preaching and the Literary Forms of the Bible* (Minneapolis: Augsburg Fortress, 1988).

23. Ronald J. Allen has carefully described the movements in contemporary biblical interpretation and how they influence and aid in the homiletical task in his *Contemporary Biblical Interpretation for Preaching* (Valley Forge, Pa.: Judson, 1984). Cf. D. Moody Smith, *Interpreting the Gospels for Preaching* (Philadelphia: Fortress, 1980).

24. Cf. Edgar V. McKnight, *Post-Modern Use of the Bible: The Emergence of Reader-Oriented Criticism* (Nashville: Abingdon, 1988).

# 9   Preaching the Parables

In his article "Listening to the Parables of Jesus" philosopher-theologian Paul Ricoeur talks about the challenge of preaching the parables.

> To preach today on the Parables of Jesus looks like a lost cause. Have we not already heard these stories at Sunday School? Are they not childish stories, unworthy of our claims to scientific knowledge...? Are not the situations which they evoke typical of a rural existence which our urban civilization has made nearly ununderstandable? And the symbols, which in the old days awakened the imagination of simple-minded people, have not these symbols become dead metaphors, as dead as the leg of the chair? More than that, is not the wearing out of these images, borrowed from the agricultural life, the most convincing proof of the general erosion of Christian symbols in our modern culture?[1]

At the same time, the various versions of the three-year lectionary treat us to a generous sample of these "childish stories." Clergy would be hard pressed to "preach around" them, even if that were desired. It is at least comforting to know that making sense of these narratives has a long history.

Preachers have been at work proclaiming the parables for nearly two thousand years. Scholars believe that the earliest attempts to interpret them are preserved in Scripture itself. The addition of brief sayings to parables may reflect the hermeneutic of early preacher-teachers. Expanded efforts to make sense of Jesus' stories, such as the explanation of the "sower" (Matt. 13:18-23), are a further development.

A number of possible approaches to interpreting and preaching the parables can be heard from pulpits on any given Sunday. My intention is to discuss a number of the ways these simple metaphors have been used and abused through the centuries, focusing on what contemporary scholars are saying about the "like sayings" and the possible implications of their probes for proclamation.

## ALLEGORIZATION IN STUDY AND PULPIT

Influenced by the delay of the parousia, the early church began to apply the parables to its own situation. Stories that had as their primary referent an immediate crisis, the event of the inbreaking of the kingdom in Jesus' own ministry, came to be applied to the future return of Christ in glory. Stories intended to arouse listeners to the crisis of the moment were allegorized to address a future calamity.

In the parable of the pounds/talents in Matt. 25:14-30/Luke 19:12-28, the journey of the merchant, mentioned to explain why the servants were left in charge of their master's money, is made the focal point of the story. In Matthew the merchant is Christ, whose departure is the ascension and whose return corresponds to the parousia. In Luke the merchant becomes a king who, at his return, has his enemies slain before him.

This tendency to allegorization was carried to bizarre extremes by the early fathers of the church. Augustine identified the innkeeper in the Good Samaritan (Luke 10:25-37) as the apostle Paul, while Tertullian equated the fatted calf slain for the feast with the crucified Christ. Of course, we must remember that allegorizing the text was the accepted higher criticism of the period, and the search for a "spiritual meaning" extended the use of allegory through the Late Middle Ages. Indeed, some have contended—justifiably—that allegorical interpretation has been the operative hermeneutic for most of those who have preached the parables right down to our own day, whether they were aware of this or not.

How is this possible? Preaching in homily fashion on key moves in a biblical parable remains the traditional way of handling these stories in many Christian denominations. Predictably the text is broken into three-point sermons. These "message sermons" usually instruct, inspire, and exhort on the basis of Scripture.[2] The preacher moves back and forth from the Bible to the present, drawing parallels and making applications wherever possible. More often than not, such sermons fall into allegory at many points and sometimes dreadful moralism.

It is easy to lampoon this style.

1a. The traveler going from Jerusalem to Jericho fell among robbers who beat him and departed leaving him half dead.
1b. The road of life is narrow and dangerous, with trouble waiting for us at every turn.
2a. A priest and a Levite passed by on the other side.
2b. How sad it is that people fail to aid those in distress!
3a. A Samaritan stopped and helped.
3b. We too must love others by stopping and helping them. Isn't it too bad more people don't?

This is obviously awful. However, even as we chuckle we have a sense of *déjà vu*. If only we hadn't heard that sermon so often! Dare we admit that we have preached it?

## PREACHING THE SINGLE MESSAGE OF THE TEXT

Scholars of the Reformation period such as Luther and Calvin stressed the principle of discerning the literal or grammatical sense of Scripture. Luther dismissed allegorizers as "clerical jugglers performing monkey tricks."[3] At the same time, Luther's own expositions and sermons reveal a receptivity to the allegories of the Fathers.

Primary credit for change away from allegory must go to Adolf Jülicher, who at the end of the last century finally brought the allegorical method of interpretation into disrepute. His two-part work on the parables of Jesus chronicles the centuries of allegorical distortion these metaphors have suffered.[4] While Jülicher's own stress on drawing from each parable a single idea of the widest possible generality was itself a distortion of the form, his method did result in a new quest for the original meaning of the parables. This quest proved a boon to exegetes and preachers alike.

The approach to interpretation that has dominated biblical studies in much of the last half-century is the so-called historical-critical method. This method seeks to determine the meaning of the text by determining the original intention of the speaker or author of the text.

After Jülicher, parable research tended to focus on the meaning of a given parable in the life and ministry of Jesus, the *Sitz im Leben Jesu*. Jesus' original intention in telling the story became the key to interpretation for our day. Following Johannes Weiss and Albert Schweitzer, C. H. Dodd showed that the eschatological context of the parables was the inbreaking of the kingdom of God in and through the ministry of Jesus.

The most important name in this movement is Joachim Jeremias, whose seminal work *The Parables of Jesus* has instructed and influenced generations of preachers.[5] Since the early 1950s it has been printed and reprinted in many languages. Jeremias's so-called laws of transformation enabled preachers to identify possible embellishments of the stories, including hortatory applications, and to focus on the impact of these conflict stories in Jesus' own confrontations with hostile leaders of his day.

Form criticism contended that the parables were transmitted first of all as independent units complete in themselves. Later on, as the words of Jesus were collected for preaching and instruction, these parables were often given contexts or were linked to other parables with similar themes. Jeremias and others have assisted preachers to zero in on (what they viewed as) the original context and message.

The name of the German theologian-preacher Helmut Thielicke is firmly linked to this quest. For example, the focus of the parable in Luke 15:11-32 was traditionally said to be the vain and proud prodigal whose lust for independence ended in the far country and who found his way home. However, in his 1959 book of sermons *The Waiting Father,* Thielicke dramatized the insight that the center of the story is really the father whose grace-ful love moves him to run and embrace his younger son.[6] Thielicke's understanding of Jesus' preaching about a grace-ful Abba enabled him to see the father at the center of the story. Likewise, Thielicke's understanding of the context of Jesus' ministry enabled him to link the elder brother to members of the household who pridefully presume that their place in the family is earned. The German preacher's treatment of the parable in companion sermons ends with both sons judged and both as recipients of grace.

This approach remains exciting in congregations that have experienced primarily three-point preaching. Preachers typically begin with the text, find the single meaning, and then relate that to the situation today.

Another way, espoused by Fred Craddock of Candler School of Theology, is to recapitulate in the sermon the preacher's journey of discovery in the study. Craddock observes that climbing the hill of discovery is dulled by the fact that the preacher does it alone, but re-creating the quest in the pulpit is one way to bring excitement to the preaching moment.[7] Never dull, Craddock frequently moves to peel away layers of false, misleading, or only partially true interpretation, leading listeners to uncover new insights in text and life. He calls this method of guiding listeners to a moment of insight at or near the end of the sermon inductive preaching. Clearly this inductive plot line is more faithful to the parabolic form than is the traditional three-point sermon.

## THE CONTRIBUTION OF REDACTION CRITICISM

Redaction criticism has tended to focus on how the parables were adapted and interpreted, what later additions were made to them, and how they were used in the context of individual gospels.

For example, Jonathan Bishop has identified a contrast, evidently redactional in Mark, between two modes of discourse.[8] According to Bishop this pattern of speaking *en parabolē,* or enigmatically, and then *parrhēsia,* "quite openly" (8:32), can be traced through the entire Gospel of Mark. The parabolic stories and sayings are mysterious, cryptic disclosures of Jesus which tend to be followed in the Gospel by more obvious, literal interpretation.

Bishop includes most of the stories and metaphors traditionally labeled parables—though perhaps not all—in the category of *parabolē,* cryptic disclosures, while the explanations that often follow parables are labeled *parrhēsia.* Bishop argues that this pattern of parable and explanation, perhaps pre-Markan, provided the evangelist with a model for use throughout the Gospel.[9]

The rhetorical pattern of parable and explanation may provide a useful sermonic structure as well. Such a structural pattern for the sermon suggests itself particularly when a pericope includes both a parable and a related interpretation and when the preacher feels inclined to deal with both in the same message.

The seed parable in Mark 4:3-9 is a prominent example. The entire group of parables clustered in that chapter is set off by the enigmatic command of Jesus to "Listen!" The good news of this parable of the seed and sower, for frustrated evangelists who experience lack of response, is the promise of an abundant harvest of believers for the kingdom ("thirtyfold and sixtyfold and a hundredfold"). Such a proclamation in the face of poor attendance and a shrinking membership is clearly mysterious.

However, the preacher may deem it well in the same sermon to explain what hinders the germination of God's word. An investigation of the resistant soils may well be juxtaposed with the gospel that God's word will find good soil in which to grow.

Admittedly, explanation is out of fashion in contemporary preaching. In *Building the Word* J. Randall Nichols of Princeton Seminary asserts, "the purpose of preaching is not to explain anything, not even the Bible.

The purpose of preaching is to extend an invitation."[10] Granting the reality that congregations are increasingly illiterate about their biblical and theological heritage, Nichols insists that preachers are at their worst when explaining anything. In addition, explanation is useless unless listeners feel a genuine need to know the information being shared.

This is not to say that explanation is totally absent in the contemporary sermon. Indeed, even narrative preaching has recognized the need for theological reflection along the plot line, lest the sermon be perceived as just a jumble of stories.

The textual pattern of parable with following explanation need not constrain the preacher to follow the same sequence each time. The *parabolē* followed by *parrhēsia* is a commonsense sequence; enigma demands explanation. However, it must be remembered that, while they originated in oral speech, the Gospels are written documents. Thus a literary sequence appropriate for reading and study need not bind the preacher. Reversing the pattern, beginning with the explanation and concluding with the parable, may be more effective rhetorically—especially for gospel proclamation. In that way the bad news of resistance and failure, experienced in the congregation's life as well as in the soils of the lesson, may be countered by the good news of God's seed and God's eschatological promise of an abundant harvest. This good news, spoken as the sermon's final word, will elicit hope in the face of frustration.

## THE NEW LITERARY APPROACH

In a fascinating study of the implications of literary form and the dynamics of a text for biblical preaching, Thomas Long of Princeton Seminary asserts that the parables may not be as "preacher friendly" as they appear.

> Preaching on a parable is a novice preacher's dream but often an experienced preacher's nightmare.... The more we get to know the parables, the less confident we become of our understanding of them. As soon as we reach out to grasp a parable's seemingly obvious truth, a trapdoor opens and we fall through to a deeper and unexpected level of understanding. Just as we are ready to play our interpretative hand, the parable deals us a new and surprising card.[11]

The literary approach to parable interpretation has proven a trapdoor to exegetes and preachers alike. Whether we have fallen to "a deeper and unexpected level of understanding" or whether we have simply fallen remains an open question for many.

The literary approach to interpretation, over against the historical-critical method, affirms that the meaning of a text is found within itself and not in reference to past meaning and usage. Rather than seeking the meaning of a parable in what it meant to Jesus or Mark, the interpreter asks what it means as it is confronted. Put another way, the reference of the text is literary, not historical. The question is what the text means in and of itself as it stands before the reader.

In his 1967 book *The Parables* Dan Otto Via approached the parables as aesthetic objects, as literary pieces. Via argued that the parables have some independence from life. Unlike a historical textbook, a news story, or a scientific journal, parables do not first of all point away from themselves to historical events or scientific facts. Parables create an internal existential world of meaning.

Borrowing from Murray Krieger, Via asserted that parables relate to the world sequentially as window, mirror, window.[12] The listener sees into the world of the parable, attracted by identification with one of the characters or by a central image. Inside, the windows become mirrors and the interpreter gains a new self-understanding. Finally, the mirrors become windows again, and the person, now changed, has a new vision of the world.

Via's work encouraged many preachers to abandon the search for the past meaning of parables in Jesus' ministry or in Luke's community, a search they had found frustrating and believed to be futile, and to focus instead on the meaning of each literary piece as it confronted contemporary persons in study and pulpit.

The narrative preachers who discovered Via were drawn particularly to his analysis of plot structure in the parables. Via identified a whole category of parables as tragic, "plot moving downward toward catastrophe and the isolation of the protagonist."[13] Juxtaposed with these, Via argued, were an entire class of comic parables whose plot "moves upward toward the well-being of the protagonist and his inclusion in a desirable society."[14] While Via's own literary-existential analysis of individual parables proved evocative for many preachers, his analysis of plot enabled some to shape their sermons to achieve the rhetorical effect of a tragic or comic plot in proclamation.

John Dominic Crossan is another literary critic who views involvement in the world of the parable as the key to interpretation. Crossan begins with the conviction that the function of Jesus' parables is not to illustrate reality but to disclose the kingdom of God. On this view, the purpose of Jesus' parables was to challenge world. Jesus was announcing God as the one who shatters reality, challenges human pretense, and establishes a new order. The parable was a key weapon in Jesus' campaign. The hearer drawn into the parable experiences "a radically new vision of world."[15] Participation precedes information. Word creates world.

Crossan identified two parables to be studied as paradigmatic: the Treasure (Matt. 13:44) and the Pearl (Matt. 13:45). In both, the main verbs reveal the structural sequence. In the first, three critical moments emerge: finding the treasure, selling everything else, buying the field. The future the man in the Treasure parable had projected for himself is overturned by the advent of the Treasure, which opens new possibilities. At the same time this advent reverses the man's past and leads to the action of selling "all that he has." While the content differs, the plot of the Pearl metaphor is identical.

Teachers of preaching have noted that the Crossan paradigm for understanding the function of all parables is simultaneously a structural intimation for sermon design. If the function of parables is to draw people into the story so as to reverse present understandings of reality and motivate action, the design of sermons based on parables may well take this purpose into account.

How might the advent-reversal-action paradigm affect sermon design? Whenever possible, the plot line of the sermon would feature surprise resembling that found in parables. The movement of the sermon would elicit shock in listeners. Some preachers take for granted that if a parable does feature surprise and reversal, a sermon preaching it should do likewise. A recent book describes this process as "creating sermons in the shape of scripture."[16] It is one way to be faithful to the intention of the text as well as to the message of the text.

One cannot discuss narrative criticism of the parables without some mention of the contribution of structural exegesis, particularly that of Robert Funk and Daniel Patte.[17] An extensive discussion of structuralist method and terminology lies outside the bounds of this essay. But the complex method of structuralism defies use by most pastors in their weekly preaching. Many continue to ask if this trapdoor opens to deeper meaning or to the abyss of confusion.

The contribution of the *Semeia* series, an experimental journal for biblical criticism, has been to assist a few scholar-preachers to rethink some classical parable interpretations. For example, Robert Funk's analysis of the Good Samaritan might cause listeners to feel contemporary claim in this ancient story. As they heard the story from Jesus, with whom would first-century listeners likely identify? Would it be the traveler on a dangerous road? Would pro- or anti-clerical sympathies come into play as the priest and the Levite pass by? Surely, says Funk, the "hated half-brother" of the Jew would be a surprise helper to first-century listeners. So the story raises a question: Will you permit yourself to be served by a Samaritan? The preacher might assist the listener to become the victim being served in the ditch by a hated enemy, and to experience that act of grace.

## THE PARABLE BECOMES THE SERMON

Taken to its limit, the aim of creating sermons in the shape of Scripture has led some preachers to experiment with blowing up the parable into a sermon.

Retelling the parable in a detailed and elaborate way trusts the fresh detail of the picture to capture interest. At the same time it counts upon listeners to identify with people in the parable, or with the hearers of the parable, so as to find meaning. While some preachers have not been reluctant to tack overt theological reflection onto the retelling, others who recognize the danger of moralism, midrash, or allegory trust the story to do its own preaching. Longer parables especially lend themselves to such experimentation.

"Cultural translation" is yet another way that preachers have permitted the parable to speak for itself. The story line of the parable remains the same, but the characters change time zones. With a bit of practice people catch on and enjoy the translation.

Henry Mitchell shares an example of the technique from Sojourner Truth, in *The Recovery of Preaching:*

> Jesus told a story about laborers hired to work in a vineyard. I can see the story. When I was a pastor in the cotton country there was a certain block where there were people standing around all the time—any hour. And most of them were not leisure class. Leisurely folk don't dress like they did. Some had paper sack lunches, but they were looking for no picnic. But you could tell what they were about if you would go down to the block at four or five o'clock in the morning, just before day, a big old raggedy bus would pull through there, and a man would hire folks to chop cotton. If you would watch long enough sometimes, the bus would come again and fill up again. They would work a long day in the fields and the bus would bring them back to the block around six or seven o'clock at night. Well this is the way it was. Jesus said the man hired a load and took them to the field. But he saw it wasn't enough, so he came back in the block three hours later and hired some more. It still wasn't enough and he hired still some more. And again, even in midafternoon, and finally just an hour before quitting time, he came and hired some more.[18]

Listeners who knew both the world of the cotton fields and the Bible moved easily back and forth with the preacher. Such accounts could be expanded by the folk preacher into full sermons.

Other preachers have used contemporary adaptations of biblical parables to make the Bible's point. Ernest Campbell, during his pastorate at Riverside Church in New York City, preached a sermon he entitled "Reflections on a Mugging." In this modern rendering of the Good Samaritan the scene shifts from the Jericho road to a Manhattan street. The time in this true story is also altered. The listeners, at the creative bidding of the preacher, arrive with the mugging in progress and are challenged to respond.

The especially creative preacher may craft her or his own fictional parables. Richard A. Jensen calls this "story preaching."[19] Story sermons ease listeners into the world of make-believe where the "good news possibilities of the gospel are hinted at in oblique ways."[20] Story sermons based on parables attempt to remain faithful to the narrative dynamics of the text while imaginatively recasting it. Having heard a reading of Luke 15, sermon listeners will recognize Grace Simon and her prodigal son Frank.

> Frank wasn't dead after all. Only he might just as well have been. Turns out he was in jail on several counts of armed robbery. He'd been too ashamed to tell his mother so he had one of his buddies write a letter home saying he had been killed when his car crashed through a bridge and plunged into a river. Even had him send a clipping from a Colorado newspaper that verified the story. Anyhow, for some fool reason, Frank had decided to write and tell his mother the truth. Don't know why he did that. Would've been better for Grace and her family to think he was dead. Nobody wants a jailbird in the family. Lots of people in this town would sure like to wring Frank's neck for that stunt. Bad enough he'd run away from home and done all those rotten things. Let him pay for it. He did it. No use makin' poor Grace suffer 'cause of it. But he did it anyways.
>
> So Grace went out there. According to the best reports we can piece together there was quite a scene in that prison when Grace Simon and Frank first encountered each other.[21]

If published collections of sermons are any indication, this type of story sermon appears to be a passing fad. Usually the extended metaphors of Scripture far surpass our feeble efforts to contemporize them.

## PARABOLIC IMPLICATIONS FOR COUNSELING
## AND PREACHING

One final development deserves to be chronicled, even though it appears in a work on pastoral care. It extends the view of Via and of Eta Linnemann,[22] that the parables are language-events that inject a new possibility of authentic existence into the situation of listeners.

When a pastor tries to get a counselee, a committee, or an entire congregation to think about things differently, or to see a new point of view, he or she is using "therapeutic reframing." In a recent book entitled *Reframing: A New Method in Pastoral Care,* Donald Capps elaborates the method for use by pastors in caring for congregations.[23] Although he does not spell this out fully in the book with regard to preaching, at least a limited use of reframing seems feasible in the pulpit as well as in the counseling session.

To understand reframing, one distinction is crucial. Paul Watzlawick, John Weakland, and Richard Fisch in *Change: Principles of Problem Formation and Problem Resolution* (New York: W. W. Norton, 1974) suggest that there are two different kinds of change.[24] "First-order change" occurs within a given system, which itself remains unchanged; "second-order change" alters the system. Reframing, the technique of assisting someone to see an entirely new point of view, aims at system-altering second-order change.

Capps illustrates this distinction with the history in the United States of prohibiting the manufacture and sale of alcohol for drinking purposes.[25] Initial restrictions were placed on alcoholic beverages, but the desired effect of curbing consumption was not achieved. So more restrictions were added, then more, and finally prohibition was established. This is an example of first-order change, more of the same with the system unaltered. When prohibition proved to be worse than the problem it was designed to eliminate, a new frame of reference was needed to address the concern. The prohibition amendment was repealed and the production and sale of alcohol were legalized again. A campaign for temperance replaced one for abstinence at the same time as the product was heavily taxed. This second-order change did alter the system.

Capps finds support for many of the techniques of reframing in Jesus' parables and miracles recorded in the Gospels. For example, in the Laborers in the Vineyard (Matt. 20:1-16) the workers complain of unfairness.[26] To a worker who labored all day under the scorching sun it seemed unfair that those who worked but one hour should receive the same pay. The owner does not respond directly, however, to the question of fairness.

Instead, he gives the situation a new frame of reference. "Friend, I am doing you no wrong; did you not agree with me for a denarius? Take what belongs to you and go; I choose to give this last as I give to you. Am I not allowed to do what I choose with what belongs to me? Or do you begrudge my generosity?" By relabeling the issue of "fairness" (and relabeling is a key technique of reframing), Jesus challenges the worker to view the situation from the new perspective of "generosity." Relabeling is not more of the same; the cognitive frame for dealing with this justice issue has been altered.

Preachers already use relabeling, often without being fully aware of the implications of what they are doing. The technique gives a different name to behavior and attitudes than the one the congregation has applied already. For instance, preachers routinely take listeners "deeper" by relabeling psychological and sociological phenomena with theological terms. The contemporary obsession with self-realization may first be labeled "narcissism," then later in the sermon be deepened to "sinful pride," the self curved inward upon the self instead of being directed outward to God and others. For preaching purposes, the new label more adequately describes the subject. The theological frame enables the preacher to bring the message of a particular biblical text to bear on the subject without mixing "languages." Insight into a new point of view and second-order change may result.

In attempting to preach on the Workers in the Vineyard, the preacher may initially echo and reinforce the charge of unfairness. Often life in the kingdom appears unjust. Some bear the burden of the day and the scorching heat but are promised no additional rewards for their efforts. Lifetime members give a congregation stability and continuity but receive no special recognition. Silent suffering or outright griping and complaining attend the giving of an equal place to latecomers. However, after building the charge of unfairness, the preacher may find a striking way to follow the parable's own shift, relabeling the action of the owner "generosity." Suddenly a bizarre bit of behavior is recognized as grace, attitudes and feelings may be altered, and the sermon is able to conclude with a doxology to God's unmerited generosity.

Of course, not every listener will take the bait. Some may continue to resent and resist. Still other sermon-samplers have already grasped the implication of Jesus' reframing and so will not experience insight with its cognitive and emotional reframing. But because the preacher uses a parabolic technique, even as she or he is preaching the parable's message faithfully, she or he may charge an old story with contemporary claim.

At their best, sermons that preach parables call for decision, because parables make claims about reality which cannot be reflected upon at leisure. Hearers are provoked to make a decision (e.g., to sell all and buy the field). These messages of the Gospels puncture pet dreams, favorite theories, beloved styles of life, and make their own demands for change.

C. H. Dodd defined a parable as "a metaphor or simile, drawn from nature or common life, arresting the hearer by its vividness or strangeness, and leaving the mind in sufficient doubt about its precise application to tease it into active thought."[27] Even this brief survey of how parables have been interpreted and preached is evidence that these childish stories continue to tease minds into active thought.

## NOTES

1. Paul Ricoeur, "Listening to the Parables of Jesus," *Criterion* 13, no. 3 (Spring 1974) 18.

2. Eduard R. Riegert, " 'Parabolic' Sermons," *Lutheran Quarterly* 26 (1974) 24–31.

3. Cited by A. M. Hunter, *Interpreting the Parables* (London: SCM, 1960) 32.

4. A. Jülicher, *Die Gleichnisreden Jesu* (Tübingen: Mohr-Siebeck, 1899) esp. Part 2.

5. J. Jeremias, *The Parables of Jesus* (London: SCM, 1954); rev. ed (London: SCM; New York: Scribner, 1963); abbreviated version, *Rediscovering the Parables* (London: SCM; New York: Scribner, 1966).

6. Helmut Thielicke, *The Waiting Father* (New York: Harper & Bros., 1959) 17–29.

7. Fred Craddock, *As One Without Authority* (Nashville and New York: Abingdon, 1971) 124–25.

8. Jonathan Bishop, "*Parabole* and *Parrhesia* in Mark," *Interpretation* 40 (1986) 39–52.

9. Ibid. 40.

10. J. Randall Nichols, *Building the Word: The Dynamics of Communication and Preaching* (San Francisco: Harper & Row, 1980) 2.

11. Thomas Long, *Preaching and the Literary Forms of the Bible* (Philadelphia: Fortress, 1989) 87.

12. Dan Otto Via, Jr., *The Parables: Their Literary and Existential Dimension* (Philadelphia: Fortress, 1967) 84.

13. Ibid. 110.

14. Ibid. 145.

15. John Dominic Crossan, *In Parables: The Challenge of the Historical Jesus* (New York: Harper & Row, 1973) 13.

16. *Preaching Biblically: Creating Sermons in the Shape of Scripture,* ed. Don Wardlaw (Philadelphia: Westminster, 1983).

17. Robert W. Funk, *Language, Hermeneutic, and Word of God* (New York: Harper & Row, 1966); *Semeia* 2 (1974) esp. 51–81. Daniel Patte, *Structural Exegesis for New Testament Critics* (Minneapolis: Fortress, 1990) may be clearer on method than his *What Is Structural Exegesis?* (Philadelphia: Fortress, 1976), but does not particularly deal with parables.

18. Henry Mitchell, *The Recovery of Preaching* (New York: Harper & Row, 1977) 84.

19. Richard A. Jensen, *Telling the Story: Variety and Imagination in Preaching* (Minneapolis: Augsburg, 1980) 114–89.

20. Ibid. 116.

21. Ibid. 164.

22. Eta Linnemann, *Parables of Jesus: Introduction and Exposition* (London: SPCK, 1966); U.S. ed., *Jesus of the Parables: Introduction and Exposition* (New York: Harper & Row, 1967).

23. Donald Capps, *Reframing: A New Method in Pastoral Care* (Minneapolis: Fortress, 1990).

24. Ibid. 11.

25. Ibid. 13.

26. Ibid. 60.

27. C. H. Dodd, *The Parables of the Kingdom* (New York: Charles Scribner's Sons, 1958) 16.

MARGARET A. KRYCH

# 10 Biblical Theology and Christian Education

*A Partnership*

## A CALL FOR PARTNERSHIP

Biblical theology and Christian education can and should have a mutually beneficial relationship. The former gives extremely important content for teaching and scholarly tools with which to appreciate and understand the scriptural text. The latter can provide clear means of communicating the content as well as seeking in biblical theology a grounding for its task and approach.

Unfortunately, biblical theology and Christian education have not always been partners, to the detriment of both disciplines. James Michael Lee points out that, while it may seem natural that both religious educationists and biblical scholars would work together to maximize the religious instruction potential of the Bible, "it is a surprise and indeed an embarrassment to find that both religious educationists and biblicists generally have been remiss with respect to either developing or incorporating those sophisticated pedagogical research studies, theories, and practices which show special promise for effective teaching of the Bible."[1]

Both clergy and lay religious educators need good procedures that can be adapted to the material and to the age and interests of the learners. The riches of biblical scholarship are of little benefit if teachers do not have thorough grounding in methods to communicate what they know. More—and more thorough—courses in Christian education, along with biblical expertise, should be required in seminaries.

Similarly, religious educators often lack knowledge of the Bible in depth. While some religious educators have good seminary training, many others do not have formal preparation in biblical studies and feel inadequate to the task of teaching the Bible.[2] Biblical scholarship is essential for understanding, appreciating, and communicating the biblical content in teaching. It is difficult enough to communicate what one does know; attempting to communicate that with which one has only vague acquaintance is nearly impossible.[3]

In addition, biblical languages can be of great help to the Christian educator. It is a pity that even those religious educators pursuing seminary degrees sometimes elect not to study Greek and Hebrew. To be able to analyze texts in the original language is as important to the teacher as to the preacher.

What we have said of the professional religious educator may also be said of many serious lay teachers in the congregation. Biblical scholarship and even languages (at least at an elementary level, which will help in using scholarly commentaries) can be of tremendous help to the volunteer lay teacher. In fact, some lay people are better equipped than clergy to deal with languages, yet oddly we keep from them Greek lexicons and apologize for introducing linguistic points. Clergy often assume that serious biblical study is too difficult for the "average" laity. But psychological research shows that any person with normal cognitive development is capable of thinking in precisely the same way from the age of twelve right through adulthood. Therefore, after a year or two of practicing abstract, that is, typically adult, thinking, we can expect that "average" lay persons will be as capable as clergy of appreciating biblical scholarship and theological points. This does not mean that they will appreciate dry-as-dust lectures or unexplained involved technical terminology. (Neither do seminarians and clergy!) But lay persons do appreciate being treated as the intelligent individuals they are. And the more solid the scholarship and the more careful the teaching, the more it will be appreciated by those who want seriously to study the Bible and teach it to others.

A very important element in any congregation is a good up-to-date library for personal and class use by laity. Probably a minority of adults have the time regularly to attend group Bible study. But many can study well on their own with the aid of excellent commentaries and a pastor willing to discuss with them their reading and questions.

Like professionals, volunteer teachers who are given little or no training may know content well but be unable to communicate it effectively. This may be especially true at the adult level. Workshops, training courses, college courses, and school observation have long been available to those teaching children. Fewer opportunities have been available to teachers of adults. Fortunately there is an ever-widening pool of excellent resources in adult religious education which can fully be tapped both by professionals and volunteers who seek to teach the Bible with adults.[4]

## CANON AS A MODEL FOR CONTENT

The partnership between biblical studies and Christian education is continued when Christian education draws on biblical insights for curriculum development. Of course, the Christian educator may draw on a number of theological or biblical roots for a basic approach. But to have such a basis is critical for a balanced and focused curriculum.

One example of such an approach is that suggested by Walter Brueggemann, who uses "canon criticism" as a clue to education both as substance and as process that has stability and also flexibility. Brueggemann holds that a balance between Torah, prophets, and Writings must be kept, and suggests that Christian education has gone awry because the three have not always been held in tension. He suggests that the Torah, the prophets, and the Writings have different functions in Israel, proceed with different epistemologies, and make different claims.[5] And Christian education can learn from these differences and incorporate a balance into curriculum.

Brueggemann holds that Torah claims the most basic authority and is fundamental for education.[6] The question asked of the parent by the child or of the priest/teacher by the learner (Exod. 12:26; 13:8,14; Deut. 6:20-21; etc.) shows the Bible's manifest concern for the educational process.[7] The question-and-answer exchange is unauthoritarian but utterly authoritative. It is dialogical, using ritual to evoke a teaching moment. Torah is stable, known, and a normative answer for both parents and children. It lives and works in a "pre-doubt" world. Misgivings and doubts occur within the context of Torah, not outside of it. The fundamental instruction of Torah encourages belief-full naïvete.[8] In Torah, the "normative articulations of the faith are not individual, private conjurings";[9] Torah knowledge has firmness and graciousness and authority. In this sense, Torah is homecoming. Story is the primary mode in Torah—a mode that is concrete, open-ended, imaginative, and experiential.[10] Torah is the story of the intervention of God—a story of miracle and wonderment, of celebration of power and promise.[11] It reminds us of the holiness of God and the value of the brother and sister.[12]

The word of the prophets on the other hand is intrusive and immediate—a disruption for justice. Prophetic knowledge is known in the uttering; its function challenges the consensus and criticizes that which has not been questioned.[13] The prophet breaks in with new truth from God about God's acts and intent, making a link between political agenda and the word of God. There is both continuity and discontinuity between the prophets and Torah. The prophets are heirs of Torah, children of Torah, yet the prophetic canon disrupts the old consensus; it proclaims that the old world is coming to an end and a new world is coming into being.[14] Although authoritative, the prophet is not as authoritative as Torah.

Finally, there are the Writings, peripheral and subordinate. In the Writings, reasonable knowledge and passionate trust in God are held together. The Writings are faith seeking understanding. The tradition of experience is linked with the immediacy of the experience of the listener. The wisdom writers look back in confidence and forward to divine inscrutability.[15] Rather than disclosure or disruption, the Writings focus on discernment, on daily experience, on the interconnectedness of life,[16] and in so doing celebrate human freedom and responsibility. The wisdom literature has a doxology based on wonder, awe, amazement; it calls for discerning obedience in daily living.

Brueggemann wants the Christian educator to hold a balance in education content and process akin to that in the Hebrew Scriptures—to hold in tension that which is not questioned and is stable in the community together with a passionate concern for justice, disruption, and disclosure from God in the midst of contemporary experience. And with these, also to call for an obedient awe-filled response to a holy God in daily living. Education must nurture "homecoming"; it must nurture some to be prophets and others to permit and welcome them; and it must take time for speech with God, developing trust and communion which is obedience.[17] Curriculum that fails to take all three aspects into account impoverishes the educational process.

Brueggemann's thesis clearly is not the only way in which to root Christian education theory in biblical studies. But it is an example of the kind of partnership that develops when curriculum developers take seriously a biblical base for their work.

## A HERMENEUTICAL FOCUS

A critical issue for the ongoing partnership between biblical studies and Christian education is that of hermeneutics. Christian education resource developers necessarily must ask which hermeneutic will most adequately serve to interpret the Scriptures so that the message will be appropriated by the learner. And teachers who use the resources need to appreciate the operative hermeneutic in the resources. By the same token, an inadequate hermeneutic is good reason for a teacher's refusal to use a resource, notwithstanding the art work or advertised promises that it is "easy to teach."

What kind of hermeneutic may be helpful in teaching? Martin Luther in the Reformation era spoke of "law and gospel." In this century, Paul Tillich used the terminology of "question and answer" to get at the same interpretive key for grasping the biblical message, and argued that just such a hermeneutic was essential for theology and for communicating the word of God in preaching and teaching.

In teaching the Bible, it is important to relate the message to the lives of the learners. Tillich advocated a correlational methodology in which question and answer, human need and divine revelation, learner's situation and gospel, are necessarily linked. To deal with one to the exclusion of the other is to fail to teach the gospel adequately. Tillich built his systematic theology around the Reformation understanding of law as that which reveals to human beings our sinful state and thus drives us toward, opens up to us the need of, the gospel. Both law and gospel are the word of God; both are necessary in teaching and proclamation; both are intrinsic to the biblical message. But the law is the message of rebuke and condemnation which reveals the reality of the human situation before God, and the gospel is the promise of the forgiveness of sins for Christ's sake. Unless learners first perceive through the law their true state before God they will not hear the gospel. Yet there is also a real sense in which, only when the gospel is known, do we genuinely understand the law. Neither gospel nor law can be proclaimed or taught without the other.

In the law-gospel or question-answer correlation, existential questions do not give the answer, but point forward to the gospel answers and are necessary for the gospel to be received as relevant to the human situation. Both question and answer are intrinsic to the biblical message. The formulation of the human question takes essential account of God's activity on behalf of humankind. And the form of the answer takes serious account of the formulation of the question. But the content of the answer can come only from revelation; the answer is inevitably spoken to our existence from beyond it.[18] To teach the good news of God's action in Christ effectively means relating revelation to the learner's own existence. The teacher's concern is to communicate the gospel so that the learner is brought to faith. Any communication of biblical knowledge must be existential knowledge or what Tillich termed "uniting or receiving knowledge."[19]

Lee points out that, since the end of World War II, religious educators have disputed about the starting place for teaching the Bible. Those with a "Bible-centered" position have argued that the basic task is to memorize and understand the text with perhaps a few minutes at the end of the study to draw implications for one's life. Those with an "experience-centered" position have insisted on an "essential and ongoing synapse between the life-experiences and the Bible."[20] In a law-gospel approach one deals directly with the text but not in a way that tags on implications for life as an afterthought. Rather, one looks to the text to find the scriptural understanding of both the human situation and of revelation's answer to that human need.

A teacher who uses a law-gospel approach may begin a class session with the biblical text to elucidate both question and answer. Or the teacher may begin with the human question as experienced by the learner today. In the latter case, Tillich himself suggested that the teacher's role is to help the learners become aware of the questions they already have and then to show how the biblical answers correlate with precisely those questions.[21] In addition, it is the task of the teacher to help learners develop the capacity to formulate the deepest human questions to which the gospel is answer.[22] In every teaching session, then, a law-gospel hermeneutic of the scriptural text also calls for a law-gospel methodology of presentation that takes seriously both the biblical text and the learner's life situation. Neither can be short-changed.

Tillich further emphasized the importance of the teacher's "participation" in the situation of the learner. The teacher must understand and experience the culture or subculture of which the learner is a member in order to express the human question and the gospel answer in ways meaningful to the learner. "Participation means participation in *their* existence out of which the questions come to which we are supposed to give the answer."[23] This is true of the teacher working in a foreign culture, of the adult working with the world of children, of the teacher in our pluralistic society working with persons of different ethnic or regional backgrounds than his or her own, of the teacher dealing with members of the youth subculture. Making the link from the biblical formulation of question and answer to that of the learner's world may be one of the most difficult tasks for many teachers, since printed resources cannot deal with every possibility; only the teacher on the spot can take the time and effort to participate in the student's situation in a way that will enable the clear communication of the biblical message.

Feminist perspectives offer us images that often have not been used in Christian education. They raise to consciousness the experience of women, which has been underrated and underused, and call us to present the whole gamut of scriptural images for God instead of merely the masculine ones. Too often teachers have taken account only of the male formulation of the human question in ways with which female learners have found difficult to identify. The more learners feel bitterness and resentment because they do not recognize their formulations of the human question being taken seriously, the less likely the teacher will be to communicate the gospel effectively. In the United States of the 1990s the formulations of women, African Americans, Asian Americans, Hispanic Americans, Native Americans, and immigrants must be taken into account. All human beings have the basic question of sin and the resultant fear of finitude and of the ambiguities of life and of history. But different subgroups express these questions in their own ways. And the expression of the question and the experiences that lead to that expression are crucial for the teaching process.

## AN EXISTENTIAL MESSAGE

All that has been said about hermeneutic calls for an existential approach to teaching the Bible. It views the word of God as message of judgment and mercy, of law and gospel that profoundly affects the lives of learners and cuts to the heart of their very existence. This word is heard primarily in Jesus Christ, God's enfleshed Word. It is heard as the message, the good news, the kerygma, about God is proclaimed. It is heard as the Bible with its center in the gospel is read and taught.[24]

In teaching and development of resources, too often such a gospel-centered focus is missing. Biblical facts are taught in an endeavor to enable persons to become "biblically literate." Now it is true that there is a great deal of biblical illiteracy in the church in the 1990s and that such illiteracy needs correction. But to know historical dates and sociological facts about the world several thousand years ago, or to recite a string of narratives or passages, is not true biblical literacy. Real biblical literacy asks: What is the central meaning of the narratives? Why did the authors incorporate them into these books? What are they trying to say? What might they have said long ago? And, most important, what might they be saying today, to the church, and to me?

Rudolf Bultmann saw that what was crucial was not the world view of the first century and the mythological framework in which the kerygma was couched, but rather the central message itself,[25] which addresses us personally at the very center of our existence.[26] "To hear the Scriptures as the Word of God means to hear them as a word which is addressed to me, as *kerygma*, as a proclamation. Then my understanding is not a neutral one, but rather my response to a call."[27] Bultmann insisted, however, that for the message to be heard, the historical-critical questions must be dealt with:

> It is true in the case of religious instruction that on the ground of truthfulness the kerygmatic character of the text must not be separated from the complex of historical-critical questions. In a word, the pupils must be given the opportunity to ask questions. Only in this way can they find the way to an understanding of the text for themselves.[28]

Teachers need to communicate basic principles and applications of exegesis and hermeneutics so that learners can, first, make sense of the Bible in terms of their own lives within the community of believers and in the world and, second, respond in faith to the word.

## HISTORICAL CRITICISM AND TEACHING

Religious education has often hesitated to face the consequences of historical criticism[29] to the detriment of the partnership between the disciplines. Even at the adult level, too few resources offering full and thorough treatment of scholarly biblical views are available. And at the youth and children's level the paucity is even more remarkable. To teach the Bible as though it were literally true for the first eighteen years of life and only then to introduce historical criticism is inviting trouble.

But when does one teach historical-critical method? Certainly not formally in early childhood. However, the way in which material is presented to even young children is crucial in laying either helpful or detrimental foundations. Wise Christian educators state openly and often that there are many biblical writers who had different points of view. They encourage children to question and to wrestle with the text.

A hermeneutic of storytelling is inevitable in presenting the Scriptures: the very way in which a story is told is in itself a theological statement, even for very young children. For example, teachers who present stories of Jesus' healings primarily as stories of "Jesus the Magician" should not be surprised at the odd Christology that children display as they develop into youth and adulthood.

It will help young children if teachers highlight not the "moral" of the story, but a carefully considered theological theme: for example, "Today's story tells us what a kind and caring person Jesus was." Such highlighting encourages the child to listen for the christological significance of the story (or whatever theological theme the teacher has chosen).

About the age of six or seven years, children can be taught formally about the Bible in a way that will help develop a "kerygmatic" attitude to the Scriptures. A teacher might say, for example, "This is a book written by many different people; it is about God and the ways in which God has dealt with people; it tells us about God's love for us and about Jesus who told us of God's love."

Early in the elementary school years children can also understand the principle of selection used by, for example, the Gospel writers. They can understand that the Gospels do not contain a minute-by-minute account of Jesus' life, but rather that the authors chose stories and sayings that they thought were the most helpful so that people might know about Jesus and believe in him.

Around twelve years, children reach the age of abstract thinking[30] when they can grasp the notion that statements can be true in different ways. For example, a poem may express truth even if it does not make scientifically verifiable statements about the world. This skill enables students to appreciate truth in religious statements without concluding that all the myth in the Bible is literally true. Students of this age can also appreciate that observers and writers can perceive different ways of looking at events and hearing arguments. They can understand that there may be no way to verify exactly "what happened" historically. They can appreciate the development of documents from a variety of earlier sources. Teenagers are also ready to deal with literary forms, images and symbols, story structure, and differences between translations. Such skills enable teenagers to deal with source criticism and form criticism, to appreciate efforts to examine documents historically, and to consider how the documents have been used by the church through the centuries. As early as seventh or eighth grade, students can be introduced to the sources of various biblical books and can learn how, when, and why the books came to be written.

Even the way in which the Bible is handled in class can contribute to a good or a bad sense of what the Bible is about. The teacher who, because the copy of the Bible is expensive, says quickly, "Don't touch the Holy Bible with dirty fingers; don't write in the margins; don't ever drop it," may be communicating a "bibliolatry" that will last a lifetime. By all means let children treat the Bible like other books—if all books should be treated with respect, then put the treatment of copies of the Bible in that framework. Writing in the margin, underlining, and generally "making one's copy of the Bible one's own" can often be very helpful for children.

Children and youth must not be shielded from the fact that the Bible contains historical, scientific, and even grammatical errors and discrepancies. Sometimes busy and well-meaning teachers, harassed by questions and too tired to look up the answer, respond quickly with, "Are you daring to question the Bible? Don't ask that kind of question." Such a response discourages the child from questioning the Scriptures and lays the groundwork for literalistic interpretation in adulthood.

Sometimes, for young children particularly, to teach biblically will mean actually avoiding the use of biblical texts. In the preoperational and early concrete thinking stage, because of intellectual immaturity the child will take parables literally—for example, the story of the lost sheep in Luke 15 taken literally is a story of a human being's joy at finding a lost "pet." For the young child who cannot deal with analogy or metaphor, the story has nothing to do with God—even when well-meaning teachers try to insist that it does. The best that such a teacher may hope for is that the child will agree that God is also glad that the shepherd found his pet! To teach biblically will mean communicating the good news, the kerygma, in the passage. And so, instead of telling the parable it may be more appropriate and helpful to say directly to the young child, "Even when we do things that are not what God wants us to do, and even when we are the kind of people God doesn't want us to be, God still goes on loving us. God is like that all the time."[31]

## NORMATIVE ROLE IN CHRISTIAN EDUCATION

A basic tenet of the Reformation was the authority of Scripture. As the record of the apostolic witness to Christ, Scripture offers all that is necessary to salvation and the church must measure all that it does and says by this authority. This normative role of Scripture can and should apply to curriculum development and teaching resources. The developer or teacher must ask whether the latest psychological gimmick or the newest intriguing classroom procedure actually contradicts biblical teaching. If so, no matter how attractive or "successful" the approach, it must be rejected.

Along the same lines we should be clear and consistent with students that there are norms in beliefs. Occasionally educators endeavor to encourage students, especially teenagers, to think for themselves by implying an "everything goes" attitude with regard to doctrine. Far more helpful is encouragement of the teenager to measure his or her ideas (and those of the teacher) against the standard of the scriptural message. We miss teaching moments and confuse students if we imply that there are no norms.

## CONTENT THAT RESPECTS THE BIBLE

An issue that has seriously threatened partnership between biblical studies and religious education has been the failure of some teachers and curriculum developers in recent decades to use the Bible seriously in teaching. Curriculum developers too often give in to fads, usually due to expressed wishes of buyers. In the 1960s and early 1970s, for example, serious reflective content tended to give way to sharing of feelings. Some religious education courses had tangential or negligible relation to the Scriptures. In the 1980s we saw the resultant backlash and cry for "basics." And so the 1990s may be precisely a good time to hope for increased emphasis on solid biblical content reflecting a partnership between informed biblical scholarship and religious education.

In any era, regardless of popular trends, solid scriptural content is applicable and appropriate in Christian education. Of course, historical theology, sociology of religion, and a host of other important study topics (even the students' feelings!) may routinely be examined. But Christian educators may rightly preserve a healthy suspicion of a curriculum that seems to have tenuous relationship to the Bible.

Moreover, it is appropriate for educators to respect the scriptural content—to seek the help of biblical scholars in ascertaining the "authentic" meaning of a passage and then making the judgment at which age that meaning is most appropriately taught to children or youth. Too often, especially in young children's material, we have persons either teaching material that is beyond the child, or alternatively, watering down the meaning of the passage so that it is "suitable": a prime example of the latter is the session for kindergarten students in which the feeding of the five thousand was presented as a story about "Jesus—the man who loved outdoor picnics"!

From the earliest years children should be aware of the Bible, identify the stories they hear with the Bible, and look forward to reading it for themselves as they grow older. An unfortunate approach in teaching preschoolers is to avoid mentioning the Bible because the children are too young to read. Even a three-year-old can benefit when the teacher says, "I am going to tell you a story. It is written right here in this book we call the Bible. Some day you will be able to read the story for yourselves. Today I will tell it to you."

A good library for children, youth, and adults is important in help-ing all age levels appreciate and respect the Scriptures. Sometimes even when congregations recognize the need of solid biblical commentaries for adults, they continue to stock poor, inaccurate, and outdated Bible storybooks for children. If children are to appreciate the Scriptures, then poorly written stories, doggerel poetry, and paltry art should find no place on congregational library shelves. The Bible deserves better and so do our children.

## METHODOLOGY AND CONTENT

A final point on partnership between biblical and educational disciplines is the need for congruence in teaching between biblical content and teaching methodology. It is impossible to separate what we teach from how we teach—in other words, the methodology itself communicates content. "Method is a content in its own right; method is structural content.... The only proper way to teach the Bible is for the teacher to make sure that the substantive contents and the structural contents are as fully congruent with one another as possible."[32] Unless content and methodology are congruent, the message we teach may actually be opposed to the official content.

This principle is true in terms of procedures and also teacher attitudes, to which students of course quickly respond. If a teacher attempts to communicate the good news of God's unconditional acceptance of us in spite of our sinfulness without accepting students in spite of who they are or what they do, then the students are likely to learn of rejection rather than of God's love. Of course, teachers are simultaneously sinful as well as saved persons and so cannot love their students unconditionally all of the time. But Tillich suggests that, in the grasp of the Spirit, we can be prototype, although only fragmentarily, of the acceptance that God has for sinful human beings in spite of their sinfulness. The Spirit enables learner and teacher to mutually respect each other and share together in the learning task.[33]

The method-content congruence is also important in balancing cog-nitive and affective dimensions of teaching the Bible. James Michael Lee correctly notes that "the religion teacher who uses cognitive instruc-tional procedures almost exclusively is thereby suffocating the affective and lifestyle essence of the Bible's substantive content."[34]

The challenge of seeking appropriate methodologies that will mirror and reinforce the content calls for biblical scholars and religious educators to work together. Excellent scholarship and carefully selected procedures in curriculum could do much to enhance the teaching of the Bible in congregations. Such an enterprise may be done denominationally but will probably be most fruitful when already well-advanced ecumenical cooperation within each discipline is reflected also in joint endeavors between the disciplines.

## NOTES

1. James Michael Lee, "Religious Education and the Bible: A Religious Educationist's View," in *Biblical Themes in Religious Education,* ed. Joseph S. Marino (Birmingham, Ala.: Religious Education Press, 1983) 2.

2. Joseph S. Marino, "Religious Education and the Bible: A Biblicist's View," in ibid. 62.

3. Lee, "Religious Education," in ibid. 7.

4. Two of the most helpful are Nancy Foltz, ed., *Handbook of Adult Religious Education* (Birmingham, Ala.: Religious Education Press, 1986), and Linda Jane Vogel, *Religious Education of Older Adults* (Birmingham, Ala.: Religious Education Press, 1984). Also see Marvin Roloff, ed., *Education for Christian Living* (Minneapolis: Augsburg, 1987), and Norma Everist, *Education Ministry in the Congregation* (Minneapolis: Augsburg, 1983).

5. Walter Brueggemann, *The Creative Word: Canon as a Model for Biblical Education* (Philadelphia: Fortress, 1982) 9.

6. Ibid.

7. Ibid. 14–15.

8. Ibid. 16–17.

9. Ibid. 17.

10. Ibid. 22–25.

11. Ibid. 28–32.

12. Ibid. 36–37.

13. Ibid. 40–41.

14. Ibid. 56–61.

15. Ibid. 74–75.

16. Ibid. 84–86.

17. Ibid. 99–102.

18. Paul Tillich, *Systematic Theology* vol. 1 (Chicago: University of Chicago Press, 1951; Digswell Place: James Nisbet & Co., 1953) 72 (the British ed. is cited below).

19. Paul Tillich, "Reply to Interpretation and Criticism," in *The Theology of Paul Tillich,* ed., Charles W. Kegley and Robert W. Bretall (New York: Macmillan, 1964) 332.

20. Lee, "Religious Education and the Bible" 30–31.

21. Paul Tillich, *Theology of Culture* (New York: Oxford University Press, 1964) 154.

22. Ibid. 206.

23. Ibid. 205.

24. Tillich points out that "God does not use a particular language, and special documents written in Hebrew, Aramaic, Greek, or any other language are not as such words of God. They can become the Word of God if they become mediators of the Spirit and have the power to grasp the human spirit.... The Bible does not contain words of God ..., but it can and in a unique way has become the 'Word of God.' Its uniqueness resides in the fact that it is the document of the central revelation, with respect to both its giving and its receiving sides. Every day, by its impact on people inside and outside the church, the Bible proves that it is the Spirit's most important medium in the Western tradition." *Systematic Theology* vol. 3 (Chicago: University of Chicago Press, 1963; Digswell Place: James Nisbet & Co., 1964) 132.

25. Rudolf Bultmann, *Jesus Christ and Mythology* (London: SCM; New York: Scribner's, 1958) 14–18.

26. Ibid. 40, 53, 63, 66–70.

27. Ibid. 71.

28. Rudolf Bultmann, "Reply," in *The Theology of Rudolph Bultmann,* ed. Charles W. Kegley (London: SCM; New York: Harper & Row, 1966) 287.

29. Martin Stallmann, "Contemporary Interpretation of the Gospels as a Challenge to Preaching and Religious Education" in Kegley, ed., *Bultmann* 251.

30. On Piaget's stages of cognitive development, see Jean Piaget, *Six Psychological Studies,* trans. Anita Tenzer (London: University of London Press, 1968) 8–70. Piaget's theory is summarized well in Richard M. Lerner, *Concepts and Theories of Human Development,* 2d ed. (New York: Random House, 1986) 245–62.

31. On using parables with youth see A. Roger Gobbel, Gertrude G. Gobbel, and Thomas Ridenhour, Sr., *Helping Youth Interpret the Bible* (Atlanta: John Knox, 1984) 113–17, 137–39.

32. Lee, "Religious Education" 34.

33. Tillich, *Systematic Theology* 3:225–26.

34. Lee, "Religious Education" 34–35.

JOHN REUMANN

# Afterword

## Putting the Promise into Practice

**B**iblical theology is alive, and its theologies lively, again, even after two hundred years, as the essays above show. As "a form of theological activity, or of theological inquiry," it has, indeed, recently been declared "robust," in terms of publications, not at all "in crisis."[1]

Currently whole journals[2] as well as individual articles are devoted to "bib theo," as students call it where curricula include courses in it. Books on it continue to appear, such as the recent, ecumenically oriented one by Hans-Ruedi Weber on the currently pertinent theme of power in both Testaments.[3] Granted, there has been a tendency in the last decade or so to concentrate on individual themes such as law, righteousness, peace, blessing, or presence, or to experiment with "overtures" for biblical theology, rather than to attempt a "total theology of the entire Bible."[4] But to the question of the "possibility" of a biblical theology, indeed, even in the face of those who dismiss the whole effort, there is a new and considerable affirmation that it is both important and needful to call for it. But biblical theology, it is usually added, should not be an enclosed system, and should allow for considerable variety and even countercurrents from within Scripture itself.[5]


## MAPPING A ROAD STILL TRAVELED

In the Introduction and ten chapters of this volume, examples have been gathered which reveal the academic and ecclesiastical vitality and the intellectual and practical vigor of biblical theology as a discipline in its various forms. In particular, evidence has been cited pointing toward its continuing existence and even growth in Europe, among Roman Catholics and Conservative Evangelicals, and in the Third World.[6] It survives also in the black churches, with their traditional rootage in the Bible and continued concern to "let it speak" to God's people in their present condition. Perhaps it has been chiefly in a declining mainline Protestantism that we have heard cries of its eclipse and demise.

Why has biblical theology been considered in desperate straits for twenty years or more? What has happened is that one particular type of biblical theology on the American scene, the so-called biblical theology movement, has suffered severe decline. Its own proponents are in part responsible for this impression, first by their somewhat overblown claims for its uniqueness, then by their use of such words as life and death, and crisis and eclipse when it fell upon times of testing.

This movement came on the scene after World War II and flourished into the 1960s, and then declined. Why this was so can be grasped by recalling certain characteristics attributed to it. The American phenomenon of biblical theology was (1) a reaction to Protestant Liberalism, usually (2) allied with Barthian Neo-Orthodoxy; (3) it championed "Hebrew mentality" over against "Greek thought"; and in (4) stressing Israel and the New Testament against their cultural environments (sometimes invoking the aid of archeological discoveries), it insisted on (5) the unity of the Bible and upon (6) "revelation in history."[7] To quote one of its supporters in the 1960s, biblical theology, while it was sometimes conceived of as descriptively articulating the theological significance of the Bible as a whole and then building a system of theology (as Barth assayed), meant above all "exposition of biblical books, texts, or words, which is based upon the presupposition that there is a common biblical (or Hebraic) viewpoint which is shared by various authors of the scriptural writings."[8]

The biblical theology movement that burst upon many of us, students and teachers, in or around 1950 was fresh air and new life. So much so that many old-time liberals were moved to fight it with caricatures, such as the gibe about its Great Commandment—"Thou shalt love the Lord thy Dodd, and thy Niebuhr as thyself"—or the description of it as a silver screen, cinemascope substitute for reality.[9] The claims of the movement were often exaggerated. But for some two decades, biblical theology captivated theology and church.

What happened to this enterprise, which had thus taken shape primarily in North American (and British) Protestant circles, and was connected with venerable theories of salvation history and "covenant theology," frequently along Calvinist lines? In brief, it fell victim to changing times.

The course somewhat parallels developments with the theology of Karl Barth: it was widely influential, adapted by successors, rejected by opponents, superseded in many quarters by new schools (such as process theology), or confronted by the revival of old rivals (neoliberalism).

The biblical theology movement's general alliance with Barthianism, although a short-term advantage, was soon affected by the changing fortunes of Neo-Orthodoxy itself. It is well known that biblical theology's dichotomy concerning "Hebrew though compared with Greek" (always to the latter's detriment) soon came to be regarded as oversimplified, because detailed historical study showed how, even in Palestine, Greek culture interpenetrated Judaism.[10]

The hostility to environment—whether Israel's or that of the early church—which characterized the biblical theology movement gave place in time to an emphasis on social setting and positive linkage with the world of the ancient Near East or the Greco-Roman culture. The archeological connections that G. Ernest Wright or W. F. Albright made with the Bible became a two-edged sword. While never intended to show (as others put it) that "the Bible is correct," such connections were sometimes so interpreted. But soon the very notion of "biblical archeology" was challenged in favor of "Syro-Palestinian archeology" or general "Mediterranean culture."[11] Unity gave way to pluralism, not only in biblical studies, as the pendulum swung again, but in contemporary church life too. Inclusivity increasingly reigned, not denominational particularities. Not only was "revelation in history" challenged by "revelation in nature," but the notion of revelation itself came under attack. This happened, at least in part, because the biblical theology of the 1950s, following neoorthodoxy, used "revelation" (in history) through the Bible (alone) to fend off all claims of other religions and of "nature."

Indeed, a real issue with which the American biblical theology movement never fully came to terms was one that has plagued biblical theology since its inception: the relation to systematic/constructive/foundational theology. In seeking to deal with "history," the American movement failed to work out the love-hate relationship that Gabler had noted between biblical religion and dogmatic theology. Is the "defining horizon" for theology to be simply the Bible or God in Jesus Christ or gospel or election or justification or some other organizing principle? To what extent and how does theology include postbiblical creeds, church, and philosophy? How is biblical theology to relate to wisdom, knowledge, or revelation outside the covenant community and Scripture? How is the Bible to connect with subsequent developments in Christian thought, which were cast, unfortunately for the movement's Hebrew/Greek dichotomy, chiefly in Hellenic terms? Is there not, people began to ask, a continuum from biblical criticism to biblical theology and then to doctrinal theology?[12]

Noteworthy also are the societal shifts in the United States in the late 1960s and 1970s. The civil rights movement, the Vietnam War debate, and environmental issues raised questions about social ethics and God's activity today, for which the biblical theology movement had no unified answer or even methodology. In Old and New Testament studies, as elsewhere in academia, "restless scholarship" was soon "restlessly engaged in efforts to understand their literature as social... and cultural phenomena" as well as past history or traditional theology.[13]

The particular strand of biblical theology that was developed in Europe in this period by Oscar Cullmann—akin to but somewhat different from the American version—attracted a considerable following and provided important influences on the work of the Second Vatican Council.[14] But it too receded, as Catholic theology developed along new (and old) lines and as many German-speaking and U.S. faculty appointments went to scholars trained in the Bultmann School, instead of along salvation-history lines.

In addition to all the new, previously described exegetical approaches, there was a general shift in many quarters from preoccupation with history and "the events behind the biblical narrative" to "the narrative itself," that is, an emphasis on "story" and on the biblical books as literary entities. At the same time a tendency developed to claim that the biblical writings are "secondary—the expression of a faith which was located in the communities of Israel and then the church; and that the theological understanding of the documents must depend upon a grasp of the realities of life as experienced by those communities."[15]

These changes notwithstanding, biblical theology of varying and often new sorts continued to be done. In Barr's words, it is "difficult to maintain that biblical theology had somehow come to a stop"; it "continued on rather smoothly," even if with less prestige.[16] Although certain models suffered eclipse or death, new impulses have arisen. All sorts of possibilities exist today for approaching biblical theology.

Any cartographer sketching the highways and byways of biblical theology since 1950 would surely have to include what seemed for a decade or two the "way of the Lord," the superhighway of American biblical theology. This notable enterprise, seeking to link the vast territories of Old and New Testament, emerged from the jungles of historical criticism and the untilled land or morass of atomistic liberalism, as a smooth expressway. But in time it grew bumpy, ran into design flaws, and divided, subdivided, and in some cases seemed to come to an end. In other instances it went on, but as a shadow of its former self, with fewer and fewer travelers.

The Liberal Protestant Highway, once the main road, experienced rough going in the 1950s and 1960s. But in the next twenty years some people sought to rebuild it. Meanwhile, new construction crews and radical engineering designs began to appear. Sociological and history-of-religions paths emerged from tunnels or swamps as new ways to get to a goal. The Historical Highway was abandoned by many in favor of a configuration of literary/narrative roadways, not to mention structuralist foundations, cloverleafs, and flyovers, a Liberation Boulevard that opened new vistas, and local and international networks designed for, and increasingly by, women. Sometimes easy interchanges existed between roadways, such as feminism and liberation. Sometimes they seemed like rival ways to go across the biblical and theological landscapes—signs were posted on the Literary/Narrative Expressway to use the Historical Highway as little as possible or to avoid it completely.

Where will all these old routes and newly blazed trails lead us?

## ASSESSING SOME OF THE PROPOSALS

The claims in Dean Mauser's lecture (chap. 5) about the future of biblical theology will strike many as basically a continuation of the line of thought found in the American biblical theology movement of three decades ago. Here, with full knowledge of such developments, Mauser makes a case for "a Hebraic understanding of events in time," in contrast to a "Greek approach" to "what constitutes human history." His argument achieves scholarly depth by appealing to scientific study of the Greek word *historia* and the Hebrew word *dābār*.[17] They are contrasted as, respectively, "critical inquiry" and Yahweh's personal will, disclosed with power to create historical reality, indeed through the person of the prophet or Jesus. Mauser draws analogous parallels between much Old Testament "history" and the New Testament climax in Christ. He claims that biblical unity is thus achieved, and a "hermeneutical sign-post" is also set up in the incarnation as the "unsurpassable apex."

Mauser, in my judgment, is correct not to abandon history but to try to discern its workings in the face of both scriptural testimony and the hard-nosed principles of research articulated by a historian such as Troeltsch. Mauser's approach contrasts with biblical theology as it was done under the American movement thirty years ago in his willingness not to quarrel with the approach of historical criticism. Instead, the several ways in which different sets of eyes see things are to be held in tension. "History" plus "the word of God" both have a place. Thus, while the critical historian may appear at first glance as foe to the biblical theologian, the former's method of investigation does have its place. But it is not the only one.

Some will find this option a helpful restatement of familiar views about *Historie* (past events) and *Geschichte* (past events with ongoing significance, under the power of God's word). A biblical theology based on historical events, has a chance, again.

At the opposite end of the spectrum is the answer Professor Strecker implicitly offers: no "biblical theology," not even a New Testament theology, is possible. This position has often been advanced, indeed by my teacher and predecessor in New Testament at Philadelphia Seminary, Russell D. Snyder.

This position decrying attempts at constructs called biblical theology arises, first, because the evidence in the canonical books is so complicated. For instance, one must distinguish Matthew's view on the law from that of Jewish-Christian sources that the evangelist inherited, and both from what Jesus taught. The evangelist's level is, of course, clearest, that of sources or the Jesus-level more problematical. And all of these differ from Paul's idea of the law, to say nothing of Paul's sources, opponents, and successors (as in the Pastoral Epistles), or the Fourth Evangelist, or Hebrews. To arrive at the Pauline view of the law is not easy. There have been several conflicting analyses offered recently, and even a book refereeing the various positions.[18]

Strecker posed, secondly, the problem of distinctions between the New Testament and later views about the law. A prominent example involves the contrast in Reformation theology (but not only there) between law and gospel. Thus, the problem of dogmatic development is raised. Such later views have often been read back into the biblical situation. Both these factors discourage much confidence in our ability to do biblical theology at all objectively. Strecker's critique of a specific type of current German biblical theology, emerging in the "New Tübingen School," has been noted above.[19]

Examples of this stance against biblical theology, could be multiplied by appeal to others besides Strecker or James Barr, who has campaigned not only against the "word study" method but also against "canonical criticism" and other approaches.[20] Even Bible-friendly theologians concerned for the life of the church, such as Dietrich Ritschl, have attacked "the fiction of a 'biblical theology'" on the basis of what theology is or ought to be. For compared with doctrines like the Trinity, Paul presents "theology" only in "the inauthentic sense of the word."[21]

Of the three new impulses toward biblical theology presented in chaps. 2–4 above—feminist hermeneutics, Christian-Jewish relations, and canonical criticism—feminist approaches probably span the widest spectrum of options between the extremes of no biblical theology and biblical theology as embodied in the American movement of thirty years ago.

In Trible's survey (chap. 2), she notes how some women would repudiate all biblical theology because they reject Scripture itself as "hopelessly misogynous." Others, employing the "conventional methods in studying the text," vary in their strategies for using the Bible. It is not impossible for women to do biblical theology along the classical lines of the American biblical theology movement. Women have put into practice literary as well as historical analyses. Among the feminist approaches in our introductory list, several slightly different combinations of methods were cited, all of them employing Scripture in historical and literary ways to liberate women and recover their stories from centuries of patriarchal interpretation.[22]

A "feminist biblical theology," according to Professor Trible, would be constructive (not just descriptive), reflective of diverse communities (academia, church, and synagogue), and varied in formulation, as it articulates biblical faith while being fully cognizant of issues concerning gender and sex. Its wrestlings would go beyond traditional meanings, and would seek to subvert "androcentric idolatry" and authority. To change the nature of the reader, from patriarchal and androcentric to feminist, "alters the meaning and power" of the text. These remarks seem to commit the program to "reader-oriented" criticism *and* to conventional historical-literary methodologies.

All this points to a fairly specific program for a different sort of biblical theology, one not yet written except in overture or preview form, but plainly envisioned by some. Mary Ann Tolbert thinks that "if New Testament theology has a future, . . . it may well be with feminism."[23]

The impact upon biblical theology from recent Jewish studies and Christian-Jewish relations can take many forms. Father Harrington's essay (chap. 3) focuses upon the Jewishness of the historical Jesus as an approach to Christology. But that includes not only Jesus' sociocultural setting and teachings, but also the cross, resurrection, and indeed incarnation, the Word as "Jewish flesh" (Karl Barth). And Christology is construed so as to include the issue of covenants in the Bible and the importance of the Holocaust in the 1940s for theology in the last decade and a half. Jewish terms and ideas are recognized as standing behind Christian themes such as justification and the sacraments.

Occasional discussion of whether Jews too might do "biblical theology," at least for the Hebrew Scriptures, has also been encountered.[24] And more could be said about Paul's Jewish roots and about the question of Jewish versus Greek influences on early Christianity. It was characteristic of the biblical theology movement in the 1950s to regard the Hebraic as "good," so to speak, and the Hellenistic as "bad." In an oversimplified way there has been some tendency in certain types of biblical theology to view Old Testament/Jewish roots as proper and the Greek world as alien. This runs the danger of "playing Semite" with the New Testament, severing connections with subsequent church developments, and "Judaizing" the Old Testament. The Bultmann school has been accused of preferring reputed Greek, gnostic influences, and the New Tübingen School in contradistinction prefers to recover Jewish backgrounds. Shall the Hebrew Scriptures be read in a continuity with an emerging Judaism (and if so, which one and when?), or was the religion of the tenth or fifth centuries B.C.E. something different from that under the rabbis of the Mishnaic period?

In other words, studies in Judaica and findings from the Greco-Roman world have each provided certain "tilts," in one direction or another, for New Testament theology. So have predispositions for Israel against its environment or toward seeing Israel within an ancient Near Eastern setting. Such a range of questions is suggested by the Jewishness of Jesus as a trend in biblical and theological discussion.

Canonical criticism, however defined, is always closely linked to biblical theology. One can scarcely stress canon and eschew theology, because the purpose of designating a collection of books is to provide parameters for the community, thereby delimiting and lifting up content for the theological enterprise. Generally, too, any emphasis on canon has moved in a historical direction, in part because of interest in determining how there arose individual books, then small groupings of them, and finally the full company of writings in the Hebrew Scriptures or the Greek New Testament (Sanders). Yet once determined, canon provides the bounds also for certain literary approaches, as well as proving foe or friend for feminist endeavors.

Sanders's essay (chap. 4) gave attention to his two-pronged research, to treat both shape and function of the canon. He explores what he regards as the key to its shape, namely theocentric monotheism. Israel's one God, what Sanders called "the Integrity of Reality," an ontological and ethical oneness, is his clue for dealing with texts that were at times "polytheizing." If biblical authors thus proceeded with a "monotheizing thrust," so should we, even with texts that threaten to make Christ a Christian idol. If the biblical writers in the wisdom literature adapted the wisdom of nonbelievers, should we not learn from others also about God? Here on Sanders's part a theologizing process is going on where a view of God and the extent of divine activity determine meaning in the canon.

But this sort of canonical criticism—and, as sketched, it does judge what the Bible says by an understanding of God—is not the only one possible. A rather different approach, which gives the biblical books themselves greater weight and does not allow for direction by any outside or by any single hermeneutical key (even God), has been briefly sketched above from the extensive work of Brevard Childs.[25] The canon, on this reading, provides context, contents, framework, and material (*die Sache* or substance) for what is construed for dogmatic theology.

No one can pretend that any one of these new impulses for biblical theology is by itself carrying the day. But in the future few are likely to do theology in either Testament without some attention to feminist hermeneutics, Jewish concerns, or canon questions. As a rough-and-ready way of assessing each (and any other approach as well), one may ask about the methodology, vantage point, applications, and connection with systematic theology in each approach.

Feminist approaches can employ all historical and literary methods, from the standpoint of women (usually understood as oppressed or persons repressed by culture and society over the centuries). Feminist hermeneutics is open to "a theology that subverts patriarchy," although for a systematics along these lines one must for the time being turn especially to the various liberation theologians, unless an "ecclesia of women" writes its own.

Studies on Jewish aspects of the New Testament (or ancient Near Eastern backgrounds of the Old) of course employ all the critical methodologies. The standpoint varies: one works as a Jew, as a Christian (of varying sorts), or with *religionsgeschichtlich* openness. There has been wide application of Jewish backgrounds for Jesus in such areas as teaching in churches (especially catechetics and Sunday school materials), preaching, and interfaith discussions. The Harrington essay notes Borowitz's response as a Jew to recent Christologies. Systematic theologies can be cited that are written from an avowedly "Jewish perspective," such as that by Paul van Buren.[26]

Sanders's canonical criticism invokes the full range of methodologies. Childs, while skilled at sketching the form, source, and redaction of a passage,[27] prefers in his canonical context approach to emphasize the completed book and its exegetical history and intertextual associations within the canon. This "book" emphasis lends itself to certain types of literary analysis. For both Sanders and Childs, the canon is the vantage point. Sanders is more interested in its development, Childs in the finished product. Each scholar has dealt with both Testaments, Childs through systematic examination, Sanders through preaching.[28] Neither relates directly to a systematics as yet, but Childs could claim Barth and much classical Protestant theology as concomitant.

## CHARTING THE LITERARY/NARRATIVE "REVOLUTION"

From the Introduction on, much has been made of a paradigm shift from historical to now a literary or narrative approach for the Bible and therefore biblical theology.[29] Proponents often see such a move as a sharp contrast to any emphasis on history, as in the American biblical theology movement. Some see it as the major (or only) alternative to historical-critical methodology, which, it is implied, is "bankrupt."[30] In our outline of possible approaches to biblical theology the literary/ narrative one was deliberately grouped with those with which it sometimes overlaps (canonical criticism, social setting, feminist, and rhetorical criticism come especially to mind).[31] The essays by Phyllis Trible, Daniel Harrington, and James Sanders at times reflect the use of literary methods. But it is chap. 7, by Robert Robinson, that directly tackles narrative and biblical theology.

The concatenation of the adjectives "literary" and "narrative" above is deliberate, suggesting a broad trend, a wide-ranging movement in recent exegesis and theological activity. As Robinson makes clear, "The emergence of narrative theology . . . bears a relationship to a major shift" in American literary criticism. It is a move from extrinsic to intrinsic analysis, that is, away from factors outside the text, such as history or social conditions or even the author, toward concentration on plot and other features within the work itself. One discerns narrative by literary observations, though without hitching the exegetical wagon to any one "literary critical star."[32]

To characterize some common features in the current literary/ narrative approach, one may call attention to the exaltation of literary insights and the minimalizing of historical emphasis (thus "literary-critical," not "historical criticism"); focus on the finished biblical book, not its development from events in Israel's history or the life of Jesus, through oral accounts, sources, and redaction; the document "as it stands," not in light of author, social setting, or its contemporary circumstances; and, for some literary critics, the interrelatedness of biblical books with each other and the whole of the narrative collection (thus making common cause with canonical approaches and even the old biblical theology movement).

Professor Robinson makes a case for the type of narrative theology that is proffered by Hans Frei, his associates, and pupils. We are rightly told that "narrative theology is hardly monolithic," and then our attention is directed toward this one version. The choice is an important one, with considerable ramifications.

The cover of *The Christian Century,* November 8, 1989, featured a map on the theme, "Where Is the 'Mainline' Headed?" in Protestantism.[33] While "Established Thinking" and "Missions Road" were still significant highways on this map (the latter, however, passing through "Funding Crisis"), "Institutional Loyalty" was a lesser route, marked "Closed for Repairs." Running toward "Baby-Boomer County" (with such place names as "Individualism," "Community," and "Spirituality") were two somewhat parallel roads, the "Liberal Protestant Highway" and, a lesser ribbon of concrete (here and there blacktop), "Liberal Culture." Between them ran the "Post-liberal Interstate," with two places indicated: Frei Township and Lindbeck City.[34] High tribute to two Yale professors! Never mind that "Evangelical Interchange" is only pointed to off the map, and Catholics and Jews are not indicated at all in the state of The Mainline. Hans Frei's importance and work are singled out in this map, as in Robinson's essay.

Chapter 7, above, presents Hans Frei's contribution as the narrative theology response to what is termed the crisis over the clarity of Scripture today. The solution is a return to the "self-evident sense of Scripture" that comes from a "realistic reading of the text," so as to point up "the history-like nature of biblical narrative and the church's understanding of the nature of the incarnation." For biblical theology the result would be the church's seeing of "its own story in part as . . . continuation of that same biblical narrative," without any hiatus. This would be accomplished especially through the use of typology. The biblical text, it is claimed, is clear; no outside key is needed. Use of critical practices is therefore ad hoc. Historical research, following its own set of rules, may give us bits and pieces of information to "reinforce the history-like character of the biblical narratives," but the aim of narrative theology is to restore the "clear and self-interpreting sense of Scripture" to "every member of the community of faith."

This attractive proposal obviously has a number of positive features. With Frei it wishes to restore the "precritical realistic reading" of the Bible which went into eclipse beginning in the eighteenth century.[35] It lifts up, with Frei, the incarnation of Jesus Christ.[36] Emphasis is placed on the entire Bible, the narrative in which is taken to embrace also the church and its development. The authority of a perspicacious Scripture is raised on high.

As one pupil of Frei has put it, this status of a text as a component of Scripture (1) "may inform an interpreter's judgment as to the sort of text it is." Whatever the genre, any text is to be construed within the whole. Thus (2) "a new context for interpretation" is provided (the canon, with its *inter*textuality). (3) "The hermeneutical priority of the text" is supported, for in its *intra*textual role it "serves as an interpretive medium for the extratextual world."[37] As Robinson phrased it, Scripture judges the words of all others. It can also be claimed that narrative, literary emphases lend themselves to a current stress on "story" in theology and preaching, and beckon the reader/teacher/preacher to unfold the biblical narratives, especially in the Old Testament "historical books" and the Gospels, for our day.

Frei's slim legacy of two books and a dozen major articles, plus his ability in teaching as well as in writing to bring "the results of patient and rigorous historical scholarship to bear on systematic theology" and to pursue his vision, obviously proved moving and influential for his students and colleagues, as tributes show in a 1987 festschrift, published shortly before his death.[38] He is compared with Freud in "recovering for us a portion of our own intellectual history" and thus laying bare "the roots of some contemporary quandaries" and providing "new energies" for further work. These associates have sought to carry on some of his insights along systematic theology and ec- clesiology lines, as well as in at least one case employing the social sciences.[39]

Nonetheless there are problems for a biblical theology with Frei's stance. First, what exactly is the "biblical narrative"?[40] Frei himself re- ferred to the temporal "sequence told by the biblical stories," set forth by such Christian preachers and theological commentators as Augustine.[41] His own account, however, lingers longer over Erich Auerbach's idea of "realistic narrative" than a precise summary of the scriptural narra- tive, and when Luther and Calvin are discussed, their versions emerge as somewhat different, Luther reading Scripture in light of a law/gospel or preserving-justice/divine-love contrast, Calvin seeing "the subject matter of scripture . . . identical with its narrative."[42]

A good case can be made for a "grand design" by God, in the Christian, Bible-based view of history which took literary form in the patristic period and endured pretty much intact until the eighteenth century.[43] But this schema was to a great extent a post–New Testament one, heavily influenced by dogmatic decisions about the church and Israel, the Trinity, the two natures of Christ, and eschatology. It was not just "biblical," the Scriptures read in their own terms. Creeds counted. Moreover, this design for dogmatic history has never gone into more than a partial eclipse, for its symbols endure in dogma, liturgy, church art, and hymnody. The eclipse was no doubt more total in rationalist circles and in whitewashed unadorned Free Church chapels, but in much of Christendom the biblical(-dogmatic-creedal) narrative has continued in various ways.

What is more, the various schools of *Heilsgeschichte* continued this narrative and at points made it more biblical, as Frei himself at points noted.[44] And as the old "grand design" broke down, new narrative versions came to the fore. This occurred, for example, in the "quest for the historical Jesus" and the retelling of Israel's history in light of fuller analysis of conflicting accounts such as Kings and Chronicles. "Eclipse" is a not inappropriate term, since the narrative never died out but rather waxed and waned, frequently changing form, as indeed it had done under the church fathers, medieval theologians, Reformers, Protestant Orthodoxy, and Pietists. But the image may overstate both the unity of the narrative throughout the centuries and what happened to it.

Second, Frei's "favored term," *history-like,* suffers from ambiguity. It has an interesting prior history.[45] It translates the German *Geschichtsähnlichkeit,* "history-likeness," and stems from the eighteenth-century debate in Germany over "the factuality of revelation and the credibility of the Bible." In this "literary-historical debate" both positivists and Deists or rationalists could agree on the "history-likeness" of the biblical narratives. Whereas C. G. Heyne (1729–1812) used such language in Latin to refer to pagan accounts from antiquity about the gods intervening (stories about Jupiter would thus be "history-like"), Schelling and J. J. Hess in 1793 spoke of biblical materials as possibly *"geschichtsähnlich"*: is what is narrated really to be understood as a historical report (*Geschichtsnachricht*) "or only as something *Geschichtsähnliches* (analogon historiae). . . . " Such discussions were usually carried on within the context of an understanding of "myth." David Friedrich Strauss, in his *Leben Jesu* (1835), developed his well-known theory that the myth-making propensity of early Christianity led to a "history-like (*geschichtsartige*) clothing of early Christian ideas" in narrative accounts (such as the story of Jesus' temptation).[46]

With such a pedigree, "history-like" is a strange word to use today to underscore the reality of, for example, the incarnation, or historicity of biblical accounts. It straddles a seeming commitment to historical facticity and an apparent awareness that stories may literally never have happened. It thus throws sand in our eyes, blinding us, by the use of the word "history," to the likelihood that the narrative is quite likely fictional—although some members of a community may still suppose the clear and self-evident meaning is factual. To speak thus of the coming of Jesus Christ would, in the view of classical Christianity, be fatal to the enterprise.

Third, by its very nature, "narrative" fits only some books of the Bible, such as those on Israel's history-like kings and prophets, the Gospels, and Acts.[47] How the approach can do justice to law codes, wisdom literature, or epistles remains unclear. True, portions of Paul's letters are autobiographical, but doctrinal slogans and paraenesis or ethical injunctions are scarcely amenable to "narrative theology."

Apocalyptic writings, which are a problem for all interpreters, pose special difficulty for narrative, because the Books of Daniel and Revelation do have plots and sequence, of sorts. How are we to take their "narrative"? It is stock-in-trade for Armageddon evangelists to read Revelation "as is," applying details in the future plot line to events about to happen in the preacher's own day. Historical-critical scholarship has rescued us precisely from such crude "reader-oriented" self-interpreting, by setting the document in the seer's own situation.

The Passion narrative in the Gospels is another example posing dangers for a straight narrative approach. A reading of the text with concern for the Jewish people will alert us to it. Read "as they are," Matthew and John can stir up and have produced anti-Semitism. The historical approach, setting them in the evangelist's own day, when church and synagogue were going their own ways, has countered much of that misuse.

Fourth, for all the authority seemingly given to Scripture by this approach, there are nonetheless disquieting limits to the resulting narrative theology. Charles Wood, whose three points (that Frei's view suggests) on the status, context, and standpoint in Scripture for interpreting the world have been cited above, goes on to pose three limits: the status given the text may lead to one construal, but others are possible; interpreters are not obliged to accept as true what the texts teach; interpreters are not committed "to the proposition that what scripture, thus construed, conveys is normatively Christian."[48] Robinson speaks of the ad hoc nature of the procedure. One is left guessing what authority the findings from a self-evident reading really have for us. Is it up to the community (the church) to decide?

Fifth, a great deal seems tossed into the lap of the community. Its members are to be competent interpreters. The church continues the biblical story. But *which* church?[49] What kind of ecclesiology is masked here? And is not some sort of magisterium called for, even though the model tries to avoid an interpretative elite?

Sixth, it seems tempting, for some, to turn the clock back to pre-critical days. Modernity can be avoided through narrative. But as one reads the books and articles of the narrative critics, the complexity in their thought, the contrasts in their views on a passage or book, and the range of their proposals threaten to become every bit as varied as under any other kind of approach.

Seventh, one may ask whether, in Frei's narrative approach or Childs's canonical criticism or Lindbeck's treatment of doctrine, there is here a "Yale school" at work. These and other scholars in New Haven readily acknowledge the influences of one on another. But lines of demarcation must also be drawn, despite certain commonalities (against the "historical-critical method" pure and simple; in favor of "the scriptural story"; an important role for "the church"). There are, after all, divergencies, as each writer makes clear. Childs has denied there is any "new Yale theology,"[50] but readers will want to look for interchanges and overlapping route numbers when mapping the highways in current biblical theology.

All in all, literary/narrative criticism has become a major avenue of approach to the Bible. Its many forms, including that initiated by Frei's research, deserve attention.

## DOING BIBLICAL THEOLOGY TODAY

Within this mass of proposals promising new and lively versions of biblical theology, the reader/teacher/preacher who cares about Scripture and about seeing it whole will find ample opportunities for new beginnings. Surely, a roadmap is needed to overview the possible routes, old and new, but the crucial thing is to get on the road—practical engagement with the process, not abstractly but in praxis.

In an article on situating the discipline, B. C. Ollenburger has argued that biblical theology relates "to the concrete life of the church" and is to be seen as an activity "helping to engage in critical reflection on its praxis through a self-critical reading of its canonical texts."[51] Stendahl's description of biblical studies as a sort of "Public Health Department for theology and church"[52] is helpful. But such descriptions seem to give biblical theology more of an ivory-tower post or watchdog role, to stay the plague or keep everything sanitary. In reality it is the day-in, day-out application of biblical theology in the community's regular tasks that will justify time spent on choosing roadways on the map and traveling them in order to get somewhere with the Bible.

The essays in Part Two exemplify, in various ways, how some members of a seminary faculty see the praxis of biblical theology functioning. Each speaks for her- or himself, reflecting on the lectures in Part One, each person's discipline and trends in it, and some joint discussion.

Margaret Krych sets the tone for the whole enterprise in her "call for partnership" between biblical theology and Christian education. She makes clear how in churches the two have often been anything but that. But the enterprise can and should provide canonical content, an operative hermeneutic that is more theological than often occurs otherwise, and an existential approach, while using historical (and literary) criticism in the teaching task. Her observations not only reflect the chapters on biblical theology in Part One but also draw on biblical scholars such as Brueggemann for reflection on canon and education (cf. also Sanders in chap. 4 on the canon's stability and flexibility) or Bultmann for observation on how the Bible's message addresses us. Will the 1990s bring together the emphases on "feelings" from the 1960s and 1970s with the 1980s' cry for "basics" and even with the 1950s' quest for an American biblical theology, by taking up the rich methods (the how) and contents (the what) now available?

This call for partnership also applies to biblical theology and systematics, biblical theology and ethics, preaching, worship, mission, stewardship, and pastoral care, as well as with Christian education.

Robert Kysar's chapter deals firsthand with how one who is schooled in exegetical techniques and who reflects on the use of the Bible goes about preaching in a congregation. He presents a method that in an exciting way dares to compare the preacher's task today to that of the biblical authors themselves. Its steps reflect the classical disciplines and subdisciplines of biblical studies, according to "tradition history,"[53] but there is also attention to communal, social setting in today's church and world. The proposal is exemplified not merely by some passing biblical illustrations but concretely through an epistle passage in the church-year lectionary. Such a passage lends itself to the historical-critical approach, but not without awareness of the literary side; indeed, the mood of the sermon may seek to reflect the literary form of the text (see Kysar's note 22).

Jesus' parables have long provided a parade ground and a testing ground for new forms of interpretation. Robert Hughes's chapter outlines a good deal of this long history, and in particular moves beyond "the criticisms" of the 1960s to the "new literary approach." Here not simply "narrative" but type of narrative (comedy, tragedy), involvement with the world (vividly exemplifying Frei's point as to how a text can reshape our extratextual world), structuralism, and shaping the sermon to the form of the text (cf. Kysar's point about the "mood" of the sermon) all come into play. Hughes's essay well reflects the sprawling breadth of literary interpretation.

Another aspect of Hughes's study is the link to pastoral counseling through "reframing." It has been observed that an understanding of what a human being is, according to Scripture—what once was called "biblical anthropology"—is important as a framework for pastoral counseling and ethics. Biblical theology can also prove important in these disciplines, although relating biblical narrative and theological anthropology is no simple matter.[54]

A link also exists between biblical theology and lectionary. A specific but not impeccable theology underlies the three-year system widely adopted in the United States and Canada from the Roman Catholic *Ordo*.[55] Biblical theology is related to liturgy, as well, whether by selection of biblical materials for frequent public use or pervasive development of biblical symbols in worship and art.[56]

The practice of biblical theology in church life requires, however, not only repeated exemplification in all these areas of functional or practical theology (to use academic terms), in activities such as preaching and teaching (to use parish ones). There must also be persons in biblical studies who put together a theology from scriptural data and make it available to would-be users. All sorts of models exist. Some have been listed in the Introduction, and new trends in Part One. It is appropriate to have Bornemann's succinct attempt (chap. 6) to move "Toward a Biblical Theology," as he modestly terms it.

Academia and churches, locally and internationally, need people who will periodically venture to state what a reading of the Hebrew Scriptures, New Testament, or the whole Bible involves in and for the current scene. Contrary to Gabler's hopes in 1787, biblical theology can scarcely provide "unchanging concepts" once and for all. Its precise value is the assertion that what this or that student of Scripture finds here and now can be a useful structure for doing biblical theology in a given time. Borne-mann, in light of what religion, theology, biblical theologians, and the Scriptures are, has dealt with what we thus say about God, ourselves, the world, and the neighbor. Such an outline—which can serve for both Testaments, provide links to later theology, but reflect the Scriptures in their own right—has provided his students over the years with a concep-tual structure and "the excitement of the quest: seeking and being found by God who enables us to live with our neighbors in God's world."

Such biblical theologies promise opportunity to grasp Scripture anew with some sense of its totality. What then does "practice" mean for those who read/teach/preach or deal with the Old and New Testaments and hope to use them fruitfully? We begin with some propositions for consideration (and debate) about biblical theologies in general.

1. There exist many attempts at biblical theology, a plurality of proposals, all of them seeking to be true to Scripture and to be "the-ological"—though understandings differ how on to be faithful to the text and on what theology itself is.

2. All attempts reflect, to some degree, later views on the part of bibli-cal theologians, the church community of the day, systematic theology, or the spirit of the age.

3. Use of the Bible is fraught with subjectivity, whether of the indi-vidual or of the different communities of faith or of scholarly approach. This is especially so when the approach is oriented to the reader and to subjective feelings about literary features.

4. Historical criticism, while also marked by subjective use of meth-odologies, provides some attempt at stating rules for interpretation of a more objective nature.[57]

5. The academic community and the ecumenical world provide im-petus and locus for formulating principles for historical and literary procedures regarding religion, in addition to principles for theologi-cal procedure. Thus, by their corporate nature and variety, they guard against the extremes of subjectivity.

6. The resulting biblical theologies exist in tension, sometimes with each other, sometimes with their age, and sometimes with the past.

7. Biblical theologies will continue to appear, and their variety will increase.

8. Users therefore need a roadmap or series of them or periodic brief-ings or reports on the state of the discipline to ascertain possibilities for themselves.[58]

Practical suggestions follow, to put promise into practice.

1. One should choose some approach to biblical theology and read in it. It could be of the "classical" variety to begin with, even from the American biblical theology movement of the 1950s, a landmark volume such as von Rad's or Bultmann's, a challenging one such as Terrien's, or a new approach suited to one's situation or concerns (for example, feminist or canonical).

2. Any biblical theology should include a data base of texts, structure of organization, and possibilities for further reading and study (footnotes or bibliography) to expand and deepen the endeavor.

3. Adopting such a biblical theology should not preclude a related systematic theology but might actually lead to fuller postbiblical articulation of the faith by dogmatic, foundational, or systematic theologians.

4. One's biblical theology should be tested by reading biblical passages and books in light of it and by reexamining the overall biblical theology in light of these passages and books in the Bible.

5. A biblical theology should be applied, using its contents in preaching, teaching, worship, and one's self-understanding and activities as a believer and in community.

6. It should also be applied as a framework for understanding persons, events, world, past history, present, and future.

7. One's biblical theology should be checked in ecumenical and interfaith contacts for faithfulness to the text of Scripture as others understand it and in light of the tenets of other community understandings of the Bible.

8. As new approaches to biblical theology are encountered, consideration might be given to grafting in their insights or even to a paradigm shift of one's own, in order more adequately to comprehend what the Bible says. If prayer is more than continuing to say, "Now I lay me down to sleep...," biblical theology will be more than repeating what one absorbed even in a good college or seminary course years ago.

The ultimate test for any biblical theology will be whether it enables faith and obedience to God's word. George Lindbeck, with regard to narrative and related theology, has objected that "there is much talk... but little actual performance."[59] His criterion is whether advocates are absorbing the universe into the biblical world! A more modest goal might be to relate a biblical theology with one's personal existence and church life, and to God's world in which we live.

The ancient collect in the Book of Common Prayer asked the Lord to grant that we may hear, "read, mark, learn, and inwardly digest" the word. A biblical theology makes bold to add that we use Scripture holistically, in all its parts—kerygma, instruction, wisdom, vision, judgment—connectedly, prophetically, and outwardly applied, in the practice of the promise.

## NOTES

1. B. C. Ollenburger, "Biblical Theology: Situating the Discipline," in *Understanding the Word: Essays in Honor of Bernhard W. Anderson,* ed. J. T. Butler et al., JSOT Supplementary Series 37 (Sheffield: JSOT Press, 1985) 37.

2. *Horizons in Biblical Theology* (Pittsburgh, Pa.), *Biblical Theology Bulletin* (Jamaica, N.Y.), *Jahrbuch für Biblische Theologie* (Neukirchen-Vluyn).

3. H.-R. Weber, *Power: Focus for a Biblical Theology* (Geneva: WCC Publications, 1989).

4. So Otto Merk, *Biblische Theologie* 471. On law, H. Hübner, "Das Gesetz als elementares Thema einer Biblischen Theologie?" *Kerygma und Dogma* 22 (1976) 250–76, and his monographs, *Das Gesetz in der synoptischen Tradition* (Witten: Luther Verlag, 1973) and *Law in Paul's Thought: Studies in the New Testament and Its World* (Edinburgh: T. & T. Clark, 1983). On righteousness: H. G. Reventlow, *Rechtfertigung im Horizont des Alten Testaments,* Beiträge zur Evangelische Theologie 58 (Munich: Kaiser, 1958) and J. Reumann et al., *"Righteousness" in the New Testament: "Justification" in the United States Lutheran-Roman Catholic Dialogue* (Philadelphia: Fortress; New York: Paulist, 1982). On peace: H. G. Reventlow, "Friedensverheissungen im Alten und im Neuen Testament," *Friede über Israel* 62 (1979) 99–109, 147–53. On blessing: Westermann. On presence: Terrien. See the Fortress Press series, "Overtures to Biblical Theology" (over 25 titles, 1978– ).

5. S. Wagner, "Zur Frage nach der Möglichkeit einer Biblischen Theologie," *Theologische Literaturzeitung* 113 (1988) 161–70.

6. Cf. Houlden, "Biblical Theology," in *Westminster Dictionary* 70. O. Merk, *Biblische Theologie* 468, sees the shift among Roman Catholic scholars to a new orientation in biblical theology to have come with the work of R. Schnackenburg.

7. G. Hasel, "Biblical Theology Movement," in *Evangelical Dictionary of Theology,* ed. W. A. Elwell (Grand Rapids: Baker, 1984) 149–50.

8. A. Richardson, "Biblical Theology," in *A Dictionary of Christian Theology,* ed. A. Richardson (Philadelphia: Westminster, 1969) 36.

9. So, for example, one of my teachers, Morton S. Enslin. The references were to C. H. Dodd, who emphasized the unity of the New Testament and its kerygma, and the theologian Reinhold Niebuhr.

10. Houlden, "Biblical Theology," in *Westminster Dictionary* 70, with reference to M. Hengel, *Judaism and Hellenism: Studies in Their Encounter in Palestine during the Early Hellenistic Period,* 2 vols. (Philadelphia: Fortress, 1974), among other works.

11. Cf. W. Dever, "Syro-Palestinian and Biblical Archaeology," in Knight and Tucker eds., *The Hebrew Bible* 31-74, and on "Mediterranean culture," B. Malina, *New Testament World*.

12. Barr, "Theological Case," in Tucker et al., eds., *Canon, Theology* 5-13.

13. Mack, *Rhetoric* 13. Once rhetoric is understood as the art of persuasion, its practice can be seen as advocacy, even in the New Testament. This contrasts with supposed objectivity, which many considered characteristic of the biblical theology movement, and the disdain by some for "prophetic advocacy," noted in the Trible essay (above, chap. 2 n. 10).

14. G. Müller-Fahrenholz, *Heilsgeschichte zwischen Ideologie und Prophetie: Profile und Kritik heilsgeschichtlicher Theorien in der ökumenischen Bewegung zwischen 1948 und 1968*, Ökumenischen Forschungen 2, no. 4 (Freiburg: Herder, 1974) 137-92.

15. Houlden, "Biblical Theology," in *Westminster Dictionary* 70, makes both points: from history to literary documents, from writings to the community; i.e., literary criticism and social setting.

16. Barr, "Theological Case," in Tucker et al., eds., *Canon, Theology* 4.

17. Cf. ibid. 8, and Houlden, "Biblical Theology," in *Westminster Dictionary* 69, on the impression the biblical theology movement made by offering "scientific evidence to support neo-orthodox points of view," especially through "Hebrew roots and meanings of Greek words"—a particular target of Barr's critique.

18. Cf. Hübner, "Das Gesetz," Moo, "Paul and the Law," and specifically E. P. Sanders, *Paul, the Law, and the Jewish People* (Philadelphia: Fortress, 1983); H. Raisänen, *Paul and the Law* (Philadelphia: Fortress, 1986); and S. Westerholm, *Israel's Law and the Church's Faith: Paul and His Recent Interpreters* (Grand Rapids: Eerdmans, 1988); P. J. Tomson, *Paul and the Jewish Law: Halakha in the Letters of the Apostle to the Gentiles,* Compendia Rerum Iudaicarum ad Novum Testamentum, 3, no. 1 (Assen/Maastricht: Van Gorcum, Minneapolis: Fortress, 1990).

19. Literature cited above, Introduction n. 27.

20. Ibid. nn. 10 and 29.

21. *The Logic of Theology: A Brief Account of the Relationship between Basic Concepts in Theology* (Philadelphia: Fortress, 1987) 68-69.

22. Above, Introduction, p. 18, approach # 14.

23. "Defining the Problem: The Bible and Feminist Hermeneutics," in *Semeia* 28: 126. Cf. Phyllis Trible, "Biblical Theology as Women's Work," *Religion in Life* 44 (1975) 1-13.

24. Above, Introduction n. 16.

25. Above, Introduction, p.16, approach # 11, and n. 33.

26. Borowitz, *Contemporary Christologies*. Paul van Buren, *Jewish-Christian Reality*.

27. Childs's commentary on Exodus (*Book of Exodus*) thoroughly treats such elements in tradition criticism.

28. J. A. Sanders, *God Has a Story Too: Sermons in Context* (Philadelphia: Fortress, 1979).

29. Above, Introduction, pp. 7–8, 16–17, approach # 12.

30. The judgment of W. Wink, *The Bible in Human Transformation: Toward a New Paradigm for Biblical Study* (Philadelphia: Fortress, 1973). Such a widely echoed contrast between "historical" and "literary" criticism is overstated, for historical criticism has regularly included literary aspects. Much of what is regarded as the heart of historical criticism, the distinction of forms, source, and redaction in a document, is based on literary observations. For a defense of the historical-critical method, sometimes under fire in recent years, see J. Fitzmyer, "Historical Criticism: Its Role in Biblical Interpretation and Church Life," *Theological Studies* 50 (1989) 244–59. That the literary/narrative approach had antecedents in G. E. Wright's emphasis on "recital" or "narrative" in the American biblical theology movement and in Barth is indicated by D. H. Kelsey, *The Uses of Scripture in Recent Theology* (Philadelphia: Fortress, 1975) 32–55.

31. Above, Introduction, pp. 16–18, approaches 11–15.

32. **Bibliography on literary theory,** in English studies and world literature, then brought over into biblical scholarship, is enormous. See, for starters, titles listed above, Introduction n. 58, and chap. 7 n. 9, and for a brief overview Catherine Belsey, *Critical Practice,* ed. T. Hawkes, New Accents (London and New York: Methuen, 1980).

33. *The Christian Century* 106, no. 33 (Nov. 8, 1989).

34. The reference is to the related works by Hans Frei (treated below) and George Lindbeck, *Nature of Doctrine.*

35. *The Eclipse of Biblical Narrative.*

36. *The Identity of Jesus Christ.*

37. C. M. Wood, "Hermeneutics and the Authority of Scripture," in *Scriptural Authority and Narrative Interpretation,* ed. G. Green (Philadelphia: Fortress, 1987) 14–17.

38. Ibid. 199–201 for Frei's bibliography; p. x for the quotations about his work.

39. Cf. K. E. Tanner, "Theology and the Plain Sense," ibid. 59–78; G. Lindbeck, "The Story-Shaped Church: Critical Exegesis and Theological Interpretations," ibid. 161–78; and S. Hauerwas, "The Church as God's New Language," ibid. 179–98.

40. M. Wiles, "Scriptural Authority and Theological Construction: The Limits of Narrative Interpretation," ibid. 48: "even if the concept of reading the Bible as one story is allowed, it is not at all clear what that one story is."

41. *Eclipse* 1, cf. 2: "if the real historical world described by the several biblical stories is a single world of one temporal sequence, there must in principle be one cumulative story to depict it. Consequently, the several biblical stories narrating sequential segments in time must fit together into one narrative." This is achieved by "figuration" or patristic typology.

42. Ibid. 18–37, esp. 23.

43. C. A. Patrides, *The Grand Design of God: The Literary Form of the Christian View of History* (London: Routledge & Kegan Paul, 1972).

44. *Eclipse* 1, 46–47, 173–82. Frei's objection to counting *Heilsgeschichte* as a continuation and expression of "the biblical narrative" is that salvation history is set within world history, not vice versa. But was not Luke 3:1-2, to cite just one example, already doing precisely that, with its sixfold secular chronology as setting for the coming of the word of God to John the Baptist? For a recent attempt at Old Testament salvation history, see R. Gnuse, *Heilsgeschichte as a Model for Biblical Theology: The Debate Concerning the Uniqueness and Significance of Israel's Worldview,* College Theology Society Studies in Religion 4 (Lanham, Md.: University Press of America, 1989).

45. *Eclipse* 59, cf. 54, citing C. Hartlich and W. Sachs, *Der Ursprung des Mythosbegriffes in der modernen Bibelwissenschaft,* Schriften der Studiengemeinschaft der Evangelischen Akademien 2 (Tübingen: Mohr-Siebeck, 1952) 15, 59, 135, where references for Heyne and Schelling are given.

46. Strauss, *Das Leben Jesu kritisch bearbeitet,* 2d ed. (Tübingen, 1836) 1:75. Cf. the translation by George Eliot, from the fourth German edition of 1840, reprinted in the Lives of Jesus Series, *The Life of Jesus Critically Examined,* ed. P. C. Hodgson (Philadelphia: Fortress, 1972) 52–92, on the rise of "historical mythi" as well as other types of myth, a debate in which Gabler had a role; Hodgson's summary, xxv–xxxvi. But the section in the second edition from which the quotation above comes was revised for the third and fourth editions, and the exact wording does not appear in the translation.

47. Wiles, "Scriptural Authority" 47 poses the question by quoting R. Thiemann, *Revelation and Theology: The Gospel as Narrated Promise* (Notre Dame, Ind.: University of Notre Dame Press, 1985) 86: "Narrative is one of a number of possible images around which the diverse materials of the canon can be organized." But as Wiles adds, many elements "do not easily fall within such a category," and, when applied to the whole of Scripture, the term "has been stretched beyond the point at which such precise description is appropriate."

48. Wood, "Hermeneutics," in Green, ed., *Scriptural Authority* 18–19.

49. Lindbeck, "Story-Shaped Church," in ibid. 162, moves for a variety of reasons, including "historical-critical awareness," toward an "Israel-like church." Hauerwas, "God's New Language," in ibid. 189 and n. 11 laments in a sermon the failure of Frei's community tradition and structure "to specify the liturgical context" through which consensus is formed. The ecclesiology called for by Frei's approach is vague.

50. Childs, *New Testament as Canon* 541–46, "Excursus III: The Canonical Approach and the 'New Yale Theology.'" He deals especially with Lindbeck's approaches to religion and doctrine: cognitive-propositional, experiential-expressive, and cultural-linguistic models. Childs finds himself in the third category, but draws lines at three points. First, the Bible provides more of "fixed propositional content," the rule of faith, for Childs than for Lindbeck. Second, "intratextuality" need not mean denying "realities outside the text." Third, the Bible calls for "continuous exegesis" of itself "as the indisputable ground for all Christian theological reflection"; it is not just a "source of imagery."

51. Ollenburger, "Biblical Theology," in Butler et al., eds., *Understanding the Word* 51.

52. "Ancient Scripture in the Modern World," in *Scripture in the Jewish and Christian Traditions: Authority, Interpretation, Relevance,* ed. F. E. Greenspahn (Nashville: Abingdon, 1982) 205.

53. Cf. above, Introduction, p. 15, approach 8.

54. D. H. Kelsey, "Biblical Narrative and Theological Anthropology," in Green, ed. *Scriptural Authority* 121–43.

55. Cf. above, Introduction n. 40; *The Use and Sense of the Scriptures in Liturgical Celebration,* Concilium 102 (1975). The use of the Old Testament in the Roman Catholic *Ordo Lectionum Missae,* where it is regularly in a subservient position to the Gospel for the Day, reflects an unfortunate hermeneutical decision, namely, that the Old Testament is neither "gospel" nor word of God in its own right. To illustrate the influence of traditional Roman Catholic dogma on the *Ordo,* the selection of Exod. 19:2-8 to be read along with the sending out of the Twelve in Matt.9:35—10:8 (for the Fourth Sunday after Pentecost, Year A) was no doubt an attempt to picture the apostles (clergy) as priests. It misfires because the phrase "priestly kingdom" in Exod. 19:6 refers to the entire people of God. But a hermeneutic and theology are at work.

56. To illustrate: churches, especially those in the West, often adorned the west end of the building, over the door(s), with a painting or mosaic of the last judgment (*Dies Irae,* "day of wrath"), to remind those leaving the building of death and God's judgment, sure to come. The bliss of the saved was also depicted. The early mosaic in the cathedral at Torcello (Venice) even includes the heretic Nestorius in the lap of the devil! How many modern churches include much emphasis on judgment in art or liturgy? Does this mean the Middle Ages overdid God's wrath but that we overdo God's love and a universalism of a positive sort?
Rather than speak of simply one "biblical narrative," one should consider how and why the story of salvation (and judgment) varied from time to time and place to place. A crucial item if, with Frei (*Eclipse*), one assumes Augustine as a norm for "the narrative," is how "(original) sin" is handled. Attitudes have varied in Bible, church history, doctrine, and liturgy.

57. Fitzmyer, "Historical Criticism" 258: while literary criticism may hold that a text takes on "a life of its own" and may convey "a meaning beyond that of the original author's intention," this meaning "beyond" ought "never be understood as losing all homogeneity with the meaning of the original author," which historical criticism helps us ascertain. Further, R. E. Brown, "The Contribution of Historical Biblical Criticism to Ecumenical Church Discussion," in *Biblical Interpretation in Crisis: The Ratzinger Conference on Bible and Church,* ed. R. J. Neuhaus, Encounter Series (Grand Rapids: Eerdmans, 1989) 24–49.

58. As in surveys noted above, Introduction n. 2, such as those by Coats and Fuller, Donahue, or this volume.

59. *Nature of Doctrine* 135.

# Bibliographical Index

Bibliography on specific topics is usually gathered in one chief footnote and is indicated in boldface type below. Full data on titles are usually given in the first footnote reference.